Lauer Series in Rhetoric and Composition

Series Editors: Catherine Hobbs, Patricia Sullivan, Thomas Rickert, and Jennifer Bay

LAUER SERIES IN RHETORIC AND COMPOSITION
Series Editors: Catherine Hobbs, Patricia Sullivan, Thomas Rickert, and Jennifer Bay

The Lauer Series in Rhetoric and Composition honors the contributions Janice Lauer Hutton has made to the emergence of Rhetoric and Composition as a disciplinary study. It publishes scholarship that carries on Professor Lauer's varied work in the history of written rhetoric, disciplinarity in composition studies, contemporary pedagogical theory, and written literacy theory and research.

Other Books in the Series

1977: A Cultural Moment in Composition, by Brent Henze, Jack Selzer, and Wendy Sharer (2008)

The Promise and Perils of Writing Program Administration, edited by Theresa Enos and Shane Borrowman (2008)

Untenured Faculty as Writing Program Administrators: Institutional Practices and Politics, edited by Debra Frank Dew and Alice Horning (2007)

Networked Process: Dissolving Boundaries of Process and Post-Process, by Helen Foster (2007)

Composing a Community: A History of Writing Across the Curriculum, edited by Susan H. McLeod and Margot Soven (2006)

Historical Studies of Writing Program Administration: Individuals, Communities, and the Formation of a Discipline, edited by Barbara L'Eplattenier and Lisa Mastrangelo (2004). Winner of the WPA Best Book Award for 2004-2005.

Rhetorics, Poetics, and Cultures: Refiguring College English Studies (Expanded Edition) by James A. Berlin (2003)

Writers Without Borders

Writing and Teaching Writing in Troubled Times

Lynn Z. Bloom

Parlor Press
West Lafayette, Indiana
www.parlorpress.com

Parlor Press LLC, West Lafayette, Indiana 47906

© 2008 by Parlor Press
All rights reserved.
Printed in the United States of America

SAN: 254-8879

Library of Congress Cataloging-in-Publication Data

Bloom, Lynn Z., 1934-
  Writers without borders : writing and teaching writing in troubled times / Lynn Z. Bloom.
       p. cm. -- (Lauer series in rhetoric and composition)
  Includes bibliographical references and index.
  ISBN 978-1-60235-059-5 (pbk. : alk. paper) -- ISBN 978-1-60235-060-1 (alk. paper) -- ISBN 978-1-60235-061-8 (adobe ebook)
 1. English language--Rhetoric--Study and teaching. 2. Essay--Authorship--Study and teaching. 3. Report writing--Study and teaching. I. Title.
  PE1471.B54 2008
  808'.042071--dc22
                              2008019682

Cover image: World Wide Web XXL © 2007 by Kativ. Used by permission.
Cover design by David Blakesley.
Printed on acid-free paper.

Parlor Press, LLC is an independent publisher of scholarly and trade titles in print and multimedia formats. This book is available in paper, cloth and Adobe eBook formats from Parlor Press on the World Wide Web at http://www.parlorpress.com or through online and brick-and-mortar bookstores. For submission information or to find out about Parlor Press publications, write to Parlor Press, 816 Robinson St., West Lafayette, Indiana, 47906, or e-mail editor@parlorpress.com.

To writers worldwide in this universe unbounded,
especially Martin Bloom

Contents

Acknowledgments *ix*

Introduction *3*

Part I On Essays and Other Heartbreaking Works of Staggering Genius *9*

1 Academic Essays and the Vertical Pronoun *11*

2 The Essay Canon *25*

3 The Essayist in—and behind—the Essay: Vested Writers, Invested Readers *56*

4 Compression—When Less Says More *71*

Part II: Teaching Writing in—and Out of—Troubled Times *77*

5 Writing Textbooks in/for Times of Trauma *79*

6 The Great Process Paradigm and Its Legacy for the Twenty-First Century *92*

7 The Ineluctable Elitism of Essays and Why They Prevail in First-Year Composition Courses *108*

8 Good Enough Writing *123*

Part III: Ethical Issues of Teaching and Writing   *137*

9 The Good, the Bad, and the Ugly: Ethical Principles for Dealing with Students and Student Writing in Teachers' Publications—and in the Abyss Beyond   *139*

10 Insider Writing: Plagiarism-Proof Assignments   *163*

11 Negotiating the Grading Contract: No More Lobbying, Bullying or Crying   *172*

Appendix 1 (Ch. 2, The Essay Canon): Shortened Version of Bibliography of Canonical Readers   *181*

Appendix 2 (Ch. 2): Table 1. The Essay Canon   *183*

Appendix 3 (Ch. 10): Writing in the Manner of Thoreau (and Other Nature Writers)   *187*

Appendix 4 (Ch. 11): The Grading Contract Itself   *189*

Notes   *195*

Works Cited   *205*

About the Author   *221*

Index   *223*

Acknowledgments

One of the acknowledgments that composition studies has changed from a narrowly bounded field to one without borders was the creation of the Aetna Chair of Writing at the University of Connecticut, which has been my privilege to hold since its inception in 1988. I have enjoyed particular support from UConn colleagues and administrators, among them Veronica Makowsky, Ross MacKinnon, Robert Tilton, and Thomas Deans. Penelope Pelizzon read the manuscript with a keen eye and generous spirit.

The Aetna Endowment, the English department, and the College of Liberal Arts and Sciences of the University of Connecticut have provided a series of superb research assistants during the decade of work on this book: Kathrine Aydelott, Denise M. Lovett, Matthew Simpson, Valerie Smith, and Jenny Spinner. Their exacting work, including unerring research accuracy, unsparing critical sense, and their own experience as teachers and writers, has made my work infinitely easier and much better. Lori Corsini-Nelson, Writing Programs Specialist, has helped throughout the decade of this research in compiling and refining the essay canon data, keeping the paper flow on target and on time, and the intricate nuances of computer usage up to date. The essay canon research was partially funded by a research grant from the National Council of Teachers of English.

Editors of journals and books in which many of these essays have appeared include Elizabeth Blackburn-Brockman, Shane Borrowman, John Boe, Barbara Couture, Robert Con Davis, Donald A. Daiker, Caroline Eisner, Patricia M. Gantt, Thomas Kent, Lynn Langer Meeks, Louise Z. Smith, Patrick Sullivan, John Paul Tassoni, William H. Thelin, Howard Tinberg, Martha Vicinus, and Edward M. White. Several have been friends and collaborators over the ever-changing course of our professional lives; all have enlarged the range of the field, and perspectives on it.

Parlor Press has been a pleasure to work with. David Blakesley, Catherine Hobbs, and Tracy Clark managed the various stages of editing with perspicacity, precision, and wit.

Martin Bloom, social psychologist, professor, and now artist, has been my best critic and best friend even before we married at the beginning of our doctoral work. That he has remained so for the fifty happy years that have followed indicates not a marriage of true minds but a recognition that debate and dissension are the basis not only of a humanistic dialogue but of conversation exhilarating enough to last a lifetime.

University of Connecticut
November 2007

Credits

The author gratefully acknowledges permission to reprint or adapt essays in this book from these sources:

"Compression--When Less Says More." appeared originally in *Pedagogy* 4.2 (Spring): 300-304. © 2004 by Duke University Press. Used by permission. All rights reserved.

"Academic Essays and the Vertical Pronoun" appeared originally in *LIT: Literature Interpretation Theory* 16.4 (2005): 417-30. © 2005 by Taylor & Francis Group. Used by permission.

"The Essay Canon" appeared originally in *College English* 61.4 (Mar. 1999): 401-30. © 1999 by NCTE. Used by permission.

"Good Enough Writing" appeared originally in *What Is 'College Level Writing?* Ed. Patrick Sullivan and Howard Tinberg. Urbana, IL: NCTE, 2006. 71-91. © 2006 by NCTE. Used by permission.

"The Great Process Paradigm and Its Legacy for the Twenty-First Century" originally appeared in *Composition Studies in the New Millennium: Rereading the Past, Rewriting the Future.* Ed. Bloom, Daiker, and White. © by the Board of Trustees, Southern Illinois University; reproduced by permission of Southern Illinois University Press.

"Writing Textbooks in/for Times of Trauma" is reprinted by permission from *Trauma and the Teaching of Writing* edited by Shane Borrowman, the State University of New York Press. © 2005 State University of New York. All rights reserved.

"The Essayist In—and Behind—The Essay: Vested Writers, Invested Readers" originally appeared in *The Private, the Public, and the Published: Reconciling Private Lives and Public Rhetoric.* Ed. Barbara Couture and Thomas Kent. Logan, UT: Utah State UP, 2004. 94-111. © Utah State University Press. Reprinted by permission.

Continued on page 222.

Writers Without Borders

Introduction

> *"For the survivor, writing is . . . a duty. Camus calls it 'an honor.' . . . Not to transmit an experience is to betray it. . . . I write to help the dead vanquish death."*
>
> —Elie Wiesel, "Why I Write"

A word on the title. Writers Without Borders can be conceived of in many senses. Creative writers, the writers whose work we read, remember, quote, and read again, set the agenda and determine the arena—the entire world, the universe unbounded to be created ever anew. In this respect, writers without borders—you guessed it—are analogous to Doctors Without Borders—free-spirited, principled risk takers willing to send their edgy writing to "the most remote or dangerous parts of the world" in order to end suffering and promote justice and human understanding, independent of vested "political, economic, or religious interests" (Doctors without Borders). In a similar spirit, the phenomenon of writing in a digital age means that writing itself is never permanent, never finished; it is a fluid medium without and beyond the borders of conventional print documents.

The literary canon, too, is destabilized and reshaped by political and social issues, as well as concerns of ethics, aesthetics, and pedagogy. What we teach and write and how we perform these most meaningful endeavors assume very different dimensions in today's world dominated by post 9/11 politics and the Internet than they did in the previous quarter-century. "For the survivor, writing is," indeed, as Wiesel says, "a duty," and "'an honor.'" The book's eleven chapters provide a contemporary dialogue—and the basis for debate—on the nature of essays, and on the political, philosophical, ethical, and pragmatic considerations that influence how we read, write, and teach them.

Part I. On Essays and Other Heartbreaking Works of Staggering Genius

"Never lose a holy curiosity," said Einstein, and indeed we in the academy take little for granted. For instance, we continually question the premises underlying our work. What is an essay, anyway? How do we ourselves write? What is it we're teaching, exactly? What do we want our students to know and learn and be able to do? The essays in Part 1—and indeed throughout this book—address these interrelated issues.

Chapter 1, "Academic Essays and the Vertical Pronoun," explains how academic writing is currently transcending its conventional boundaries, as writers in many disciplines have begun in the past two decades to write academic prose in what Scott Russell Sanders calls "the singular first person," with a distinctive human voice and individual personality. This engaging writing is particularly important when the prevailing alternative is voiceless, faceless academic prose born, as essayist William H. Gass says, for "immediate burial in a Journal" (26). As my analysis reveals, lightening up in style does, however, not mean lightening up in thought or in seriousness of purpose or subject; only that the writing is accessible to a much wider audience, and more memorable. Indeed, as I elaborate in Chapter 3, "The Essayist in—and Behind—the Essay," even though the personae and voices of superstar essayists, such as Virginia Woolf and George Orwell, seem individual and intimate does not mean they are necessarily either autobiographical or confessional. The intensely felt presence of the distinctive essayist within the essay is under the writer's firm control, as is any aspect of an exceptional artistic production—an ethos comprised of the author's ethical and intellectual stance toward the subject and perhaps the world, manifested in the essayist's characteristic voice and literary style.

Writers whose work presents the voices and personae we remember have a shot at becoming canonical. Chapter 2, "The Essay Canon," addresses my identification and analysis of the essay canon. Essays are reprinted primarily in college textbooks. Thus, the essay canon is a pedagogical canon, empirically derived, consisting of the 175 essays most frequently reprinted in America's most widely used textbooks; *Readers 1946–1996* covers the fifty-year span extending from the end of World War II to the beginning of the widespread use of the Internet. Here I identify the canon and its superstars, including E. B. White, Joan

Didion, Henry David Thoreau, Annie Dillard, and Martin Luther King, Jr. I explore the attributes that make these writers the textbook editors' and teachers' perennial favorites because their work is not only memorable in subject and distinctive in style, but eminently teachable to the millions of American college students exposed to this core of a liberal education. In Chapter 4, "Compression," I analyze a 252-word section of one of my own essays, compressed from the original twenty-one pages of preliminary writing, to demonstrate to students one way to attain authorial command—and power. Saying less trusts readers to understand more.

PART II. TEACHING WRITING IN—AND OUT OF—TROUBLED TIMES

Anything can happen, the tallest things
Be overturned, those in high places daunted,
Those overlooked esteemed.

—Seamus Heaney, "Horace and the Thunder"

"We tell ourselves stories in order to live."

—Joan Didion

Canonical boundaries, no matter how eclectic, how elastic, can never contain the subject matter of composition courses, which indeed encompass the world. Chapter 5, "Writing Textbooks in/for Times of Trauma" discusses the rationale for expecting students to read and write about inescapable issues of international terrorism, leavened by commentary on international peace, as exemplified in Nobel Peace Prize speeches. We tell ourselves stories of cataclysmic events such as the events of 9/11, and now of the ongoing conflicts in Iraq, Israel, and Iran to make sense of things that don't make sense, to bring, as Joan Didion implies, order from chaos. As time passes we are still trying to figure out what stories to tell, for the narratives of that fateful day and its aftermath remain stories-in-progress, stories seen through a glass darkly with complicated beginnings, muddled middles, and ambiguous trails that are not really endings. The sense of destabilization persists, as Seamus Heaney's "Horace and the Thunder," written as a commentary on 9/11, continues to remind us.

Even as we write on this freighted topic, as teachers we must necessarily address new language and new ideas, strive to avoid polarizing attitudes, and consider ethical issues embedded in concepts which themselves need continual definition: *patriotism, freedom, humanitarianism, justice,* and *creativity.* For irrespective of subject matter, composition teachers' primary concern is now, as it has been throughout the past two centuries, how to help students write better. And better. And better still. In Chapter 6, "The Great Paradigm Shift and Its Legacy for the Twenty-First Century," I explain why the process paradigm developed in the 1960s remains the default model for teaching writing: invent-write-revise, with recursive opportunities at any stage until the final edit is reached. This model pervades the textbooks, and has generated some of the most ground breaking research, including that of Elbow, Flower, Murray, and Rose. No matter what theoretical language we use to label our current era, we are still wedded to process. Chapter 7, "The Ineluctable Elitism of Essays and Why They Prevail in First-Year Composition Courses," explains why the academy favors elitist reading matter, literature of intellectual complexity and fine art aesthetics, in freshman composition, as in more advanced courses. The belletristic essays that constitute the essay canon, actual or prospective, are an elusive, elitist genre difficult to write and nearly impossible to imitate. Although, as Patricia A. Sullivan has observed, "Class is academe's dirty little secret, its last taboo, that about which we dare not speak" (239), there is considerable counter-pressure to interpret these essays, even those that discuss working class life, in terms of middle class values and experiences. Given the conservatism of many curricula, this pervasive split-level practice, using elitist material to teach middle class writing and style, seems likely to remain normative in American college composition courses for the foreseeable future. There is no viable literary alternative in an academic culture that reinforces the upwardly mobile aspirations and values of students and faculty alike, although real-world writing assignments embedded in service learning and other community, national, even international venues provide appropriate experiential balance.

Writers Without Borders interrogates how we teach, as well as what we read. As English teachers, we often conceive of ourselves as the ultimate defenders of the standards that our professional literature endorses: critical thinking, adequate development, Standard English, conventional grammar, expression appropriate to context and audience. Yet, as analyzed in Chapter 8, "Good Enough Writing," we may be deceiving ourselves. Evidence from normative grades and grading practices nationwide indicates that, on pragmatic grounds, most teachers will settle for "Good Enough Writing," student essays sufficiently normative in substance and style to warrant B grades. These papers, often dull and conformist, are characterized by a clutch of Academic Virtues, among them Rationality, Conventionality, Order, Cleanliness, and Modesty in form and style; we reward them, as well, for Punctuality, another Virtue. If we accept these norms, have we reconceived what it means to write acceptably? Have we caved on quality? Have we stopped encouraging our students to take risks, in substance or in style? Given up trying to help students see the possibilities for humanistic understanding, social action in their writing? Are we simply taking the easy way out in an academic universe where lawsuits for higher grades lurk at the drop of a GPA?

PART III. ETHICAL ISSUES OF TEACHING AND WRITING

There are no sure-fire solutions, either, for the complicated ethical issues embedded in teaching and writing know no borders—and have no fail-safe solutions. If these are not new, then they are certainly newly-configured in contemporary times. Questions of intellectual property, for instance, have been with us since writing became a paying profession in the eighteenth century. But what does it mean to write today, in the pervasive presence of electronic media, with their ever-changing capability? Who owns the words, the literature, the images that circulate so rapidly and freely on the Internet? Often, these have no identifiable authors, multiple authors with indistinct identity, or pseudonyms. Who should be acknowledged? Under what circumstances? What if a source website gets taken down—can student authors prove its existence? How do the questions themselves, and their innumerable and complicated answers, bear on how we teach writing in the twenty-first century? Student, and perhaps faculty, understanding of the nature of writing, including use and citation of sources, have undergone changes that I address in Chapter 10, "Insider Writing: Plagiarism-Proof Assignments," and Chapter 11, "Negotiating the Grading Contract." Both provide innovative ways to enable students to concentrate on tasks essential to any writing class—thinking, writing, revising—and free the teacher to focus on these, as well, instead of becoming a plagiarism sleuth.

The contemporary climate of media candor, from confessional talk shows to blogs, Facebook, MySpace, LiveJournal, and other popular forms of instant self-representation, create possibilities for a classroom climate that is open to self-revelation. As I explain in Chapter 9, "The Good, the Bad, and the Ugly: Ethical Principles for Representing Students and Student Writing in Teachers' Publications—and in The Abyss Beyond," most teachers know most of the time how to deal appropriately with most student papers. We understand the good and the bad; these (we hope, more good than bad) comprise most of the papers we see throughout most academic terms, year in and year out. But those truly ugly papers—transgressive writings in which students confess to self- and substance abuse, or horrendous anti-social acts (assault, rape, even murder) without a sense of ethical responsibility or acknowledgment of community (if not legal) standards—present their teachers with an ethical morass. We can't restrict our comments to organization, development, and grammar. For teachers have ethical and legal obligations to deal with troublesome confession, misrepresentation, deceit, and other deadly serious issues, even though current professional guidelines, such as those provided by CCCC, are inadequate to the task. I offer ethical principles here to address these grave matters, though particularly in light of Seung-Hui Cho's massacre at Virginia Tech in April 2007, there is no closure on the subject.

And so this Introduction remains open-ended, like the subject itself. Writers Without Borders, actual writers as well as the title of this book, will continue to confront the conventional, to transcend the predictable. In the spirit of Elie Wiesel, writers retain this obligation to speak out, not for the sake of nonconformity but for the sake of humanity.

Part I

On Essays and Other Heartbreaking
Works of Staggering Genius

1 Academic Essays and the Vertical Pronoun

Welcome

A bunch of us were sitting around on the porch of the House of Theory, enjoying the cool breeze, a glass of Pinot Grigio, and swapping stories in actual words—neither langue, nor parole—of the good old, bad old days. Cathy and Jane and Marianna and Alice. Phyllis, Nancy, Sandra, Susan . . . . Carolyn would've come, but she was busy being Amanda. And many more, men too, coming out from the shadows now, into the sun. We had been laboring for long years in that stuffy house, trying to untangle miles of syntax, to define complex abstractions with other abstractions, tired of defending ourselves against interpellation, hegemony, erasure. We were missing Julia; hoping Gayatri, and Judith too, would come out, but they remained inside. After our eyes, accustomed to the interior darkness, got used to the light that flooded the porch we realized—quelle horreur—that every last one of us was wearing black. As we tore off the turtlenecks, replacing them with pastels, prints, even plaids, in a swirl of fabrics (vive la difference!) we began to talk of the novels, poetry, nonfiction, not texts, we would read, the essays we would write. I could swear that Virginia, a mote in the middle distance, was proffering a platter of raspberries and angel food cake, sweetness and light.

On Academic Essays of the Future

"Welcome" illustrates what I predict will be the ethos for scholarly writing in the foreseeable years of the twenty-first century. It depicts some of the reasons for the movement that is already underway in academia, as more and more people turn to writing essays with persona, voice, wit, panache, intelligence, and grace. In so doing, they move away from writing conventional academic articles, particularly those bearing a heavy burden of esoteric theoretical language, their "dry dull voice . . . born," as William H. Gass says, for " immediate burial in a Journal" ("Emerson" 26), to more lively works. These may be published in academic journals, to be sure, but because they are accessible and interesting to a potentially wide readership, they may and do appear in a host of magazines little and big, niche and more general, and in newspaper op-ed pages as well.

This essay will explain why, in addition to sheer theory fatigue, personal-sounding academic essays are coming into the light. Today's essays—I am referring here primarily to short works of literary criticism—reflect a literary climate in which changes beginning in the late 1970s-early 1980s have converged in the early twenty-first century. These include: the disappearance of the New Critical ethos, whose views on the depersonalization of the author reinforced deconstruction's death of the author; the blurring of literary genres in various fields; the stylistic influences of New Journalism; the powerful presence of the personal in the mass media, including the Internet that, coupled with an argument for clarity, has carried over into the personal presence of either superstar critics or personal publication in prestigious journals. If the tastemakers can come out in the first person, so can everyone else. But, make no mistake, the vertical pronoun is not a foolproof guarantee of quality any more than a plethora of footnotes; writers whose tin ears can't hear the jazz of language, its sounds and rhythms, need to listen up.

Disappearance of the New Critical Ethos

Modernist aesthetic dominated critical taste from post-World War I to well after World War II. In "Tradition and the Individual Talent," T.S. Eliot presented the manifesto of Modernism, including the principle of authorial self-effacement and detachment from the completed work: "The progress of an artist is a continual self-sacrifice, a continual extinction of personality," a process which operates much like that of a catalyst, in which "the mind of the poet is the shred of platinum. . . . The more perfect the artist, the more completely separate in him will be the man who suffers and the mind which creates; the more perfectly will the mind digest and transmute the passions which are its material" (539–40). That this stance misleadingly presents knowledge (whether critical, historical, or scientific) as an objective phenomenon, independent of its human origin, is a deception so ingrained in the habits of writers and readers that they forget the fact that all knowledge is generated, interpreted, filtered, and shaped by personal agency and personal agenda. Nevertheless, this concept of ordered, highly structured, depersonalized writing provided the critical aesthetic for many strands of the critical movements in the 1970s to 1990s, epitomized in Gerald Graff's 1985 summary of the complaints against the 10 percent of academic professionals who constituted the overpoweringly influential "vanguard" literary critics in the 1980s to 1990s:

> Today, one hears the complaint that literary theory has taken over the literature departments and is distracting students and professors from literature itself. It is said that the traditional study of literature as a humanistic enterprise is in jeopardy. Instead of advancing humanistic values, literature professors are cultivating opaque jargon and pseudoscientific systems. Hiding behind smoke screens of esoteric terminology, theorists turn their backs on outsiders, including most students, and carry on endless private conversations with other theorists. Literary works have been demoted to secondary importance, serving as mere occasions for displays of theoretical agility. ("The University" 62)

But the critical landscape has changed in the twenty-first century, with the de-frocking of deMan for his Nazi sympathies, irritation with Lacan, the death of Derrida and, some argue, the death of theory itself. Faculty and students alike are eager to return to passionate readings of the literature they were once enamored of, rather than to approach beloved works through a thicket of theory (see Phyllis Rose, passim). As we shall see, their own writing now seems decidedly Romantic in self-expression and sensibility, the Wordsworthian "spontaneous overflow of powerful feelings," with the twist that the emotion is recollected not necessarily in tranquility, but in the heat of the moment.

Blurred Genres

Academics should be receptive to blurred genres; they invented them in the latter twentieth century. In "Blurred Genres" (1983) Clifford Geertz observed the "enormous amount of genre mixing in intellectual life": "philosophical inquiries looking like literary criticism (think of . . . Sartre on Flaubert), scientific discussions looking like belles lettres *morceaux* (Lewis Thomas, Loren Eiseley) . . . documentaries that read like true confessions (Mailer) . . . theoretical treatises set out as travelogues (Lévi-Strauss) . . . methodological polemics got up as personal memoirs (James Watson)" (19–20). To which we could add the crossover experiments of Barthes's *Mythologies* and *S/Z*, and Federman's *Critifiction*. As Geertz implied, no single set of literary features (persona, form, style, and a host of narrative techniques) remained the exclusive property of a particular genre; contemporary authors could pick and choose among genres as they wished. As Geertz explains in *Works and Lives,* memorable anthropologists of the twentieth century—Lévi-Strauss, Evans-Pritchard, Malinowski, and Benedict—so individually and distinctively "transfigure their observations of other people and places into such persuasive rhetoric" that afterward the subjects are "unimaginable except through the texts of their authors" (Behar, "Vulnerable Observer" 7). So powerful is the effect of the anthropologist's writing on the subject that, says Geertz, "One can go look at Azande again, but if the complex theory of passion, knowledge, and causation that Evans-Pritchard said he discovered there isn't found, we are more likely to doubt our own powers than we are to doubt his—or perhaps simply to conclude that the Zande are no longer themselves" (*Works and Lives* 5). Do not such powerful readings of other cultures strive for the same effect that critics aim for in their "strong readings"?

The New Journalism

A number of the literary features apparent in what Tom Wolfe labeled as "The New Journalism" are conspicuous in these blurred genres. What made journalism "new" from the 1960s onward was, says Wolfe, "not simply the discovery that it was possible to write accurate nonfiction with techniques usually associated with novels and short stories" (21), but the opportunity to use these techniques in dramatic and radically new combinations to make the writing intensely realistic and superlatively exciting. These devices include whole scenes and "scene-by-scene construction," extended dialogue, shifting "point-of-view, and interior monologue." Wolfe's conspicuous contribution, in addition to a mannered style that includes "the lavish use of dots, dashes, exclamation points, italics . . . interjections, shouts, onomatopoeia" and more (21), is to provide a superabundance of details symbolic "of people's *status life*" (32), thereby recording "everyday gestures, habits, manners, customs, styles of furniture, clothing, decoration, styles of traveling, eating, keeping house, modes of behavior toward children, servants, superiors, inferiors, peers" (32), what Geertz would call "thick description." By reminding readers of the distinctive, ubiquitous, ever alert authorial presence in and behind the writing, these techniques in combination give contemporary nonfiction a human angle of vision, a human voice, however demure or outrageous its register, whatever its subject.

The devices of New Journalism, particularly writing from a distinctive, identifiable personal point of view that pays excruciating attention to minutiae of the "status life" that earlier writers had previously ignored, make the writing sound extremely intimate; the writer appears to be confiding private (and not necessarily flattering) observations and telling secrets, his own or another's, to a privileged audience. Wolfe has identified multiple voices in which the characters, or the narrator, speak: dialogic, polyphonic, cacophonic, all distinctive, individual, and sounding personal even though they are carefully constructed personae revealing neither more, nor less, than the author wants the readers to know. Truman Capote, Wolfe notes with approval, employed these literary techniques throughout *In Cold Blood* (1965), his "nonfiction novel," and Wolfe exploited them with deliberate excess in *The Electric Kool-Aid Acid Test* (1968) and other nonfiction of the 1970s. Other belletristic nonfiction writers, including many essayists, have continued to use them, with varying degrees of moderation and exuberance, from that day to this. These authors range from the relatively restrained Annie Dillard (who is not above an occasional "Yikes!" in *Pilgrim at Tinker Creek*) to David Foster Wallace's strobe-lit essays on virtually everything, such as "A Supposedly Fun Thing I'll Never Do Again."

In "Getting Away from Already Being Pretty Much Away from It All," Wallace's account of ten days at the Illinois State Fair in 1993, his reportage about attending the Open Poultry Judging is characteristically Wolfean:

> now my nerve totally goes. I can't go in there. Listen to the untold thousands of sharp squawking beaks in there, I say. . . . It's 93° and I have pygmy-goat shit on my shoe and am almost weeping with fear and embarrassment. . . . I've never before realized that "cacophony" was onomatopoeic: the noise of the Poultry Bldg. [sic] is cacophonous and scrotum-tightening and totally horrible. I think it's what insanity must sound like. No wonder madmen clutch their heads and scream. There's also a thin stink, and lots of bits of feather are floating all over. And this is *outside* the Poultry Bldg. . . . When I was eight, at the Champaign County Fair, I was pecked without provocation, flown at and pecked by a renegade fowl, savagely, just under the right eye, the scar of which looks like a permanent zit. (109)

Wallace's sharply detailed rendering of the Poultry Building as Grand Guginol, where the insane noise of "untold thousands of sharp squawking beaks" and noxious smells strike fear not into the narrator's cowardly heart but his scrotum, is a reminder of his "savage" victimization by "a renegade fowl" when he was eight. Why is the author, whose trust and authority readers expect to esteem, presenting himself not as an anti-hero but as a wimp? Why does he tell us these humiliating details? Certainly not as a warning to stay away from domestic poultry; in fact, the very specificity of the account re-creates the scene so exactly that the readers are cheek-by-fowl with Wallace as tour guide through State Fair hell, and must perforce take his side, sharing his values for the moment if not for all time.

The Powerful Presence of the Personal in the Mass Media

Nonfiction of all sorts, including many straight news pieces even in the formerly staid *New York Times,* incorporates many of the New Journalistic techniques, though they are often more restrained than in David Foster Wallace's work. There are cultural reasons why personal-sounding nonfiction—whether exaggerated, as is Wallace's, or more subdued—is so pervasive and so popular. Nonfiction is being written today from a human perspective with a sense of human presence; such writing, including academic writing, appears both more informal and more personal than ever. As in dress, essays have moved from modernist three piece suits with matching hats and handkerchiefs to jeans and t-shirts; from "trousers rolled" by one who dares to "walk along the beach" to bikinis and bare feet. Contemporary essays leave a trail of footprints rather than footnotes. The essay, the most informal, always, of genres has become—in some ways—even more informal in its contemporary presentation of the authorial persona as the reader's intimate friend and confidante. Of comparable influence to the pervasiveness of New Journalistic techniques in print media is the personal orientation of television and many Internet sites.

We live in an age of media intimacy; personal exposure is now the normative mode because of the invasive influences of television and the Internet. The private has become public, as attested by the sad but inspiring autobiographies on Oprah, confessions of televangelical sin, real-time paternity tests, Judge Judy's no-nonsense interpretations of individual guilt and innocence, "extreme makeovers," "reality" television that captures people at their weakest and worst. When played out on the Internet, the individual's fifteen minutes of fame can extend indefinitely, through webcams that allow voyeuristic viewers access to a formerly private person, twenty-four hours a day for months at a time. Anybody and everybody can write their electronic autobiography, and millions do. Personal websites and blogs allow their authors to present themselves any way they want, in text, music, photographs, and video—looking for love in all the right (or wrong) places; becoming pregnant (or not) or parents; playing games; hating (rarely loving) their jobs; experiencing spirituality, disability, disaster, war; undergoing sex changes or other sea changes—divorce, homelessness, bereavement. Chat rooms extend the intimacy. That there is a sufficient amount of fiction amidst the nominal facts to keep viewers continually on their guard does not diminish the ever-increasing attraction of the media. No longer do intimate photographs appear primarily in *People Magazine* and the supermarket tabloids; larger than life images pulsate up close and personal on the 64-inch plasma screens in our very bedrooms.

Cinema, television, and the Internet have had major influences on print media, particularly in the past decade. They have influenced visual dimensions that appear in the printed text: photographs, paintings, drawings, color, white space, layout and design. In this supercharged environment it would be hard for essayists (like all other writers), even authors of academic articles, *not* to sound more personal and informal in the twenty-first century than they did in the twentieth. Even if a particular essayist never watched movies or TV and ignored the Internet, the visual and verbal influences of these media on highbrow publications, among them *Harper's, The Atlantic, The New York Times*,[1] and some academic journals, including the prestigious *PMLA*, are pervasive and inescapable. So there is more latitude, simply by means of the prevailing cultural climate, for writers who might have been more reticent in the far more discreet Victorian or Edwardian literary eras to present very human, intimate personae a century later.

What, Me, a Human Being? Personal Academic Writing

By the 1980s, academic writers—at least, some with tenure who could afford the risk—began to come out as human beings, usually in less flamboyant ways than Wallace, but in style and orientation that seemed daring to scholars trained to consider the vertical pronoun taboo. Academics who write in a personal style understand very well that their human approach does not mean that academic essays are either simple-minded or innocent of theory, just that they are far more accessible than those written with large amounts of technical jargon, or in dense theoretical language and its accompanying unending syntax. Surprisingly, a *de facto* coalition of feminist scholars, linguists, and neo-cons agree—through pronouncement and performance—that postmodern criticism, for instance, is both unintelligible and undemocratic, as Susan Peck MacDonald argues in "The Literary Argument and Its Discursive Conventions." MacDonald concludes, if "professional prose is so specialized that too small a circle of insiders can read it," if "novice professors and even seasoned professors" and students "have trouble gaining access because they find prestigious prose to be either unreadable or unwritable," "not because of the demands of the subject, but because it is professionally advantageous to appear 'difficult,' then we ought to stop awarding prestige to unreadable prose, and we ought to consider the social implications of reinforcing an elite caste system within our profession" (59).

The language itself of many contemporary academic essays is in fact returning to the clarity, simplicity, and honesty that George Orwell advocated in "Politics and the English Language," inveighing against "pretentious diction," jargon, other language designed to mask bias, sloppy thinking, bad ideas, and other forms of political manipulation. "The great enemy of clear language is insincerity," he said. "Political language . . . is designed to make lies sound truthful and murder respectable" (958–67). "What would Orwell say about X?" is a familiar, not-so-rhetorical question, of commentators of all rhetorical and political persuasions. Thus, in "So Help Me God," an analysis of fifty-four presidential inaugural addresses, Ted Widmer, National Security Council director of speechwriting during the Clinton administration, declares "Politics" as "the greatest essay on speechwriting ever written." In support of this, he quotes the "lies sound truthful and murder respectable" (40–41) sentence.

From a post-postmodernist, neo-conservative perspective, Stephen K. Roney, past president of the Editors' Association of Canada, uses Orwell's precepts, including the same "lies/murder" sentence, to undercut the stylistic propositions of postmodern critic Judith Butler, whom he is careful to identify at the outset as having not only "been charged with bad writing but also as having "won the annual 'Bad Writing Award' from the journal *Philosophy and Literature.*" In propositions adopted widely throughout the 1980s and 1990s in the writings of academics MacDonald labels "vanguard" or elitist literary critics (such as Frederic Jameson and Gayatri Chakravorty Spivak, also winners of the "Bad Writing Award"), Butler claims that "clarity and simplicity are impossible if one is discussing a topic deeply." Difficult ideas "must necessarily be expressed in difficult language." Obscurity, rather than clarity, "is the proper medium to represent the obscure." It is "*necessary to use bad style to be a good thinker*" (all Roney's paraphrases, 13–20). Illustrating throughout this critique his understanding of Orwell's views that obfuscating language is a "rhetorical trick; a way for bad ideas to hide . . . an obscure style is always a hindrance," Roney concludes that "Butler's challenge to Orwell cannot be justified on the grounds she has stated. Obscurity of style is still . . . and necessarily, a bad thing in itself. As for the true significance of the obscurity characteristic of postmodernism, I would only suggest that it is a symptom, not of a progressive or enlightened position, but of a vested interest seeking to secure its privilege" (21). That critics from potentially antagonistic ends of the critical spectrum, MacDonald as a liberal linguist, Roney writing in the journal of academic arch-conservatives, the

National Association of Scholars, as well as Widmer in a centrist position, concur philosophically in their analyses may indeed signal, if not "the death of theory," then "the death of obscure academic discourse as we know it" and an indication that the academy is ripe for another kind of writing that is not only clear, but personal.

Recent academic essays seem smart in their intellectual range, depth of learning, and verbal wit rather than because of either obscure language or an abundance of citations, which diminish as essays grow more informal and authors trust their readers to get the point. Titles, too, become shorter. If the author relies on a few short, simple, perhaps witty or shocking words (read on!) to carry the freight, she is likely to skip the semicolon and its string of explanatory language. In "Me and My Shadow" (1987), Jane Tompkins initiated a vigorous defense of personal writing by lambasting the academic convention, "the public-private dichotomy, which is to say the public-private *hierarchy*" that had hitherto isolated her as a private person from her public writing: "I say the hell with it. The reason I feel embarrassed at my own attempts to speak personally in a professional context is that I have been conditioned [by men] to feel that way" (1104). Tompkins's prominence as a feminist critic assured notoriety to her other audacious confessions, among them that while meditating on the suicide of a young female colleague she was "thinking about going to the bathroom. But not going yet" (1107). This essay provoked a storm of controversy, neatly summed up by her champion, Nancy K. Miller, in "Getting Personal": "How can women get power from this . . . self-indulgen[ce] . . . Is [her essay] about going to the bathroom? Or is it about critical authority? Or are they the same question?" (8). Miller also sagely observes, in a biographical aside a truth that would have been taboo among New Critics and postmodernists alike: "One could argue that the [effect of the critic's authority] depends on the status of the writer. No one would care if Jane Doe went to the bathroom: it matters that Jane Tompkins is a known critical quantity, that (some) people will know that she is married" to (27) an even more prominent literary provocateur, the astute—and flamboyant—Stanley Fish. Defending such intimate personal commentary, Miller concludes that it "embodies a pact . . . binding writer to reader in the fabulation of self-truth, that what is at stake matters to others: somewhere in the self-fiction of the personal voice is a belief that the writing is worth the risk" (24). Carrying out the logical implications of her defense, Miller soon published

"My Father's Penis" (1991), thereby exceeding Tompkins' daring in her very title.

As academic critics, women in the forefront, rushed to take up the challenge, a landmark essay in a personal style appeared in 1989, Susan J. Leonardi's "Recipes for Reading: Summer Pasta, Lobster ? la Riseholme, and Key Lime Pie." Unusual for academic journals, "Recipes" is distinguished by its gracious persona, graceful style, traditionally feminine subject, unusual structure, total absence of footnotes, and paucity of sources—seven of the mere eleven "Works Cited" are primary texts. Leonardi's wit, too, is verging on mockery but not going there yet. Most important of all, however, "Recipes" is distinguished particularly by its locus of publication. That such a glamorous, groundbreaking work was published in *PMLA,* the most prestigious modern languages journal of its time in America, known for intellectual rigor and decades of male hegemony (including male editors), speaks volumes. How astonishing to find "Recipes," its intellectual daring, theory, and conceptual sophistication couched in thoroughly accessible language, dancing cheek-to-cheek with a clutch of *PMLA*'s customary, heavily theoretical articles, including " [T]he Self-Destruction of Modern Scientific Criticism," "Foucault's Oriental Subtext," and "Baudelaire's Theory of Practice."

"Recipes" begins with—quel surprise—a recipe, for "summer pasta, lovely, sophisticated, delicious,"adjectives that apply, as well, to the authorial persona. How odd—and how welcoming—to be invited to relax ("Let [the pasta] sit for a minute or two if you're not in a hurry, toss again, and serve.") and to indulge one's own tastes ("You can leave anything out of this recipe except the pasta and the olive oil.") as a way of making Leonardi's topic one's own: "the giving of a recipe" and its "interesting relationships to both reading and writing" (340). How startling for Leonardi's feminist literary analysis to begin with Irma Rombauer's use of rhetorical strategies in the canonical *Joy of Cooking.* But is a cookbook in the wrong (i.e. not literary) canon? After establishing a social community of women cooks and analyzing their behavior as readers and writers of recipes, Leonardi moves to similar considerations in E.F. Benson's Mapp and Lucia volumes and Nora Ephron's *Heartburn.* The author concludes by anticipating readers' potentially antagonistic questions: "What importance, after all, can recipes have to the reading, writing mind?"; echoing Tompkins— "Would the tensions that academic women face between the domestic and the professional make it more or less difficult for them to extend credibility toward a writer who begins with a recipe?"; and "Do I erode my credibility with male academics by this feminine interest in cooking, cookbooks, and recipes?" But her last question echoes her initial invitation, "And, finally, will you try my summer pasta?" (347). Who could resist?

The generally enthusiastic response reinforced *PMLA*'s editorial decision to publish Leonardi's essay, and gratified the author, who had taken the risk as an untenured assistant professor to submit to this "typically staid, dignified publication" a piece to which *PMLA*'s readers' initial reaction was "'the editors have gone mad'; 'this must be the April issue and it's an April Fools' Day joke'; 'they got mixed up and bound the wrong innards inside these sedate *PLMA* covers.'" However, the correspondent, R. Baird Shuman, at the time a senior professor at the University of Illinois, Urbana, and respected critic, goes on: "I was absolutely dazzled by it. The piece is brilliant in every respect, combining valuable information on literacy embedding with feminist matters, with issues of kinship, with an analysis of symbolism" and much more. Shuman ends with congratulations to *PMLA* for being "willing to take a chance on a contribution as far out of the ordinary" as this (904). M. Thomas Inge, Blackwell Professor of the Humanities at Randolph-Macon College reiterates, "The Editorial Board is to be congratulated for its breadth of vision in approving for publication Susan J. Leonardi's excellent essay. Seldom have methodology, form, style and content been so beautifully integrated in an article for *PMLA*, the first one I have wanted to read in ten years" (904).

If Leonardi could do it backwards and in high heels in *PMLA*, other academics, men, as well as women, could publish personal-sounding essays. By the early 1990s, the floodgates were opening in literary criticism (though Leonardi's triumph did not signal a revolution in the usual *PMLA* article) as in numerous other academic fields: anthropology (Clifford Geertz, Ruth Behar), law (Patricia Williams), medicine (Oliver Sacks, Richard Selzer), linguistics (Deborah Tannen), computer science (Paul De Palma), information technology (Sven Birkerts), education (Shirley Brice Heath, Mike Rose, Howard Gardner), the sciences (Stephen Jay Gould, Isaac Asimov); and the academy more generally as in such essay collections as C.L. Barney Dews and Carolyn Leste Law, *This Fine Place So Far From Home: Voices of Academics from the Working Class;* Alan Shepard et al, *Coming to Class:*

Pedagogy and the Social Class of Teachers; Deborah H. Holdstein and David Bleich, *Personal Effects: The Social Character of Scholarly Writing;* Jan Z. Schmidt, *Women/Writing/Teaching;* and Diane Freedman and Olivia Frey, *Autobiographical Writing Across the Disciplines.* These writers and many more, trained in scholarly disciplines, have become accomplished at communicating ideas, however complex, by means of a human persona who writes without jargon.

A single example must serve as a synecdoche for this extensive body of contemporary work. In analyzing the impact of parenthood on his writing, Jeffrey Nesteruk's brief "Fatherhood, in Theory and Practice," published in the *Chronicle of Higher Education* 2005, makes explicit the ways many academic personal essayists conceive of style, rhetorical strategy, subject, and nature of their intended audience. Nesteruk, a professor of legal studies at Franklin and Marshall University, explains that before he became a father he used to develop "lofty thoughts" in his "intellectual sanctuary," his den, door closed, "deepening an intellectual insight, tracing a complex chain of logic, sifting carefully through conflicting bodies of evidence." His daughter's birth, three years earlier, opened that door as it humanized the author's style and altered his rhetorical strategy. Now, he says, "both my scholarship and writing have become more personal, more revealing. I tell stories along with arguing doctrine. . . . I also say things more provisionally. I let more of my uncertainties onto the page." Echoing Leonardi's invitation he explains, "I'm less interested in winning an argument than in starting a conversation. . . . I want to give everyone, especially my critics, their due" (B5; see also Frey, "Beyond Literary Darwinism").

The existential demands of parenthood have influenced Nesteruk's choice of subject, as well. Reminded daily by his daughter of "how precious life is," he wants to concentrate on "enduring, basic questions" rather than "the latest academic trend or controversy." Thus, he now composes essays "for larger academic audiences" and—because "having a child immerses you in a world of wider connections"—"the general public." In this more interconnected world, constraining "disciplinary boundaries . . . are slowly losing their sway." Fatherhood, like the "struggles of scholarship," first fragmented the author's world and "then put it back together in new ways," making him, like his young daughter, open to seeing and learning anew (B5), exactly the way most creative writers function.

INVITATION

You're invited to join us essayists on the porch; there's plenty of room. If it gets too crowded, we'll build a House of Essays; we'll use I-beams. Anyone—theorists, included—willing to trade the language of dialogics, utterance, intertextuality, and the "anxiety of influence" for the friendly conversation of humankind, on any subject, is more than welcome. You'll need to be ready to present your specialist's knowledge with voice, panache, and a broad perspective, in language that doesn't grind gears on the uphill climb but sails up in overdrive. Feel free to bring your laptop, food, spouse, children, pets, the comforts of home and—dare I say, traces?—of life's messiness and uncertainty that may even appear in your writing, as long as they suit your subject, in style and in substance. For, like Tompkins, Leonardi and Nestruk, in the vertical pronoun you'll be inviting readers into your own wondrous world, to engage in a hospitable, collaborative dialogue rather than competition to see who can score the most esoteric points. This writing will be very hard work; "we must labour to be beautiful," as Yeats reminds us in "Adam's Curse." But it will be the best fun you've ever had, I promise you. You'll get fan mail along with citations. Write—and see.

2 The Essay Canon

This study began with two seemingly simple questions, "What essays do people read and where?"[1] The short answer—and my thesis—is, "Those Americans who read essays at all find them reprinted in Readers, anthologies intended for freshman composition." No matter where an essay first appeared—in *The New Yorker* or a little magazine or a newspaper's op-ed page—if it is to survive in the hearts and minds of the contemporary American reading public it must be reprinted time and again in a composition Reader (capitalized to distinguish it from the book's human reader). This article introduces the only essay canon to be publicly identified in the twentieth century. It is a *teaching* canon as distinct from a *critical* canon.

Canon-makers make pronouncements and they make lists. Although I am not now and never have been related to any other Bloom of canonical persuasion, either Harold ("Read my list!") or Allan ("Read Great Books!"), I make the following claims. This study is the first to define this—or any—contemporary essay canon, the first to define that canon empirically rather than critically, and the first to discuss its formation, significance, status, and implications. Whether or not critics pay attention to essays, teachers do and consequently so do their students. Thus, this contemporary essay canon has profound implications—intellectual, aesthetic, pedagogical, and political—not only for what but also for how our nation's 2.2 million first-year college students read, think, and write—and for how they'll think about reading and writing for the rest of their lives. The teaching essay canon may, indeed, constitute the core of a liberal education for many of these students.

Consequently, we must bring to the forefront of our pedagogical consciousness what has to date been shoved to the dim recesses of the shelves loaded with fiction, poetry, and drama. A few essayists were assigned canonical status by scholars focusing critical and curricular attention on particular sorts of belletristic short nonfiction prose by eighteenth- and nineteenth-century white male British writers (see Golding; Rasula; McQuade), but the empirically defined essay canon depends on the sheer frequency with which particular works have appeared in a half century of Readers. It was formed by diverse post–World War II composition teachers, acting independently or in collaboration with publishers, who compiled various configurations of short nonfiction pieces to be used as stimuli for class discussions and as models for student writing—on the whole, a democratic rather than an elitist process. By making visible what our left hands have been doing in the composition classroom while our right hands are transacting the academy's literary business, my research provides the intellectual basis necessary to reexamine the common substance of the American university's most common course.

Thus, this chapter will survey the vast territory of essays—they are all over the map—and sketch out some of its major dimensions. Part 1, "Canons and the Essay Canon," explores the relation of essays to canon theory; explains why the only essay canon is a powerful teaching canon; and defines the essay canon operationally. Part 2, "Researching the Essay Canon," discusses my research method. Part 3, "How Essays Become Canonical," shows where essays live, how they arrive in the teaching canon, and why they stay there. Part 4, "The Essay Canon and Implications for Undergraduate Education," examines how essays are taught and what that teaching implies. Part 5, "The Future of the Essay Canon," concludes with a largely hopeful observation on the current status of the essay in and out of the academy. To anticipate (and to reiterate the sentiments of Chapter 1)—it is, as Joseph Epstein has observed, "a sweet time to be an essayist" ("Piece Work" 411).

1. Canons and the Essay Canon

In "Contingencies of Value," Barbara Herrnstein Smith offers an exhaustive list of the "diverse forms of evaluation" of a literary work. Among the kinds of literary canons she identifies are critical canons (which include the *historical, national,* and *cultural* canons, such as Harold Bloom's *The Western Canon,* often presented as if they were universal); the teaching canon (sometimes called *pedagogical* or *institutional*); and the economic canon (42–53). Frank Kermode sees critical canons as "strategic constructs by which societies maintain their own interests, since the canon allows control over the texts a culture takes seriously and the methods of interpretation that establish the meaning of 'serious'" (in Altieri 42). Scholars and critics create the *critical canon* through publishing reviews and criticism, rank-orderings, evaluations and re-evaluations, and by awarding prizes (B. Smith, *Contingencies,* 45–46). Because, as Alan Golding observes, "any given period has its canonical genres; its canonical critical paradigms, or ways of seeing and reading" (59), the reinterpretations and reassessments of any powerful group, or even a single individual, can produce *revisionist canons* such as that promulgated by the multi-ethnic *Heath Anthology of American Literature,* its initial selection based, as general editor Paul Lauter explains, "not on that of previous anthologies or our graduate school training" but on a survey of "a new literary world . . . . the vast range of the literary output of this country," including a great deal of nonfiction prose ("Preface," xxxv). *Pedagogical canons* live and die in anthologies, curricula, syllabi, and reading lists (B. Smith, *Contingencies,* 46; Golding 70–113; Rasula 415–69), as this chapter demonstrates with regard to the essay canon. Finally, in the larger world, best sellers constitute what might be called an *economic canon.* For instance, Oprah Winfrey's selection of a novel for her book club ensures million-dollar sales, which may make her the single most influential force in contemporary American belles lettres, the newest canon czar.

The canon, any canon, may be viewed as a map of the territory it claims to encompass. Yet, for the canon czars who have dictated the shape and scope of the critical canon of American literature during the twentieth century, essays are nowhere. Even as recently as 1970, the critical canon included only a few essays, typically literary criticism by writers distinguished in other genres, such as Ezra Pound and T. S. Eliot. Critics pay scant attention to individual essays or even to the *oeuvre* of renowned essayists. Jonathan Swift's "A Modest Proposal," the most widely reprinted essay, has been the subject of thirty-eight critical or pedagogical works in the past twenty-five years. But between 1963 and 1998, E. B. White's classic "Once More to the Lake" elicited only five critical responses, George Orwell's "Shooting an Elephant" four; most other essayists and their works remain in critical limbo (see *MLA International Bibliography,* 1963–98). The *historical canon* of nineteenth-century essayists (Lamb, De Quincey, Ruskin, Carlyle, Mill, Arnold, Pater) did not survive in the twentieth-century pedagogical canon, and has scant likelihood of reappearing in the twenty-first century.

Teachers have more influence over the canon than they may realize. For the teaching canon is constructed, says Smith, when faculty compile anthologies, construct curricula, and draw up class reading lists (*Contingencies,* 45–46) and, I would add, doctoral prelim lists—activities calculated to ensure the replication of these lists and perpetuation of the canon in subsequent generations. A literary work gains value, as Smith explains, through "repeated inclusion" in literary anthologies and on reading lists, in addition to "frequent citation or quotation by professors, scholars, and academic critics" (46). To the extent that the critics' and the teachers' judgments are congruent—as in estimates, say, of Shakespeare, Hemingway, and Faulkner—the critical canon is the same as the teaching canon. But when teachers teach material ignored or undervalued by the critics, as in the case of essays, a canon emerges that is only tangentially related to collective critical judgment.

Given the essay's absence from a large swath of our literature textbooks ("I wanted to include a whole section on belletristic essays," says the editor of one 2,500-page literature anthology, "but there wasn't enough room."), and the fitful attention essays receive from critics, how can there be an essay canon? Students in the nation's three thousand or so colleges and universities, even those who never meet a literature anthology, are almost sure to encounter essays in required composition courses, most likely in Readers. With the exception of obvious works of fiction and poetry that occasionally appear in essay anthologies, for the purposes of the subsequent analysis I am including the entire contents of these Readers—all the variant forms of nonfiction and satire that they publish. In these Readers, then, an *essay,* for practical purposes, is any piece of relatively short nonfiction prose that the book's editors select for their essay anthology—just as any piece of writing in a literature anthology is by definition *literature.* It is this operational definition that I will be using throughout the rest of my discussion of textbook Readers.

The critical definition of an essay as a short work of belletristic nonfiction that was understood throughout the formation of the nineteenth-century critical canon continues to prevail in contemporary critical discussions. From Montaigne's definition of the essay as "a trial, an attempt," through Adorno's discrimination between essays and articles, to contemporary definitions by William Gass, Wendell Harris ("Reflections"), Phillip Lopate, and others, the essay is seen as representing ideas in an associative and open-ended process of exploration and development. However, my operational definition differs from all of these. The essay canon, derived from twentieth-century canonical freshman composition Readers, contains diverse kinds of nonfiction: besides belletristic (or personal) essays and informational or programmatic essays sometimes called articles, there are a variety of other nonfiction prose forms including memoir and character sketch; travel narrative and natural history; cultural, social and political analysis or advocacy; a miscellany of philosophical statements, science writing, literary criticism, editorials, research reports; and satires and speeches. Teachers and textbooks use *essay* as a catchall term, as I do throughout this analysis. When I refer to *the essay canon*, I mean the multiple works of *essayists* rather than individual essays, with a few exceptions, following the practice used with canonical studies of poets, who are conventionally represented by multiple poems rather than single works (see Harold Bloom, 548–67; Golding; Rasula).

Indeed, most editors of canonical Readers are vague about both the term and the concept, and this is intentional. As one editor of a prominent anthology—who shall remain nameless—explained, "We try not to define *essay*. That way we don't have to debate the status of Chief Seattle's speech, the Declaration of Independence, James Thurber's fables. We're going to include them, anyway." Even those Readers, such as *The Bedford Reader* and *Subject and Strategy*, that do define *essay* typically bury the definition in a glossary. As Randall Decker laments in *Patterns of Exposition*, "[B]*ecause of the wide and loose application of the term*, no really satisfactory definition has been arrived at" (Glossary in the first 14 editions—e.g., 4th ed, 351; emphasis added). Often, editors substitute for *essay* textbooky terms such as *selections, pieces, readings, materials, prose models*.

To adopt a definition other than this pragmatic one would mean making a series of critical decisions that would override the pedagogical decisions of the Readers' editors, attempting to assess the literary merits and technical features of innumerable items treated in the textbooks as essays but of questionable status even in this protean genre. To substitute a critical canon for a pedagogical one would confound the purposes of this research. Are speeches essays? Not only the "Gettysburg Address," but "We Will Fight No More Forever"—attributed to Chief Seattle (who allegedly didn't write it)? Are political manifestos essays? Not only "The Declaration of Independence," but Martin

Luther King's "Letter from Birmingham Jail"—and is that document really a letter, even though it begins and ends like one? May parts of book chapters be treated as essays—Elizabeth Kubler-Ross's "On the Fear of Death" and Mike Rose's "'I Just Wanna Be Average'" (both titles supplied by anthologists)? What about segments of autobiographies, such as variously titled portions of Maya Angelou's *I Know Why the Caged Bird Sings* or Richard Rodriguez's *Hunger of Memory?* Or segments of essays themselves, excerpted from longer prose works, as are many anthologized pieces by Twain and Thoreau? Are editorials, op-ed pieces, straight news stories—such as Martin Gansberg's "38 Who Saw Murder and Didn't Call the Police"—essays? Are discipline-based academic articles (almost always excerpted) essays, among them Stanley Milgram's "The Perils of Obedience"? According to a strict (or even loose) belletristic definition, none of these works would "count" as essays. However, were I to be such a strict constructionist, I'd be basing my study on my *personal canon,* not a sound basis for the comprehensive scope of this analysis. So, for the operative purposes of this study, whatever is in essay anthologies that isn't poetry or fiction is an *essay*—even material that in contexts other than Readers would have a different label. That's what textbook editors and teachers call this material, an unacknowledged convention.

Length, like other dimensions of size (height, weight), has a culturally-determined sense of what is right. In an era of shrunken newspaper editorials and sound-bite-sized newsmagazines, students often feel that an essay is long if it's over ten pages. Just as contemporary poetry anthologies favor lyrics over epics, most Readers favor material that is either short to start with or that can be custom-excerpted to fit the anthology's format. (Two anthologies, *A World of Ideas* and *Ways of Reading,* are atypical, using extremely long excerpts from even longer essays and book chapters.) In practice, the possibility of excerpting means that any prose work of any length is (un)fair game. Although Woolf's *A Room of One's Own* and Thoreau's *Civil Disobedience* rank high in the canon, these long works are invariably excerpted.

Abridgments are a staple of all sorts of anthologies, not only in literature but in every academic discipline. Truncated readings appear to perturb neither students, nor teachers—perhaps themselves educated via anthologies, given the pervasiveness of "the Nortons" and "the Oxfords" in all realms of literature. In fact, Arthur Eastman, editor-in-chief of the first eight editions of *The Norton Reader,* held firm to the principle that no essay in the book should exceed 5,000 words and excerpted accordingly, although thirty-one years later his successor as editor-in-chief, Linda Peterson, abandoned this practice with the ninth edition (personal communications with Eastman and Peterson). Nevertheless, the practice of editorial surgery—and in some instances, dismemberment—continues to flourish in Readers as it does in anthologies of other literary modes. Although teachers who dislike abridgments can assign entire works, in practice it's easier to stick with the anthology *du jour*. Students fed a diet of Works Lite through elementary and high school have learned to accept abridgments as the literary norm; it is whole works that are anomalous. It could be argued that when coverage—of a period, a canon, a field, even the long works of a single author—must be accomplished in a semester or a year, a hefty anthology does the job better and cheaper than the alternatives. But can blades of grass suffice for *Leaves of Grass?*

A good case can be made, however, for reprinting integrated, relatively self-contained, sections of book-length works—most commonly, excerpts from treatises on particular subjects such as Carl Sagan's *Nuclear Winter,* Rachel Carson's *Silent Spring* and Deborah Tannen's *You Just Don't Understand,* and from autobiographies. For instance, Thoreau's "Where I Lived and What I Lived For," Frederick Douglass's "Resurrection" (recounting his liberating fistfight with the oppressive overseer, Covey), Mark Twain's "Uncle John's Farm," Malcolm X's "Hair/My First Conk," Maya Angelou's "Graduation," and Richard Rodriguez's "Aria" (can you guess which titles editors have supplied?) are typographically set off from the rest of the autobiographies in which they appear. Yet, this practice leaves us with a bizarre textual synecdoche, in which a small part of a long text attains canonical status as a self-contained work.

Researching the Essay Canon

Basis of Reader selection. To find out which essays have constituted the teaching essay canon during the last half-century, my research assistant, Valerie Smith, and I looked at Readers intended for use in freshman composition of several kinds: basic writing, regular freshman composition, discipline-based, or writing-across-the-curriculum courses.

Time span. In order to obtain complete runs of some of the most enduring Readers and thereby to assess their changes over time, we needed to go back at least to the 1960s, when the first editions of Gerald Levin's *Prose Models* (1964), Arthur Eastman's *The Norton Reader* (1965), William Smart's *Eight Modern Essayists* (1965), Randall Decker's *Patterns of Exposition* (1966), and Muscatine and Griffith's *Borzoi College Reader* (1967) appeared. However, one book led to another, and another, and another, until we decided to study Readers published throughout the entire half-century, beginning with the end of World War II. This fifty-year span was the period of many major changes in higher education: the shift from prewar elitism to postwar democracy—in admissions and ultimately in curriculum; the opening up of community colleges, urban universities, and evening and weekend programs alongside traditional four-year schools; the expansion of a college education as a right for all—including women, minorities, immigrants, first generation college students, and the underprepared. This time span also encompasses the major conceptual reorientation in teaching writing, from imitation of prose models to an emphasis on writing processes, reading, and critical thinking. It ends, in 1996, with the beginning of widespread Internet usage. Because Internet access allows teachers to compile and download their own course materials, under the radar range of researchers wanting to study their choices, 1996 is a fitting time to stop.

These changes in twentieth-century education, we reasoned, would be reflected not only in the individual Readers but also in major changes in the essay canon itself. To our surprise, we discovered that the canon itself remained surprisingly stable over those past fifty years. Harris's observations on "the glacially changing core" of canons in general—that "authors once a part of the diachronic canon retain at least a minimal cachet; they may be relegated to a canonical attic but rarely to the trash can" ("Canonicity" 113)—hold true for essays as they do for other genres of literature.

Sample. I chose to identify the canonical essayists in Readers as those who survived in enough editions for their works to have been reprinted at least twenty times. Because, as I explain below, I used an approximately 20 percent sample of the total reprints, each reprint figure you read here and in Appendix 2 should be multiplied by 5 to determine the actual reprint total.

Thus to be canonical, an essay would have actually been reprinted a minimum of one hundred times (20 x 5) 1946–1996. This was an arbitrary decision on my part in an attempt to prevent the editors of a single book (say *The Norton Reader*, with the potential for reprinting an essay in all eighteen versions) from determining the presence of a canonical item, although perforce the influence of well-established books would be great. Twenty reprints is a figure that I expected would also allow for the emergence on the list of newer authors, reflecting current concerns such as issues of gender and multiculturalism. Conceivably new, wildly popular authors could make it onto the canonical list within a year or two—though only one author did so in the 1990s by the time the study ended. Fifty new or reissued books per year, from 1970 to 1995, would have yielded a total of 1,250 Readers, containing 81,250 essays (averaging 65 per Reader)—a daunting number of books to locate. Fewer books were published in fewer editions between 1946 and 1970: a conservative estimate suggests 500 volumes, containing some 32,000 essays. Thus a fifty-year total would be about 1,750 Readers and 113,250 essays—an unwieldy body of material even if we could have found all the volumes, fugitive, forgotten, and forlorn. To complete this study before the end of this millennium—if not the next—we needed a sample.

We reasoned that not all textbooks were equally influential, and that the canon should be derived from the most influential textbooks, those published in multiple editions, presumably with sufficient course adoptions to warrant continuing publication, and continual revision to ensure adaptation to the market. Thus, we decided to examine every edition of any Reader that had been published in four or more editions between 1946 and 1996. New editions are ordinarily published three or more years apart. Thus, a canonical Reader, according to this criterion, would have been published for a dozen or more years and would presumably have enough sales to warrant these successive incarnations. Relatively large textbook sales ranging upward from 2,000–3,000 a year (not counting the elusive used book market, by 1996 global as a consequence of Internet sales) over the long term are a rough measure of a given Reader's influence. Because publishers will not reveal their sales figures, however, the number of editions must serve as an approximation. In his *Memoir* of *The Norton Reader*, Gordon Sabine estimates that the industry leader sold an astronomical 1,500,000 copies in the first eight editions—sales approximating 43,000 copies annually (100).

This selection of Readers resulted in an 18.6 percent sample of the total number of volumes (1,750) published between 1946 and 1996 These canonical Readers, 58 titles in 325 volumes, contain approximately 21,000 reprintings of some 8,000 different essay titles by 4,246 authors ("title" is not necessarily synonymous with an individual essay, because editors often retitle the works they reprint). These authors and titles have been compiled in a database from which we have derived the essay canon. The collection of Readers is ultimately destined for a composition studies archive.

Database. Appendix I identifies all the Readers in this study, arranged alphabetically by title. For simplicity's sake, I will refer in our analysis to the first edition title, despite subsequent minor alterations of titles, a few changes of editors, and (because of acquisitions and mergers) far more changes of publishers. If a book is quoted from, it is cited, editor's name first, in the *Works Cited* list.

The Readers' contents are compiled in a database that can be sorted by author (Edward Abbey to Harold Zyskind), essay title, anthology title, anthology editor, or publication date. Analysis of these categories suggests some of the factors, implicit and explicit, that have influenced the anthologists' choice and treatment of selections. According to what principles do they decide what to include and what to delete from successive editions? How do they advise students to read and write essays, in general and in particular? What apparatus do editors provide—such as rhetorical advice, organizational schema, headnotes, suggestions for reading and writing? What's in the instructor's guide? (The span of this study ends just as various electronic adaptations of Readers appear on the horizon, their effects ephemeral even a decade later; thus they are not considered here.) Space does not permit the publication here of either the entire database, which compresses into a 64-page alphabetical listing all the 4,246 authors whose works are reprinted in the canonical textbooks, or even of the complete list of 172 canonical authors. Appendix 2 is an abbreviated list of those authors whose essays have attained the canonical status of 50 or more reprints, with the short title of their most widely reprinted essay(s).

The entire canonical list consists of Supernovas (the 19 authors whose works were reprinted 100 [actually, 500—remember, we're multiplying the 20 percent sample by 5] or more times), Stars (14 authors whose works were reprinted 70–99 times); and Luminaries (139 authors whose works were reprinted 20–69 times). Of this total, the 19 Supernovas' 534 titles totaled 3,148 reprints; the 14 Stars wrote 239 titles that totaled 1,130 reprints; and the Luminaries contributed 1,331 titles, totaling 4,574 reprints. Thus, although the 172 canonical authors comprise only 4 percent of the 4,246 authors included in these Readers, the 8,852 reprints of their essays constitute 42.15 percent of the total canon—close enough to 50 percent to warrant their stellar status. This chapter will focus on the research findings derived from an analysis of the entire list of canonical authors with twenty or more reprints.

How Essays Become Canonical

Where essays live. Today, essays live in freshman composition courses, devoted to the reading and writing of this genre. Until the publication of the first volume of *The Best American Essays* in 1986, essayists themselves were lonely travelers in an indifferent universe of literature, lurking on the edges of the mainstream territories mapped out and claimed by writers of fiction, poetry, and drama. Although the status of essayists has improved considerably since then, as I demonstrate in Chapter 1, their works are less likely to appear in whole books than in out-of-the-way locales—big and little magazines (*The New Yorker, Creative Nonfiction, The Sewanee Review*), organizational publications (such as *Sierra* and the *New England Journal of Medicine*), the odd commercial catalog (Land's End, Banana Republic), and in mass circulation magazines, and newspaper op-ed and feature sections. Yet, we seldom think of the authors primarily as *essayists* or even as writers of articles, but as philosophers, politicians, historians, humorists, scientists, physicians, clergy, or practitioners of other arts, crafts, and skills.

The common reader's biggest problem is not what to read, for essays abound, but where to find these works in bookstores, in libraries, or online. A Google search on November 4, 2007 yielded a redundant 76,100,000 hits for *essay* or *essays* in English alone, reinforcing Alexander Butrym's earlier observation on the perforce vague, eclectic, and consequently unhelpful subject heading, *essay,* in the *Library of Congress Subject Headings.* The Library of Congress jumbles together "learned treatises of all sorts with the works of classical essay writers such as Montaigne, Lamb, and Bacon," but omits the works of contemporary belletristic essayists, such as Richard Selzer, Joan Didion,

Annie Dillard, Alice Walker, Tillie Olsen, Gretel Ehrlich, and Lewis Thomas, who are catalogued under a variety of diverse genre and key word subject headings (1–2). At the other extreme, bookstores disperse belletristic essays according to key word categories, biography, travel, nature, politics, and more. Another form of obscurity is the absence of the term *essay* from Stephen North's index to *The Making of Knowledge in Composition Studies,* even though the writing of essays (which he usually calls "texts") is the subject of much of the research North surveys.

As a consequence of these kinds of fragmentation, the essay as a genre has had a furtive, if not fugitive status in twentieth and twenty-first century American belletristic writing. There are very few single-authored collections of essays relative to the numbers of novels published in the same time period; many types of nonfiction are known by subject (Civil War history, philosophy of ethics) rather than by form. Print runs of essay collections from academic presses seldom exceed 1,500 copies. At this turn of the millennium, despite the distinctive literary presence of essayistic critics such as Joseph Epstein and Susan Sontag, Americans have no tradition of buying and reading single-authored collections of what they regard as *essays* as they might have done in the nineteenth century with the works of Ralph Waldo Emerson or Oliver Wendell Holmes. Holmes could style himself "the autocrat of the breakfast table"; no essayist today claims such authority.

Nevertheless, essays—broadly conceived—are the *lingua franca* of the American academy. Even if students call their assigned reading "stories" and their assigned writing "papers," it is "essays" that they read in any of the two hundred composition anthologies on the market in any given year which collectively publish about 13,000 essays. And it is "essays" that they write. Except for Atwan's annual *Best American Essays,* and more recent series clones, *The Best American Sports Writing* (1991), *The Best American Spiritual Writing* (1998), *The Best American Science and Nature Writing* (2000), *The Best American Travel Writing* (2000), and the occasional little magazine, there is no predictable, widely-accessible gathering place for essays in twentieth/twenty-first century America other than these textbook anthologies.

How an essay arrives in the canon. To arrive in the canon, an essay must travel a long and arduous journey, "the survival of the teachable." It must first be discovered. The editors of canonical textbooks are, as a group, omnivorous yet discriminating readers, eager for new authors, new subjects, and new treatments of familiar topics. But they can't read every nonfiction piece published in English (*Writer's Market* annually lists some 4,000 publications, not including 90,000 professional journals; the on-line version updates 6,000 contacts "every business day"). So they (and significant others—colleagues, spouses, graduate assistants—they have enlisted in their quest) read around in highbrow and sometimes middlebrow periodicals. They read creative nonfiction: autobiographies by such writers as Henry Louis Gates, Jr., Esmerelda Santiago, Mary Karr; collections of essays either by individual authors, such as Anne Fadiman (*At Large*), Atul Gawande (*Complications*), Scott Russell Sanders (*Hunting for Hope*), or on particular topics—travel, sports, food, relationships, science, spirituality.

They also read each other's books. An appealing and teachable work that surfaces in one anthology is likely to appear in five to ten canonical collections, as well as innumerable others, within the next five years. A single case in point should suffice. Brent Staples, whose work was anthologized eight times between 1983 and 1989, rose to canonical status in the 1990s with 41 reprints between 1990 and 1996. His essay, "Black Men and Public Space," was originally published in *Harper's* in December, 1986. It was picked up by one reader in 1987; in 1988 it appeared in three others including, significantly, both the longer and shorter *Norton Readers*. From then on it spread until by 1996 it had been reprinted 23 times in nine canonical Readers, ranging from *Life Studies* to *Reading Critically, Writing Well*. Its longevity continues into the twenty-first century.

There's no ready way to tell whether an anthologist has obtained a particular essay from its original source or from another anthology unless an early editor prints only excerpts and successive reprintings consist of the same excerpts (or, as one astute editor told me, when that editor's silent corrections of errors in the original are picked up by later editors). It seems unlikely that all the editors who have anthologized works such as "A Modest Proposal" (160 reprints), "Letter from Birmingham Jail" (first published in *Why We Can't Wait*, 1963; 68 reprints), or Alexander Petrunkevitch's "The Spider and the Wasp" (first published as part of an article in *Scientific American,* August 1952; 63 reprints) would have gone to the original sources to find them. It should be noted that such imitation, indeed the sincerest form of flattery, is not unique to essay anthologists. As critics of poetry anthologies are wont to lament (see Rasula, Golding), it can scarcely be coincidental that the same poem or combination of poems by a particular poet is selected for inclusion in anthology after anthology.

A particularly good source of belletristic essays, elegant and efficient, is Atwan's *The Best American Essays*, invaluable not only for the two dozen essays its guest editor chooses, but also for its appended list of 150 other "Notable Essays." These comprise the remainder of Atwan's original list, winnowed from hundreds of submissions, published in the predictable big and little magazines, and in such out of the way locations as *Adolescent Psychiatry, Family Therapy Networker,* and *New York Law Journal*. Virtually all are by experienced essayists, as Jamaica Kincaid's selections for the 1995 volume illustrate, although some are better known as poets (Maxine Kumin, Charles Simic), as fiction writers (Edna O'Brien, Grace Paley, John Edgar Wideman, Tobias Wolff), or as academic critics (William H. Gass, Henry Louis Gates Jr.). The entire list of works identified in the successive volumes of *The Best American Essays* might constitute an aesthetic canon, if one existed, for as Atwan says, they are "admirably written" "works of high literary quality intended as fully developed, independent essays on subjects of general interest," demonstrating an "awareness of craft as well as a forcefulness of thought" (*Best,* 2nd College ed., xv). Or it might be called, simply, Atwan's canon, though he told me in an email message that he is wrestling with a "strong definition" of *essay* that encompasses the common elements of the "two major branches" of essays that he selects—"one that's more literary (the personal, familiar, reflective, or informal essay) and the other less literary (articles, criticism, journalism)." Atwan, in effect, does the preliminary searching and screening for all the anthologists who subsequently examine his list—much as, say, a major newspaper's book review editor funnels to reviewers one or two percent of the published books received.

Why do some essays remain in the canon? My understanding of the survival factors that result in the teaching canon is based not only on my current research, but also on my long experience as editor of five Readers (one canonical, four not, sigh). It is also derived from interviews—engaging and candid—with the editors and publishers of a number of the most widely used canonical anthologies currently on the market. Indeed, the 119 editors of contemporary freshman essay anthologies—many college English teachers, a few professional editors

(Jane Aaron, Robert Atwan) and writers (including canonical essayists Donald Hall and X.J. Kennedy)—became the compilers of the American canon of twentieth century essays.

For an essay to remain in subsequent editions of a Reader, it must survive repeated scrutiny from the anthologist and the ever-changing in-house editors. Every edition of a canonical Reader is also vetted by multiple reviewers—among them, classroom teachers who adopt the book and other teachers whose responses are either volunteered or solicited by the publisher. Although such editorial Darwinism does not automatically ensure the survival of a canon of distinguished essays, it does favor the pedagogically sturdy.

Another survival factor lies in getting there first; editors of the anthologies that began the earliest and have the longest life-spans also exercise the greatest influence over canonicity. Four of the five most influential are Readers with a liberal arts orientation; *Patterns of Exposition* alone among these emphasizes modes of discourse. The leader is *The Norton Reader*, where 25 of the 172 canonical authors first appeared. The ubiquity of *The Norton Reader* and the propensity of other editors to copy its selections make it the industry point of reference. Next is *Readings for a Liberal Education* ("Locke, Gibson, and Arms"), published in five editions 1948–1967, and contributor of 21 authors to the canon. *A Collection of Readings for Writers* (Shaw, Bryan, and Wykoff), published in six editions 1946–1967 introduced 14 canonical authors, and *The Borzoi College Reader* published in seven editions 1967–1992 added 10, as did Decker's *Patterns of Exposition* (1966–1995). Essayists, like other authors who attain canonical status, tend to remain ensconced, as Willie van Peer demonstrates in "Two Laws of Literary History," so over time the canon expands. Only Jacques Barzun (1948–1983), Bergen Evans (1948–1978), Maynard Hutchings (1948–1988), Lewis Mumford (1948–1982), George Bernard Shaw (1957–1987), and X. J. Kennedy (1965–1989—whose "Who Killed King Kong?" was consistently published in the *Norton Reader* during this period) disappeared from the list before 1990.

Professional writers contribute 58 percent of the canonical pieces: journalists (29 in number), belletristic essayists (27), novelists (25), satirists and humorists (10), and poets (9). Most of the other authors are distinguished scholars or other professionals, whose writing is clear and accessible to a general readership: critics (12); educators (9); scientists (9); theologians (8); politicians (8); psychologists or psychoanalysts (8); linguists (7); historians (4); and others (7). Nevertheless, an essay is not necessarily canonical because its writing is distinguished, intellectually brilliant, or the work of a distinguished figure. Nor is an essay necessarily canonical because it is critically esteemed; as we've already established, critics generally ignore essays. This doesn't mean that essays *can't* be distinguished, brilliant, or excellent models—just that such criteria are not essential for an essay to arrive in the canon or to stay there.

Once an essay has been discovered, to attain canonicity it must not only be liked, but sufficiently well-liked to have been reprinted, according to my criteria, twenty or more times over a fifty year period in this 20 percent sample. This is not an exorbitant standard of affection. Most publishers have a broad spectrum of Readers: the equivalent of a stripped-down economy vehicle; a general purpose model; a minivan; a truck; a sports car; and an elegant, fine-tuned top-of-the-line model. The sponsoring editor usually determines the type of Reader to meet the competition. For example, will it be brief or bulky? Will it be arranged according to modes of discourse, contemporary issues, or a particular theme—such as ecology or civil rights? The Reader's niche profoundly influences the anthologist's choice of essays. In theory, the more features that make an essay appealing to an anthologist, the greater its chances for canonicity. In actuality, the importance of any given feature in a particular textbook depends on the anthologist's taste, judgment, and experience and on the textbook publisher's in-house editorial influence, supplemented by external reviews of the manuscript-in-progress.

To become a candidate for canonicity, an essay first must satisfy the anthologist's criteria for teachability; then it must balance intellectually, politically, and rhetorically with the rest of the book; it must contribute aesthetically; and its permission-to-reprint must be affordable. The consistent exception to the following analysis is *Ways of Reading*, with its deliberate focus on "long and complicated texts" (4th ed., v), many highly theoretical, and on highly innovative ways of reading them.

1. Criteria of teachability. Whether and how an essay will (or is imagined to) work in the classroom is the overriding concern for including it in a Reader of any type, and for re-assessing its reprinting in subsequent editions.

… The Essay Canon

a. *Level of difficulty.* How much do teachers have to know or learn in order to teach this work (a particular concern for administrators of courses with multiple sections, new TAs or teachers assigned to sections on short notice)? Will students understand its concepts, vocabulary, with or without a lot of explanation in class? Is it intellectually appropriate for them? Is it too technical, too allusive, too arty for students to stick with it?

b. *Suitability for the level and type of course the anthology is targeting.* Is the essay amenable to a particular teaching philosophy or method? Does it suit the orientation to reading and learning that the anthology is intended to promote?

c. *Length.* Is the essay short enough (say, under 5,000 words) to be discussed in one or two class periods? If not, can it be excerpted—and with how much violence to the text? Well-written short works of any genre (think of lyric poetry) are tightly and conspicuously structured. To leave out the opening paragraphs forces a later segment to serve as a beginning, despite argumentative or rhetorical devices that signal "middle." Nor can a midsection double rhetorically as a conclusion; the author didn't set it up to end the piece, and it will invariably sound sawed-off, as if the author had stopped in mid-. Moreover, omissions throw off the proportioning of the entire work; excerpting violates the delicate balance between beginning, middle, and end.

2. Balance with the rest of the book.
    a. *Intellectual and political resonance.* In what ways does the essay's topic, point of view, moral or ethical stance, contribute to the kinds of dialogue or debate the Reader hopes to engender? Will this essay, either by itself or in conjunction with other essays (a major reason that rivals clone entire sections of engaging books) abet the students' critical thinking and their understanding of the world or of a particular issue? Does the essay represent views and values that anthologists believe students should consider, confront—and either challenge or adopt? (A telling case in point is Judy Syfers/ Brady's feminist manifesto, "I Want a Wife," whose uppity

stance drew gleeful applause in 1972 but is so, well, over for twenty-first century readers.) But—moderation in all things—does the piece nevertheless avoid offending readers?

b. *Author's reputation and personal characteristics.* What characteristics of the author contribute to the book's balanced perspective? (Literary reputation in the 1950s and 1960s has been to an extent supplanted in the 1980s and 1990s by gender and ethnicity.) Does the essayist's life, if perceived to be relevant, as is Martin Luther King Jr's combination of Christianity and civil rights activism, reinforce the essay's point?

To attain canonicity, the work must be written by an author of reputation, either as a professional writer, or as a scholar or notable practitioner in the field the writing addresses. The sole exception is "I Want a Wife" by the otherwise unknown Syfers/Brady. (Non-canonical works anthologized only once or twice in fifty years are of much more diverse, often unknown ancestry. In contrast to the canonical Woody, which authors do you recognize among the six noncanonical Allens—Charlotte, Frederick Lewis, Gina, Jennifer, John L., William?)

3. Aesthetic qualities. While no anthologist would admit aesthetic indifference, anthologists whose books are explicitly oriented toward the essay as exemplifying modes of discourse (X.J. and Dorothy Kennedy's *Bedford Reader,* Joseph Trimmer and Maxine Hairston's *The Riverside Reader)* or as a belletristic genres (Sheridan Baker's *The Essayist,* William Smart's *Eight Modern Essayists*) are especially concerned with aesthetics. Readers that contain a high proportion of autobiographical writing, as do multicultural Readers, are also well-written, as a rule.

a. *Form.* Is the essay a good rhetorical model—for example, of argument or comparison and contrast? Does it provide appropriate ballast with other selections in the book? An essay usually exemplifies a multitude of rhetorical techniques; a definition, of *love* or *truth,* for instance, might contain illustrations, examples, comparison and contrast, description, even narrative replete with characters and dialogue. Thus, a particular piece might work equally well in a rhetorically-oriented Reader if categorized under any of these terms; or in a belletristic Reader classified, say, as both satire and autobiography. The more versatile a work is perceived to be, the more places it will turn up.

b. *Technique.* Is the essay technically interesting, sufficiently well written to serve as a good model for organization, style, vocabulary, tone, even wit? Does the author "make it new," enabling readers to see the subject afresh?

Contemporary canonical essays, on the whole, have to sound contemporary—in language, syntax, relative briskness and brevity. Whether the subject, style, or other features (such as length) account for the disappearance of the canonical nineteenth-century essayists from the twentieth-century canon—Newman is the sole exception—is difficult to determine, though their absence is conspicuous.

As they fulfill multiple criteria that ensure their pedagogical longevity, extremely popular canonical essays also satisfy a felt sense that they are not only canonical but inevitable. These include such works as Swift's "A Modest Proposal" (160 reprints); Orwell's "Politics and the English Language" (127 reprints) and "Shooting an Elephant" (119 reprints); "The Declaration of Independence" (106 reprints); White's "Once More to the Lake" (91 reprints); King's "Letter from Birmingham Jail" (68 reprints) and "I Have a Dream" (50 reprints); and Thoreau's "Civil Disobedience" (40 reprints). Multiplying the numbers roughly by 5 to get a realistic estimate of the actual pervasiveness of the canonical writers' work, I estimate that "A Modest Proposal" has been anthologized some 800 times during this 50-year span, "Shooting an Elephant" 595 times, and so on. Thus, our sense of the essay canon is dominated by three belletristic essays (four if you include the satire, "A Modest Proposal"), a political manifesto, a philosophical treatise, a speech, and a sermonic letter that combines qualities of all of these other forms of writing—a blurred genre indeed. All of these works offer political commentary, even "Once More to the Lake," with one reading as quietistic balanced against another that sees the work a harbinger of World War II (Ned Stuckey-French in conversation, Nov. 2, 2007). Nevertheless, like the other essays that endure, all of these pieces have a humanistic relevance for discussion and writing that can transcend their own contexts of time and culture. For comparable reasons, essays that narrate the experiences of a particular life in ways that can be generalized, such as Angelou's "Graduation" (44 reprints), Thurber's "University Days" (34 reprints), and Rodriguez's "Aria" (23 reprints), stand a better chance of becoming canonical than do essays laden with information that quickly becomes dated, as do most newspaper editorials and sociological treatises.

4. Cost. An essay must be affordable. Supply and demand govern permissions prices for anthology selections, as for any other commodity. *Norton Reader* permissions rose an inflated 24-fold, from $4,200 in 1965 to over $100,000 in 1992 (Sabine 66). Some well-established authors, and others in the ascendancy, charge over $1,000 per essay (or even $1,000 per printed page), a few charge by the word, and the cost continues to rise. Since pricey canonical authors, such as Orwell and Walker, continue to be anthologized as briskly as ever, the costs of their work must be balanced by writings in the public domain—"The Allegory of the Cave," "A Modest Proposal," *The Declaration of Independence,* "The Gettysburg Address."

Assuming even a modest $40,000 in contemporary permissions costs, half borne by the publisher, half by the anthology's editor, a Reader earning a 10 percent royalty would have to sell 5,000 copies at $40 a copy before it would even begin to compensate for the editor's effort. That a scant 10 percent of all Readers published go into second or subsequent editions implies that most don't recoup the initial investment. Thus, permissions costs provide the most significant counter-canonical pressure on anthologists to dilute the cost of copyrighted canonical essays by including works in the public domain, reprints from scholarly journals with modest permissions fees, and essays by emerging, relatively unknown authors. Kevin Dettmar's analysis of the economic constraints operating on textbook anthologists, "Writers Who Price Themselves Out of the Canon," is right on target.

In any given year, some two hundred essay anthologies are marketed for freshman composition, including some fifty new titles, half brand new, half new editions, as the *WPA Annual Bibliography* reveals. Assuming that the anthologies published in a given year average 65 selections, of the 13,000 annual essay slots (200 x 65), around 3250 (50 new Reader titles x 65) have the opportunity to be filled anew every year (see Martin, Smitten, Webb). However, as the database reveals, except for student writings most of these essays will not be new. Even if 25 percent of these were new in a given year, the actual number of new arrivals into the canon will be much smaller, about 4 percent. Thus, only 32 of the 812 essays newly anthologized in 1990–1995/96 have a shot at canonicity. (Although this number seems small, it is on par with the odds for all literary genres, as van Peer, 121–27, and Golding, Ch. 1, demonstrate). The other 780 newcomers will remain on the periphery, included in the first edition, perhaps in the second, out thereafter.

A case in point: of all the authors new to these books in the 1990s, only Deborah Tannen has attained canonical status during the decade in which her work was originally published. Her example perhaps characterizes the sensibility of current anthologists. She is a woman linguist of international distinction; her writing is lucid, informed, politically sensitive, and on a topic of perennial interest—human relations. Moreover, her books intended for a general readership, such as *You Don't Understand: Men and Women in Conversation*, from which most of the 26 excerpts, reprinted in 19 anthologies between 1992 and 1996 are taken, are divided into brief sections with catchy titles. The 21-page Chapter 3, for instance, "'Put Down That Paper and Talk to Me!': Rapport-talk and Report-talk" has thirteen sections ranging from two to eight paragraphs. Although the book as a whole is well-integrated, many of these short sections appear to be self-contained, and can thus be excised as single, free-standing units that require little or no editorial intervention. Clearly, a book born to be anthologized, as is Tannen's 2006 best-seller, *You're Wearing That? Understanding Mothers and Daughters in Conversation*.

The ten or fifteen additions to the canon in any decade will come from a pool of writings in various disciplines that share the features of

Tannen's work. Or else they will be self-contained essays or op-ed pieces by belletristic writers and journalists, particularly women, minority, and ethnic authors of diverse class backgrounds, political allegiances, sexual orientations, and disabilities (for predictions see Chapter 2, pp. 53-55). The increasing prominence of graphic essays will add author-artists such as Lynda Barry, Scott McCloud, and Art Spiegelman.

Shelby Steele's essay, "On Being Black and Middle Class," a well-written argument from a controversial (but not *too* controversial) perspective, offers an almost irresistible case in point. First published in *Commentary* in 1988, reprinted by Atwan in 1989, then widely anthologized between 1991 and 1995, it headed straight for the charts. Because Sucheng Chan's "And You're Short, Besides!" (1989), on overcoming discrimination as a self-described "physically handicapped Asian American woman," is not of comparable literary quality, it is less likely to endure. I would, however, lay even money on such exciting writers as Hilton Als, Chang-rae Lee, Azar Nafisi, Arundhati Roy, Luc Sante, Zaidie Smith, and Lê Thi Diem Thúy—and I am not a gambling woman.

The Essay Canon and Implications for Undergraduate Education

Why is the freshman textbook enterprise, with its opportunity to transform dramatically the ways students participate in the world as readers and writers, so essentially conservative? The perseverance of the canonical essayists in the canonical textbooks confirms Thomas Kuhn's observations on the normative state of scientific textbooks, as conservators of received knowledge rather than as innovators. Each sales representative is promoting books that compete not only against the comparable works of other publishers, but against other works in the publisher's own line—a practice intensified by mergers that combine, for instance, Little Brown HarperCollins, Addison-Wesley, Longman, and the textbook lines of each. This competition, as well as editors' human inertia, exerts conservative pressures.

The winnowing never stops, but it does conserve. New editions of a book appear every three or four years, not because the contents or the pedagogy are outdated, but because the extensive recycling of used books and publishers' sample copies extinguishes the bulk of new book sales at this point. To justify the publication of a subsequent edition, 25–35 percent of the selections in the previous edition must be replaced, but not necessarily with new works; material from earlier editions may be reinstated, and readings may be imported from the anthologies of others. Publishers solicit reviews of the tables of contents from instructors who have used or might use the book, and from a few who have rejected it, but seldom if at all from actual student readers. Essays that are taught and will be taught again remain. The rest are discarded, irrespective of merit, unless the anthologist can convince an in-house editor to retain a favorite ugly duckling. Because most reviewers indicate that they don't use most new authors and published student essays in class, there is pressure to replace the rejected fare with tantalizing new morsels—authors and topics *du jour* to tempt the prospective adopter. Thus, the chances are high that an earlier edition's familiar material will be retained, and that its new material will be replaced by even newer material that fits into the slots vacated by its temporary predecessors (see my "Making Essay Connections" and "Once More to the Essay"). These practices have an inescapably conservative bias in favor of familiar canonical works.

Teachability is, however, not replicability. If these books enabled students to re-create canonical essays, they'd create a new generation of potentially canonical essayists—but then, students who read *Moby Dick* and "The Waste Land" don't write works like these either. Anthologized essays that depend on the sophisticated writer's depth or breadth of understanding of an issue ("Letter from Birmingham Jail") or disciplinary field (anything by, say, Lewis Thomas, Stephen Jay Gould, Bertrand Russell, William James, Karl Jung, or Sigmund Freud) are intended not for replication but for the intellectual stimulation of student writers. It usually takes more years than student writers have experienced to attain the technical finesse and stylistic and emotional daring that characterize the work of belletristic essayists—though their subjects, organizational patterns, tone, and perspective are nevertheless expected to provide students with models of thinking and writing.

All anthologies, not just Readers, deracinate their material—old or new—from its original context and replant it in the anthologist's soil. There, the anthologist usually cuts, espaliers, grafts, and otherwise trims the added work to fit in with the rest of the selections, on which s/he has performed comparable operations. These normative activities of the anthology editor make what Golding says of the teaching canon in poetry equally applicable to the essay canon:

> The teacher-editor needs to accommodate extracanonical work if he or she is to represent the current state of poetry with any accuracy. When a textbook anthology such as *The Norton Anthology of Poetry* canonizes poetic outsiders, however, it renders their work culturally and intellectually harmless. What one might call this detoxification of potent work has its sources in the interpretive community's survival instinct, and the fact that if a pluralist literature is to be taught, it must be systematized. (36)

Thus, any essay in a Reader is recontextualized by being juxtaposed with other essays of the anthologist's choosing, in the anthologist's arrangement, according to the anthologist's logic, aesthetic, and pedagogy. For example, Susanne Langer's "Signs and Symbols" (originally published in *Fortune*, January 1944), Nancy Mairs's "On Being a Cripple" (*Plaintext: Deciphering a Woman's Life,* a 1984 doctoral dissertation before being published in 1986), and Charles Darwin's "Understanding Natural Selection" (a small portion of *On the Origin of Species,* 1859) each had a particular range of meaning and resonance in its original context. They acquire new, potentially very different coloration when transplanted, especially if they illustrate rhetorical modes in belletristic anthologies, which always emphasize form and subordinate history and culture.

Moreover, most anthologists reinforce their new contexts by providing an extensive rhetorical matrix for each essay—including discussions of how to write, biographical headnotes, and suggestions for reading and writing. Reader editors seem uniformly to assume that student writers can use the textbook's rhetorical or thematic concepts to write about—or in the manner of—even the most abstruse and complex works in the anthology. Hence, the common writing assignment, to imitate "Once More to the Lake" or "A Modest Proposal." These assignments are usually exercises in civil obedience, but sometimes a sophisticated assignment "takes," as in University of Connecticut student Nicole Estvanik's Aetna prize-winning essay, "Babysitter: A Study in Power Relations" (1998) among sitter, parents, and children, a Foucauldian analysis stimulated by an assignment in *Ways of Reading.*

Given that many individual readings are engaging, even exciting, and as a rule well written, why do so many of these anthologies seem so dull? Would more exciting books incite students to the civil disobedience that many of the anthologized essays discuss, and even encourage? How much more excitement, indeed incitement, do students need for social activism than the inspiring, confrontational words of the anthologists' darlings—Frederick Douglass, Henry David Thoreau, Virginia Woolf, George Orwell, Alice Walker, Martin Luther King, Jr.? Yet, many American college students read essays in Readers as they learn to read everything in school, through the clouded lens of having been there, been doing that for a dozen grades before they get to freshman English. Thus, the textbook context modulates what in other settings emerged as a high-minded zeal for death and transfiguration, blunting the knife edge of the individual essays into a conservatism their authors never knew.

However—and this is an important caveat—for students not jaded by their journey through American primary and secondary schools, essays such as these have the potential to retain their original incendiary power. One of my doctoral students, Ning Yu, born in Beijing in 1955, had been denied an education during the Maoist regime. His father, a professor of Chinese literature, was imprisoned, his family sent far from home, and Ning forced to work as a bricklayer. When the political winds shifted and Ning was finally allowed to attend Beijing University, he took an English course taught by an American (and therefore by definition subversive) who smuggled in copies of "The Declaration of Independence," "Civil Disobedience," "I Have a Dream," and other American freedom documents. Through the purple smudge of tattered dittos, Ning read these incendiary words in much the same spirit as their original audience did and found in the American dream his dream. He vowed to study these authors in their native context, came to America, wrote his doctoral dissertation on Thoreau, and has since become an American citizen.

Ning's exceptional reader response notwithstanding, a problem even bigger than the recontextualization of a Reader's essays lies in the very reductive ways in which editors' study questions encourage students to read them. For the most part, these questions have throughout the fifty-year period of this study embedded a philosophy of reading and writing that encourages students to be passive, obedient, and reverent; they read to unlock the meaning of the text, and write to understand and appreciate its meaning or replicate its matter, mode, or manner (see Scholes, Ch. 1). Editors create a distinguished canon but undermine it by surrounding its constituents with interpretive apparatus. It's not the essays' fault if the apparatus clings to them as lint to velcro, marking them as textbook fodder rather than as freestanding citizens of the once proud literary genre to which in other times, other contexts, they belonged.

It's hard to talk about study questions, let alone write them, without succumbing to parody, as Frederick Crews reveals in *The Pooh Perplex: A Freshman Casebook*—a collection of a dozen hilarious essays on *Winnie-the-Pooh* from the critical perspectives of a Marxist, a Freudian, and others whose names betray their profession. The "Questions and Study Projects" for "A Bourgeois Writer's Proletarian Fables" are:

1. In our Freshman English courses we try to show that everyone, within certain very broad limits, is entitled to his opinion on any subject. Do you feel that Tempralis [the alleged author] was entitled to his 1939 opinions about Pooh? Why not?
2. Tempralis seems obsessed with "fascism," doesn't he? Look up this difficult word in your dictionary and explain its meaning to the class (26).

That these parodies sound remarkably like the real thing is not surprising, given that the trend-setting Readers of the quarter-century after World War II reflected the liberal arts, New Critical orientation pervasive in the teaching of both composition and literature during this time (see Sabine 25–31). That these study questions are today seen to undermine the very qualities that led certain essays to be canonized in the first place reflects a changed sensibility in today's pedagogy of reading and thinking (see Slevin, Faigley). The fault, if fault there be, lies not in the canonical selections themselves, but in the passive relation between reader and text that these questions—and, let's face it, many classroom teachers—continue to encourage. We have met the teachers of what Scholes calls "the proper consumption of literature ... 'interpretation'" (5), and they continue to be us.

The Norton Reader's apparatus illustrates what appears in literally hundreds of other Readers. All of the nine editions in the canonical research include similar study questions for E. B. White's highly metaphorical "Democracy," two brief paragraphs originally published anonymously in *The New Yorker* "Talk of the Town" on July 3, 1943. Democracy, says White, is "the line that forms on the right. It is the don't in don't shove. It is the hole in the stuffed shirt through which the sawdust slowly trickles; it is the dent in the high hat. Democracy is the recurrent suspicion that more than half of the people are right more than half of the time. It is the feeling of privacy in the voting booths, the feeling of community in the libraries, the feeling of vitality everywhere" (in Eastman et al, 1st ed, 767). Here's how the editors' "Questions for Study, Discussion, and Writing" encourage students—and their teachers—to approach this text. They are brief enough to quote in full:

1. White's piece is dated July 3, 1943, the middle of World War II. How did the occasion shape what White says about democracy?
2. Look up "democracy" in a standard desk dictionary. Of the several meanings given, which one best applies to Becker's definition [in another essay]. Does more than one apply to White's?
3. How does Becker's language differ from White's? What does the difference suggest about the purposes and audiences of the two men?
4. Translate White's definition into non-metaphorical language. (For example, "It is the line that forms on the right" might be translated by "It has no special privileges.") Determine what is lost in the translation, or, in other words, what White has gained by using figurative language. (Eastman et al, 1st ed, 768)

From interviews I conducted with Arthur Eastman in 1995 and 1996, as well as from my experiences of auditing his Shakespeare course and taking his graduate course in expository writing at Michigan in the 1950s, I know him to be a superb teacher. He was concerned with careful and precise reading, not only the letter of the text, but the spirit—of the author, of the age, of the nature of the work, its music, its silence. Long before "process" became the mantra of writing teachers nationwide, for Dr. Eastman we wrote and rewrote and rewrote until we got it right: sense, sensibility. As general editor of the first eight editions of *The Norton Reader,* he was responsible for writing most of the book's apparatus. These study questions reflect his liberal arts orientation, his love of essays as a genre (Sabine 31), his orientation to reading and writing, and also the New Critical orientation of the early postwar years when he came of age as a teacher.

Today's Marxist and postmodern critics, such as John Trimbur ("Articulation Theory"), Paul Lauter (*Canons,* Chs. 3 and 4), Lester Faigley ("Coherent Contradictions,") and James Slevin would ask "What version of whose world?" White's essay represents. The *Norton* apparatus for "Democracy" says Slevin in "Reading and Writing in the Classroom and the Profession," implies that reading is "passive and obedient: the reader's role is simply to understand—by acts of consulting (a dictionary [#2]), translating (updating examples [#4]), and comparing (with the definition of another writer [#3])." Student writers, too, are conceived of as "ahistorical and passive"; the questions invite "stereotyped notions of the Fourth of July and World War II" and require "no serious research or historical inquiry." The students, "appreciative and uncritical," are invited to "consider what White gains by metaphor but not what he might lose or conceal." Moreover, "the text's relevance to other writers is also, in the sense used here, only occasional: White's essay is to be used as a model for composing a similar text on a different abstraction. Writing is thus seen as a form of uncritical imitation." Reading according to this apparatus, concludes Slevin, "means understanding the point and appreciating the technique. Writing involves reproducing the qualities that get exhibited in White's style." Thereby reading and writing become "acts of attentive acquiescence" (55).

There are, of course, other ways to read White's (or any) text, as Slevin points out, in a complicated analysis that addresses the upper class, "corporate personality" of White's persona; his easy assumptions that upper class privileges are everyone's privileges; his complacent vision of America as "owning" democracy; and his idealized construction of a "purified version of the American polity" that "suspends his critical judgment and implicitly encourages his readers to suspend theirs." Slevin favors instead critical literacy "that is historical and contextual," removing readings of texts from the formalist literary theory that pervades the *Norton Reader* into the realm of "poststructuralist cultural theory's historicizing and problematizing of texts and textual studies" (65–71). Faigley's postmodern analysis of "The Conflicting Rhetoric of Writing Textbooks" reaffirms Slevin's perspective (132–62), although neither Faigley, nor Slevin, offers alternative study questions that would encourage, for instance, discussions "of whose interests are at stake in a particular conflict," or "how the language writers use is related to those interests" (Faigley 161–62). Whether the adoption of alternative "powerful conceptual models" in composition textbooks across the board would elevate the essay from the *declassé* status to which twentieth-century formalist criticism consigned it remains to be seen. But in the new millennium, rescue is at hand from other sources.

THE FUTURE OF THE ESSAY CANON

The future of the essay canon is, of course, inextricably intertwined with the future of the essay. If essays were a dying genre, written by dead people in a dead language, their lowly status during much of the twentieth century would lead us to predict their death in the twenty-first. Happily, the millennium reveals new and abundant life in this revitalized genre.

For the essay in contemporary America "has joined the modern world," as Annie Dillard says ("Introduction" xx). No longer need essays be treated as "synonymous with literary criticism," written *about* literature rather than being literature themselves (see this book, Chapter 1; and Scholes, Textual Chapter 1). No longer need essays be considered anemic, genteel, old fashioned, written by failed novelists or trivializers of the ephemeral. Essays are now being written, as Atwan explains, "in the same imaginative spirit as fiction and poetry," and with comparable artistry by writers daring and determined to write with elegant toughness about tough subjects, determined to resist "the plodding memoir, the facile discovery of identity, the predictable opinion, the unearned assertion" ("Introduction" 6, 9). Dillard and Atwan are partisans of essays, however, and we will know the essay has truly come of age, however, when writers—essayists and critics alike—can discuss it without defining it; we should know it when we see it. What we will come to recognize as the essay canon in the new millennium is today in flux, as canons always are, however glacial their rate of change.

The essay canon, as you have seen it here, is in the process of transformation from an inadvertent to a deliberate canon, as our literary nation undergoes a process of "essay warming" (see for instance DuPlessis). The creative nonfiction categories of numerous MFA programs and writers' workshops are a sign that essays matter. Writers identify themselves as "essayists," their work is awarded prizes in "creative nonfiction" categories of contests, and is now published in *Creative Nonfiction* (1993–), *Fourth Genre* (1999–), and *River Teeth* (2000–). Essays continue to appear in magazines little and big, specialized and general;

on newspaper op-ed pages and in every freshman and upper-division writing course in the country, as well as in discipline-related courses. My work here is a sign that essays are significant enough to be thought of in canonical terms. Robert Atwan's *The Best American Essays* and related volumes, Joseph Epstein's *The Norton Book of Personal Essays* (1997), Philip Lopate's large anthology *The Art of the Personal Essay* (1994), Tracy Chevalier's mammoth *Encyclopedia of the Essay* (1997), and Jenny Spinner's comprehensive *On Women and the Essay* (2004) are signs that essays are being read—and read about in ways that respect, as Lopate says, their "density of thought," their "living voices," their ability to provide "mental adventure" (*Anchor* x). All of this is proof that essays will not, need not be ghettoized in their academic setting, reprinted in Readers treated as separate from and unequal to mainstream literature anthologies—Readers whose hospitality to this genre during a century of exile cannot be overestimated.

Indeed, in the past twenty years, our professional journals have been receptive to the genre in publishing articles about essays and writing by a variety of essayistic academicians, as I have demonstrated in Chapter 1. *College English,* for instance, devoted a special issue (January 2003) to creative nonfiction, and *LIT (Literature, Interpretation, Theory),* in a special issue on "The Future of Academic Writing" (Oct.-Dec. 2005), examined the compatible relations between essayistic and scholarly writing. Recent essayistic scholarly writing ranges from Mike Rose's groundbreaking *Lives on the Boundary* (1989) to Richard Murphy's *The Calculus of Intimacy* (1993) and Victor Villanueva's *Bootstraps* (1993); to Wendy Bishop's *Teaching Lives* (1997) and Joseph Trimmer's *Narration as Knowledge: Tales of the Teaching Life* (1997); to Rachel Hile Basset's *Parenting and Professing: Balancing Family Work with an Academic Career* (2005) and Kimberly Myers's *Illness in the Academy: A Collection of Pathographies by Academics* (2007).

There is one significant oversight that rankles. Essays might as well be written in invisible ink as far as the calls for proposals of the conferences of two of our major professional organizations, CCCC and MLA, are concerned. *Essays* are not yet included anywhere in CCCC's annual call for program proposals. Even as recently as 2006, the nonfiction forms identified in "Creative Writing" include "creative nonfiction, journalism and documentary, life writing, memoir, auto/biography, identities, pedagogy, publishing, and travel and nature writing." But no *essays*—an ironic but conspicuous oversight in an organization devoted to teaching the reading and writing of that very genre. Although in the late 1980s-early 1990s MLA formed divisions on "Autobiography, Biography, and Life Writing" and "Nonfiction Prose Studies, Excluding Biography and Autobiography," *essay* makes only cameo appearances in MLA convention programs, either by genre or by author, even though essayistic elements often appear in *PMLA*'s *Forum* section of short, sometimes personal-sounding commentaries.

Nevertheless, as we have seen in Chapter 1, essays—the Cinderella genre—have been steadily climbing up from the basement in the House of Literature to reclaim their place once again, wherever serious but pleasurable reading is done. Certainly, as long as essays are taught as the academy's lingua franca, there will be an essay canon, hardy and versatile, that students will read. If tomorrow's students approach these essays in the spirit in which they were written, or were discovered by receptive readers such as Ning Yu, they will also be inspired to understand and appreciate the ideals of a free society, a liberal education—truth, justice, the spirit of inquiry. In this ethos, they will learn to think critically, and to write with some measure, we can hope, of the eloquence and elegance that reside in the most distinguished essays they read. Whether the critical stepsisters reconfigure the critical canon to make a place for essays is far less important than that common readers and writers, and yes, composition teachers, will surely continue to take this most attractive genre to the ball.

3 The Essayist in—and behind—the Essay: Vested Writers, Invested Readers

Voice-Over. Our telephone was tapped during the eight years it took to write and publish Doctor Spock: Biography of a Conservative Radical—*my hopeful contribution to ending the Vietnam War. When I'd pick up the receiver to dial out, I'd hear mysterious clicks, breathing—sometimes even panting, but never a voice. Sometimes the line would go dead. I have never again experienced the sense of a palpitating but silent presence on the other end of the line except for a brief stay in Bucharest during the depths of the Ceausescu regime. Our approved Intourist hotel was so close to a thicket of radio relay towers that the spies could have peeped through the window, but they evidently preferred the phone. It rang at random hours of the day and night to deliver breathing and static. No voice, not even in a language I couldn't understand.*

The Prodigious Presence of Superstar Essayists

This chapter will demonstrate that the work of superstar canonical essayists is qualitatively different from that of many other essayists (including many canonical essayists of lesser luminosity) in one significant respect—the intensely felt presence of the essayist within the essay. This ethos is comprised of the author's ethical and intellectual stance toward the subject and perhaps the world, and manifested in the essayist's characteristic voice and literary style. These constitute the author's persona, distinctive and ongoing, sustained from one work to the next. Verisimilitude notwithstanding, the essayist behind the essay is not necessarily the character, the *I*, "the singular first person" who appears in the essay. This essayist-in-the-essay, apparently artless and transparent, is actually a work of art to which readers—even those sophisticated enough to know the character represented is a carefully constructed artifact—react as if it were the real person whom they know and—usually—love. As Scott Russell Sanders, himself a canonical essayist, observes in "The Singular First Person," "Brassy or shy, center stage or hanging back in the wings, the author's persona commands our attention. For the length of an essay, or a book of essays, we respond to that persona as we would to a friend caught up in a rapturous monologue" (194).

Extremely popular canonical essays, those by the twenty superstars with 480 reprints or more in composition studies anthologies since World War II (see Chapter 2; also L. Bloom, "The Essay Canon and Textbook Anthologies"), satisfy the felt sense that they have not only transcended time, if not culture, but that they are inevitable. Virtually all of these writers (except two authors of documents that are not essays, Thomas Jefferson as first author of the "Declaration of Independence," and Plato as author of "The Allegory of the Cave") convey a powerful sense of a human being within and behind the writing that many other perfectly competent nonfiction writers—including many canonical essayists of lesser ranking—exhibit less memorably or not at all, even when they are writing on subjects of comparable significance. These superstars, like the rich whom Fitzgerald allegedly told Hemingway are "different from you and me," include the following. George Orwell heads the list; with 1785 (numbers from the 20 percent sample tabulated on p. 183 multiplied by 5 to equal 100 percent) reprints of such essays as "Politics and the English Language" and "Shooting an Elephant," his work is included in virtually every Reader published during the second half of the century. E. B. White, with 1,340 reprints—including "Once More to the Lake" and "The Ring of Time," is a close second. Then come: *3* Joan Didion (1,095 reprints), *4* Lewis Thomas (1,020), *5* Henry David Thoreau (900), *6* Virginia Woolf (885), *7* Jonathan Swift (865), *8* Martin Luther King, Jr. (825), *9* James Thurber (790), *10* Mark Twain (715), *11* Annie Dillard (680), *12* Thomas Jefferson (660), *13* Russell Baker (630), *14* Loren Eiseley (605), *15* E.M. Forster (590), *16* Maya Angelou (565), *17* Ellen Goodman (560), *18* James Baldwin (510), *19* Richard Rodriguez (495), and *20* Plato (480).

A contrast of the following with the canonical superstars is illuminating. At the bottom end of the canon list are twenty authors with 100–110 reprints apiece: Hannah Arendt, Michael Arlen, Sigmund Freud, Dick Gregory, Sidney J. Harris, Jane Jacobs, Alfred Kazin, X.J. Kennedy, Robin Lakoff, Ashley Montagu, Gloria Naylor, Chief Seattle, Eric Sevareid, George Bernard Shaw, Gail Sheehy, William Stafford, John Steinbeck, Alvin Toffler, Gore Vidal, and Edmund Wilson. Try this test. Which works of these authors come to mind? Many have reputations as writers of novels, poetry, drama, psychiatric treatises, urban analysis, or theology, and it is likely you would identify their best known works first. If you, as a reader, can think of essays or longer pieces of nonfiction written by any of these authors, which works are these? I surmise that if readers do associate a specific authorial presence or persona with each or any of these writers, it will be the presence that emanates from their best known works in the genres and fields where their reputation lies—fiction for Naylor, drama for Shaw, poetry for Stafford, rather than through their essays.

"The Singular First Person": The Authorial Presence of Superstar Essayists

Simply—and subjectively—put, for an essayist to become a canonical superstar, teachers and by extrapolation, their students, have to love the performance. Readers respond vigorously to the work and, thus, to the author whose presence emerges in and through the writing. By and large, they love the writer they come to know as a more-or-less constant presence from one canonical favorite to another: the George Orwell of "Shooting an Elephant," "Marrakech," and "Politics and the English Language"; the E. B. White who emerges in and through "Once More to the Lake," "The Death of a Pig," and "Walden"; the Joan Didion of "Why I Write," "On Keeping a Notebook," and "Some Dreamers of the Golden Dream." Yet, when the narrator of a superstar essay elicits loathing, as the monstrously bland narrator of Swift's "A Modest Proposal" is calculated to do, readers are expected to recognize and respect the ethical distance between the actual author and his created character (even though some naive readers elide the two). For better or for worse, as Scott Russell Sanders explains, "It is the *singularity* of the first person—its warts and crochets and turn of voice" (196)—to whom readers respond as if that first person were a real person.

Essayists themselves are under no illusions about the illusory characters they create, and why they do so. The author's self-presentation as simple and unadorned is as old as the genre, invented by Montaigne, who artfully began the tradition of artlessness, as well. He slyly explains "To the Reader" of *Essays*, "I want to be seen here in my simple, natural, ordinary fashion, without straining or artifice; for it is myself that I portray. My defects will here be read to the life, and also my natural form...." Custom permitting, Montaigne says he would "very gladly have portrayed [himself] here entire and wholly naked" (qtd. in Sanders 195).

Contemporary canonical superstars have addressed this subject in a comparable vein. Thoreau opens *Walden*—of which textbook excerpts are treated as essays—by observing that "In most books, the *I*, or first person, is omitted; in this, it will be retained; that, in respect to egotism, is the main difference. We commonly do not remember that it is, after all, always the first person that is speaking" whether or not the pronoun is there to send that signal. "I should not talk so much about myself," adds Thoreau, "if there were anybody else whom I knew as well" (3). E. B. White introduces his own selected *Essays* by acknowledging that although the essayist "can pull on any sort of shirt, be any sort of person, according to his mood or his subject matter—philosopher, scold, jester, raconteur, confidant, pundit, devil's advocate, enthusiast," he must tell the absolute truth. Lest readers suspect that this multiplicity of roles might lead to artifice and role-playing, White—drawing again on the example of Montaigne, who "'had the gift of natural candour'"—confidently asserts that the essayist "cannot indulge himself in deceit or in concealment, for he will be found out in no time" (vii-viii). Although George Orwell in "Why I Write"—a literary manifesto written near the end of the author's short life—concludes that "one can write nothing readable unless one constantly struggles to efface one's own personality," he acknowledges that all writers—members of a small class of "gifted, wilful people who are determined to live their own lives to the end"—are driven by "sheer egoism. Desire to seem clever, to be talked about, to be remembered after death...." He writes, as well as, from three other motives that all essayists share: "(ii) Esthetic enthusiasm ... ; (iii) Historical impulse ... to find out true facts and store them up for the use of posterity; and (iv) Political purpose ... desire to push the world in a certain direction" (1082). And, in her version of "Why I Write," Joan Didion, acknowledging that she stole the title from Orwell, gets right to the point—the egoistic emphasis of the "*I, I, I*" sounds in the title: "In many ways writing is the act of saying I, of imposing oneself upon other people, of saying *listen to me, see it my way, change your mind*" (44).

Such pronouncements could easily lead readers to expect that superstar canonical essayists are writing autobiography—itself a highly constructed artifact despite autobiographers' protestations of truthfulness (see Gusdorf; Mandell; Howarth). However, the only autobiographers among the top twenty are Maya Angelou (virtually all her "essays" are editorially-selected excerpts from *I Know Why the Caged Bird Sings*) and Richard Rodriguez, with chapters or excerpts of chapters from the autobiographical *Hunger of Memory: The Education of Richard Rodriguez*. Indeed, although the essays' readers could glean occasional "facts" about the lives of the canonical superstars, these are insufficient to present even a fragmentary sketch of the writer's life. For instance, in "Once More to the Lake" White tells us about the week the narrator and his unnamed son spent an idyllic week at an unnamed lake in Maine, doing a variety of activities (boating, fishing, swimming) that White himself had enjoyed as a boy vacationing at the same lake. But however ample or minimal, such autobiographical information is beside the point. The essayist's point of view—as signaled by the "*I, I, I*"—is the focal point of authorial presence, as Sanders explains in "The Singular First Person" and Gordon Harvey elaborates on in "Presence in the Essay."

After modestly claiming that the essayist, in comparison with poets, playwrights, and novelists, "must be content in his self-imposed role of second-class citizen," E. B. White admits that "some people find the essay the last resort of the egoist, a much too self-conscious and self-serving form for their taste; they think that it is presumptuous of a writer to assume that his little excursions or his small observations will interest the reader." Acknowledging the "justice in their complaint," White adds, "I have always been aware that I am by nature self-absorbed and egotistical; to write of myself to the extent I have done indicates a too great attention to my own life, not enough to the lives of others" (vii-viii). Not so, explains Sanders, for contrary to the autobiographer's practice of looking inward, the superstar essayists are looking outward on the creation that is the world. As White says in "The Ring of Time," "As a writing man or secretary, I have always felt charged with the safekeeping of all unexpected items of worldly or unworldly enchantment, as though I might be held personally responsible if even a small one were to be lost" (143). These superstars know that—as Sanders says of his own essays—"the public does not give a hoot about my private life. . . . I choose to write about my experience not because it is mine, but because it seems to me a door through which others might pass" (197–98).

Indeed, the perspective of the first person singular that dominates the essay is that of the essayist who opens doors to others' common experience. (That all essayists are embedded in constraints of class, ethnicity, gender, physical and emotional functioning, age, time, and culture is today's truism; that no writer can claim universal connections with a universal audience does not negate the fact that the work does establish a great many significant relationships.) This perspective establishes the authorial presence within the world of each individual essay that creates the bond with the readers, the ethos that persists from one essay to another. It should be noted that presence (amplified below) is a more robust concept than voice, even as addressed in Carl Leggo's comprehensive list of ninety-nine "Questions I Need To Ask Before I Advise My Students To Write in Their Own Voices"—ranging from "What is there of desire in voice?" to "Is voice like a thumbprint—unique?" (145–50). Presence is also more robust than the concept elaborated on in Peter Elbow's thoroughgoing discussion of "audible voice or intonation in writing," "dramatic voice in writing," "recognizable or distinctive voice in writing," "voice with authority" ("Introduction: About Voice," xxiv–xxxiii). When Elbow addresses the last item on his list, "resonant voice or presence," he finds "trouble—the swamp," because this concept embeds questions of authorial sincerity, authenticity, and relationship to the "real character" of the "actual author" beyond the text (xxxiii–xlii). The answer, he says, lies in Aristotle's *Rhetoric,* which "clearly implies what common sense tells us: we are not persuaded by the implied author, as such—that is, by the creation of a dramatic voice that sounds trustworthy; we are only persuaded if we believe that dramatic voice is the voice of the actual speaker or author." Elbow elaborates: "We don't buy a used car from someone just because we admire their dramatic skill in creating a fictional trustworthy voice. If ethos is nothing *but* implied author, it loses all power of persuasion" (xlii). Yet there is more to presence than Elbow acknowledges. Although it is true that in order to trust the sentiments expressed in nonfiction readers need to sense a congruence between the actual writer outside of the text and the authorial presence within it, the latter is—and has to be—a construct, rather than a literal re-creation of the writer in real life. This presence constitutes the sense of the essayist *in* the essay; the more powerful the sense of presence, the more likely the essayist is to be a superstar.

It is this sense of presence that Gordon Harvey anatomizes in "Presence in the Essay." In an explanation that reinforces the observations of White and Sanders, he says: "If a piece of autobiographical writing *is* an essay, it has already moved beyond private confession or memoir to some shareable idea, for which the personal experience works as evidence. This move from experience to idea, and then, through painful revision, from a dull idea and simple, narrative structure to an interesting idea and structure, bringing general insights out in the particulars and erasing narcissism, is precisely the great challenge and the great value of the personal essay as a freshman writing assignment—this and the broadened sense it gives of what can count as evidence for ideas" (648). The "personal" in essays is not necessarily "represented by autobiographical anecdote and image or by explicit self-analysis and introspection," but by authorial presence. Presence, Harvey says, "is the concept we invoke when we feel life in writing, when we feel an individual invested in a subject and freely directing the essay—not surrendering control to a discipline's conventions, or to a party line, or to easy sentiments and structures, or to stock phrases" (650).

In general, readers don't know or care much about the essayist behind the essay except to assume that figure to be intellectually and ethically congruent with the writer whose perspective appears in public. By and large, this assumption is warranted, to the extent that the author's ethos—disposition, character, and fundamental values—is stable in person and in print. And this assumption holds true even when readers know that an author such as Virginia Woolf is writing on her more cheerful days rather than from depression; or that George Orwell's unverifiable accounts of "A Hanging" and "Shooting an Elephant" do not depend on "factual, historical veracity" but on fidelity to the generic experience of colonial officers in Burma (Crick 85, 95–96, 112).

> Voice-Over: *During the course of my research, Dr. Spock and four others were prosecuted by the federal government for conspiring to encourage students to resist the draft during the Vietnam War. The FBI agents who testified were to a man rigidly erect*

> in posture and testimony, literalists all—with no acknowledgment of the figurative elements that pervade the language their wiretappers would have overheard—metaphor, hyperbole, understatement. What someone said or wrote, they meant. Thus "Oh, I could just die" could be construed as an intention to commit suicide, rather than a comment of embarrassment.

"ONCE MORE TO THE LAKE" AS AN EXAMPLE OF AUTHORIAL PRESENCE

Harvey goes on to explain the process and technical means by which essays, including academic writing, can "be *informed* by personal experience without injecting personal *information*" or even the personal pronoun, "a matter of felt life in the writing rather than anecdote or self-analysis." Although presence is "everywhere" in an essay, it is particularly apparent in the five aspects of the essay Harvey identifies, which I will analyze here as they are manifested in "Once More to the Lake," using male pronouns to accommodate the male author.

Harvey's first aspect is (1) *motive*. Usually in the introduction, the writer establishes, for himself and his readers, why the subject is "interesting enough to pursue," "why it isn't simply obvious, why there's a mystery to unfold,"—in brief, why the essay needs to be written (650). At the outset, White announces that throughout his childhood his family spent every August at a lake in Maine; "none of us ever thought there was any place in the world like [it]." Although I have "since become a salt water man," says White, "there are days when the restlessness of the tides and the fearful cold of the sea water and the incessant wind that blows . . . make me wish for the placidity of a lake in the woods" like the one of the childhood summers (197). To recapture this "sacred" time and place, he returns to the same lake with his son, and the story begins. The element of the quest is subdued but omnipresent—can a father re-experience the past and transmit this legacy, and its meanings, to his son?

The second aspect Harvey identifies is (2) *development*. Presence, says Harvey, "is manifest, along with pleasure, sometimes wonder and even passion, in a willingness to pursue a topic through twists and turns: to see in it, and follow it through, its various aspects and complications and sub-ideas, which not just anybody would think of or predict." The real issue "isn't between orderly and disorderly development, or between linear and nonlinear; it's between dull, mechanical order and complex, alert order, whose creation and control manifest presence" (650–51). White signals this alertness in the second paragraph, when he explains the associative nature of the juxtaposition of past and present that he proffers throughout the essay: "It is strange how much you can remember about places [like the lake, "this unique, this holy spot"] once you allow your mind to return into the grooves that lead back. You remember one thing, and that suddenly reminds you of another thing." He reaffirms this, with a surprise—as much to himself as to the readers—in the fourth paragraph: "I began to sustain the illusion that [my young son] was I, and therefore, by simple transposition, that I was my father. . . . I seemed to be living a dual existence. I would be in the middle of some simple act . . . and suddenly it would be not I but my father who was saying the words or making the gesture" (198).

White's fifth paragraph concurrently illustrates all of the remaining characteristics Harvey describes: (3) *"Control of quotation"* [when the writer is responding to other texts] *and detail"*—through original metaphors, similes, metonymic details that indicate "the feeling of a mind engaged in the subject at hand," not grandstanding razzle-dazzle. (4) *"An awareness of cliché and what doesn't need saying,"* witty allusions to readers' shared knowledge and experiences. (5) *Broadenings of the subject.* "It's a mistake," says Harvey, to think that particulars only "particularize," when in fact they can broaden out the discussion, perhaps drawing on "the essayist's experiential grasp of human behavior, of how life tends to go." (6) *Judgments and reasons:* "Giving specific reasons for one's general impressions . . . happens also to be its most personal aspect" (651–52).

To establish the convergence of past and present, White repeats "the same" in detail upon detail of going fishing the first morning: "the same damp moss" covers the worms in the bait can; "the small waves were the same"—original detail—"chucking the rowboat under the chin"—"and the boat was the same boat, the same color green and the ribs broken in the same places, and under the floorboards the same fresh-water leavings." A dragonfly lights on the tip of his rod, convincing him "beyond any doubt that everything was as it always had been, that the years were a mirage and that there had been no years." Despite the comfortable familiarity of these phenomena, White uses no cliches. Nor does he spell out his interpretations, trusting that if he presents appropriate information his readers will understand the music as well as the words. Indeed, he broadens the subject even as he embeds his interpretations in the telling details: "I looked at the boy [whose name does not matter], who was silently watching his fly, and it was my hands that held his rod, my eyes watching. I felt dizzy and didn't know which rod I was at the end of" (198–99). White's presence here is far more profound than a voice; it is an active, engaged mind in motion, even in the stillness of the event.

The essay, originally published in *The New Yorker* in August 1941, re-created for its sophisticated, urban audience the rhythms and events of a summertime-out-of-time "pattern of life indelible, the fadeproof lake, the woods unshatterable, the pasture with the sweetfern and the juniper forever and ever, summer without end" (200). Whether or not White's readers have ever gone to the woods (with their overtone of Thoreau's *Walden,* where one could live "deliberately"), White invites them there, to that special segment of the universe in the last tranquil summer before the cataclysm of World War II, where grandfather and father and son blend in an indissoluble union. This essay has withstood nearly seventy years of intervening shifts in reading (and to a lesser extent teaching), and some critical bashing, from poststructuralist, postmodern, neo-Marxist, feminist, multi-ethnic and a plethora of other critical perspectives. Its survival attests to its resonance in human terms for generations of readers—women as well as men—who value the essay's real subject, the human connections White celebrates. Moreover, it is pedagogically versatile, and can be taught for its narrative, implied argument, comparison and contrast, illustration, characterization, tone, structure (of sentence, paragraph, and whole work), and pace, as well as this myriad of themes.

The actual person of E. B. White, the existential human being, is irrelevant to the authorial presence conveyed within the body of his work. Readers' response to the intensely felt presence of the author in this essay carries over to their reading of White's other widely reprinted essays, as well; the process is the same for all other canonical superstars, among them Orwell, Didion, Thoreau, Virginia Woolf, Martin Luther King, Jr., Thurber, and Twain. This sense of authorial presence, when coupled with other features of teachable texts identified above (such as intellectual relevance, accessibility, and length) is predictive of future canonical superstars, as well. These are the contemporary belletristic writers whose essays are beginning to appear in textbooks in significant numbers, essayists whom some critical readers already refer to as "canonical" because of the felt sense that their presence is indispensable. Tomorrow's superstar shoo-ins (some of whom are already on the canonical list) include Sherman Alexie, Diane Ackerman, Dave Eggers, Anne Fadiman, Henry Louis Gates, Jr., Jamaica Kincaid, Barbara Kingsolver, Scott Russell Sanders, David Sedaris, Shelby Steele, Amy Tan, David Foster Wallace—and Jhumpa Lahiri, if only she'd write more essays. (Gloria Anzaldúa was there until she died, usually a downer on the charts.)

> Voice-Over: *Here's what the FBI eavesdroppers in Cleveland, Indianapolis, St. Louis would have heard, colloquies in disembodied voices. Conversations with academic colleagues, editors, and students about work-in-progress. Arrangements with neighbors about car pools, play groups, peace marches, integration efforts, and the elementary school's annual geranium sale (run, of course, by the Blooms). One babysitter's routine calls—on the job—to her bookie.*
>
> *After my initial call to Dr. Spock—"I've recently finished my Michigan doctoral dissertation on literary biography and now I'd like to write a real biography—of you"—we talked only in person. Whether the FBI ever provided a context for the fragments of lives they overheard, ever sought to assemble whole presences from the auditory mosaic that tumbled into their tapes I do not know. Literalists would leave out the laughter, the fun and effort of the process, the exhilaration borne of the hope that this writer—myself—an author behind the author of America's best-known baby book—would and could change the world.*

Issues in Teaching Canonical Essayists

Teachers who distrust personal-sounding writing in the classroom respond to such texts—particularly student papers—with suspicion and perhaps with readings more literal than the writing warrants. The authorial presence sends the wrong message in an academic universe, they say, making little allowance for the literary artistry—shaping characters, establishing a voice and an individual style—that they reward in fiction and poetry (see Bartholomae "Inventing"; Bizzell "Cognition"). Not so. The essayist's human presence raises ethical problems (for innocent or forgetful readers) and possibilities for teaching writing and for re-invigorated academic writing that I have space to discuss only briefly.

Ethical considerations. Author-evacuated texts, conventional academic articles, appear objective, impartial, as William H. Gass says in "Emerson and the Essay," "complete and straightforward and footnoted and useful and certain" and "unassailable," and are therefore "a veritable Michelin of misdirection" (25). Author-saturated texts may be equally misleading. Readers expect honesty, openness, intimacy; a writer as personal-sounding as Orwell or Didion or White is trusted to tell the truth the whole truth and nothing but the truth. This trust in the personal is paramount, in spite of what teachers as well as authors know about the aesthetic necessity—and latitude—in shaping characters, setting scenes, representing dialogue, and other features common to both fiction and creative nonfiction. In a variety of circumstances—political, religious, cultural, academic—audiences trust the messenger and so they adopt the message. Thus teachers have an obligation to make it clear that like all forms of literature all essays, however personal or impersonal, are constructs. Wendy Bishop offers teachers "Places to Stand," saying as a reflective writer-teacher-writer "I still need a place to write from, a writer's identity; as a teacher, I need to ask students to question the self they are constructing in their physical texts and in the actual classroom" (22). Harvey provides practical advice in "Presence in the Essay" on how teachers can teach their students to create such constructs by employing the features of presence he has explicated (649–53) and that I have used above in analyzing "Once More to the Lake."

Pedagogical influence. Personal presence gives essayist superstars, like canonical authors in other genres, significance in the field disproportionate to their numbers. Although they are not the rock stars of the belletristic world, because their essays have been reprinted so widely their influence has the potential for being profound. Yet we can ask whether these essayists have really affected the way the millions of student readers in the past sixty years have seen the world. Have these essayists caused their readers to think and act on the subjects their works address—civil and human rights, education, culture and multiculturalism, science and technology, writing and the arts? Is the superstar influence actually as profound as its potential?

As many textbooks reveal, students are obliged to read essays as prose models to emulate, even in process-oriented courses. In courses focusing on critical thinking, argumentation, or disciplinary issues, students are expected to read critically, take an intellectual stand, and enter into the agonistic language and dialectical postures of the academy. But most of the superstars' work is reflective, interpretive instead; it invites readers to enter the writer's world, look around, deepen their understanding, and come to their own interpretations and conclusions about that world.

Some of these interpretations could, however, lead to social action—even to civil disobedience or more extreme activity—for a number of the essays by canonical superstars are revolutionary. These include Swift's "A Modest Proposal"; Orwell's "Politics and the English Language," "Shooting an Elephant," and "Marrakech"; Thoreau's "Civil Disobedience"; Martin Luther King Jr.'s "Letter from Birmingham Jail"; and "The Declaration of Independence." Yet, Americans—teachers and students alike—tend to respond to these as historical documents, rather than as incitements to social action, as I have discussed in Chapter 2 (pp. 49–50). If essays such as these will make the students more thoughtful, morally better people (perhaps in emulation of the author's presence), or move them to noble or socially responsible action, it is hard to discern such effects in any given composition class.[1] For to recontextualize any essay, no matter how inspiring or incendiary, in a textbook and a school setting is for most college students to blunt the keen edge of the excitement—intellectual, political, aesthetic—that inspired the authors to write them in the first place.

Teachers should expect to expend some effort to override the anesthetic effects of anthologization, to help transform students from passive readers of entombed works, however canonical, to active responders to living words, the lively presences within and behind the essays they read. If, for example, students read "Shooting an Elephant" only as a course requirement, or as a personal essay—in this case, an episode of junior colonial officer's humiliation before Burmese "coolies" long ago and far away—they miss the point. If they read it in isolation from other canonical works of civil disobedience, they miss the point. Teachers can help students understand a work's importance in its original and its current contexts—political, social, intellectual, aesthetic. Thereby, teachers can reinvigorate significant essays by encouraging students to make meaningful connections—among the past and present implications of a given work and among readings on related topics (say, issues of civil disobedience, human rights, or multiculturalism).

And they can apply these—through deeds as well as words—to real life. As such works come alive to the students, so will their meaning, and their invitations (implicit and explicit) to think—and to act, to change the world.

This transformative potential of literature is one of the foundational principles of Kurt Spellmeyer's *The Arts of Living*, a radical, moral argument for *Reinventing the Humanities for the Twenty-First Century* reinforced by the philosophically provocative readings in *The New Humanities Reader* (edited by Richard Miller and Spellmeyer). Likewise, Thomas Deans moves the values articulated in *Writing Partnerships: Service-Learning in Composition* into the classroom and the wider world in his textbook *Writing and Community Action*.

Reinvigorating the genre. If more teachers wrote essays, or academic articles with presence that acknowledged their authorial investment, they would be better able to teach students not only the craft but the art. Until recently, composition studies scholars took the ideas—and indeed the personae—of academic essayists with presence, such as Peter Elbow, Donald Murray, Mike Rose, and Nancy Sommers—to heart, but dismissed or trivialized the genre in which they wrote as too obvious, too easy, too confessional: "U.S. composition teachers have created a school genre that can exist only in an expressivist composition classroom" (Dixon 257). Now that more academics have begun to try such writing themselves, as I explain in Chapter 1, they have realized how hard it is, in the absence of a predictable form and conventional academic language, to present profound ideas simply, with elegance and apparent ease, and even harder to create a credible persona of the sort that appears with regularity in the best nonfiction in the *The New Yorker,* little magazines, and sometimes the *The New York Times*. As writers of the genre, teachers and other essayists can with greater authority show students ways to convey the presence that can transform their own worlds and their relationship to their readers from distance and abstraction to immediacy and engagement. As writers of personal-sounding essays, teachers could speak with authority about the inevitable disparity between the private person behind the work and ways to translate salient elements of self-characterization to the public document. They could have students try to consciously control features such as motive, voice, degree and nature of investment in the subject, with an awareness that what beats on the page is the vitality of the writer's vision, not the bleeding heart of the writer behind the work.

> Voice-Over: *In 1993 the Massachusetts Civil Liberties Union Foundation honored the five defendants of the 1968 conspiracy trial, Dr. Spock included, at its annual Bill of Rights Dinner. In attendance was John Wall, who had prosecuted the government's case twenty-five years earlier. Tight-lipped and remote during the trial, he was now genial, beaming as he introduced himself to me. "I read your book and I loved it." He added, "When I saw Dr. Spock and the others in person, and came to know them through their presence in the courtroom, I grew to admire their ethics and their courage in speaking out and being willing to go to jail—for life if necessary—to defend the principles our country is founded on. The [FBI] agents just didn't get that on the tapes."*

4 Compression—When Less Says More

Omit needless words. Vigorous writing is concise.

—William Strunk, Jr. and E. B. White, *The Elements of Style*

A literary text must . . . be conceived in such a way that it will engage the reader's imagination in the task of working things out for himself, for reading is only a pleasure when it is active and creative.

—Wolfgang Iser, "The Reading Process"

"You know what it's like when the car you're in is going to crash and you're powerless to stop the events in motion?" This question invariably compels the students' attention, and I usually introduce it about a month into the semester, after we've come to know and trust one another. "Time slows down in your mind, doesn't it?" I say, and they nod affirmatively. "And events unfold as if you're watching them happen from a distance. You're detached, even calm, yes?" We discuss the reasons why this is so, and I summarize: "This is a way of taking control when we're out of control. By focusing intently on the matter at hand, eliminating everything extraneous or distracting, we gain power over the interpretation of the event even when we can't control the event itself," I say. "But there's a big difference. In real life, we crash and have to pick up the pieces. In our writing, this concentration gives the work its utmost power."

Then—the only time I use my own writing as an example during the semester, for the focus belongs on the students' work—I tell the story of the accident that led to this discovery. I tell the students how I wrote about it, and why I cut the original twenty-one pages down to the 252 words that appeared as a short segment of a creative nonfiction essay, "Teaching College English as a Woman." Before I get to the story itself, let me tell you why I tell it.

My teaching of writing, particularly—though not exclusively—creative nonfiction, is guided in part by Strunk and White's modernist principles of prose style epitomized by "Vigorous writing is concise." They explain: "A sentence should contain no unnecessary words, a paragraph no unnecessary sentences, for the same reason that a drawing should have no unnecessary lines and a machine no unnecessary parts. This requires not that the writer make all sentences short, or avoid all detail and treat subjects only in outline, but that every word tell" (23). Yet the postmodernist view in which writing, like the life it represents, is seen as indeterminate, non-linear, allusive, and incomplete could serve as the essential definition of belletristic essays (which I am using in Chapter 2, "The Essay Canon"), including much creative nonfiction. These two perspectives, the writer's pragmatic means to gaining verbal power, and the theorist's acknowledgment of the infinite and continually evolving universe of prose (like the cosmos, as well), find a happy pedagogical blend and application in the reader response theory, particularly that of Wolfgang Iser. Says Iser in "The Reading Process: A Phenomenological Approach," "The 'unwritten' part of a text stimulates the reader's creative participation," noting Virginia Woolf's observation of the way Jane Austen "stimulates us to supply what is not there. What she offers is, apparently, a trifle, yet is composed of something that expands in the reader's mind and endows with the most enduring form of life scenes which are outwardly trivial" but dynamically suggestive of the complexities of plot, dialogue, character (Woolf 142). Drawing on this and other examples, Iser concludes that "no author worth his salt will ever attempt to set the whole picture before his reader's eyes. If he does, he will very quickly lose his reader, for it is only by activating the reader's imagination that the author can hope to involve him and so realize the intentions of his text" (57).

This theoretical blend undergirds my classroom experience when I tell the accident story or its equivalent as a cautionary tale—not about driving, but about writing. The undergraduates who have sailed through earlier creative nonfiction courses usually arrive in my advanced course in love with everything they write, eager to say more and more and still more. They have taken to heart and computer the pedagogical advice often given to novice writers—even experienced ones—to expand on events, flesh out the characters, add details and dialogue to transform bare information into a story. And they've needed to do this, for amateur writers often underexplain, expecting readers to have more local knowledge (who's who, what's where, why things happened) than outsiders would know. They have learned that they need to supply enough information so their work will be self-contained, that they must provide a context adequate to interpret or illustrate what they're saying, and sufficient evidence to advance the points they're making, whether directly or by implication. All of this argues for amplification. Indeed, such advice establishes an expansive mind set that leads students to add material when they edit, as often, they should.

Yet, paradoxically, students write too much, even when they're writing too little. Most have not yet learned to trust their readers to understand what they're aiming at, and so they offer verbal pokes in the ribs—"Get it?"—through repetition, redundancy, overt recognition of what they've already implied. Such copious explicitness signals that they don't trust themselves as writers able to get their meaning across without explaining its significance, or that they haven't learned to edit. Or both. Their writing becomes overstuffed, zaftig, when what they really need is a body of lean, muscular prose capable of heavy lifting. So it's necessary to help the students understand how to write with compression, and thereby enable them to edit for the power that comes with making every word, every sentence, every syllable, every space count. This used to seem counterintuitive for both me as a teacher and for my students, especially when their papers remain underdeveloped in critical areas, until I began to tell—and unpack—stories like this one:

> Then, on a clear crisp evening in January, tenure became irrelevant. Our family dinner was interrupted by the phone call that every parent dreads. Come right away.
> We saw the car first, on a curve in the highway near the high school, crushed into a concrete telephone pole. Next was the rescue squad ambulance, lights revolving red and white, halted amidst shattered glass. Then the figure on the stretcher, only a familiar chin emerging from the bandages that swathed the head. "He was thrown out of the back seat. The hatchback

> door smashed his face as if he'd been hit with an axe," said the medic. "I'm fine," said our son, and we responded with terror's invariable lie, "You're going to be all right."
>
> After six hours of ambiguous X-rays, clear pictures finally emerged long after midnight, explaining why Laird's eyes were no longer parallel—one socket had simply been pulverized. The line of jagged-lightning stitches, sixty in all, that bolted across his face would be re-opened the next day for reconstructive surgery. "Don't go out in a full moon," sick-joked the doctor, howling like a banshee, "People will mistake you for a zombie."
>
> Laird had to remain upright for a month so his head would drain, and our family spent every February evening on the couch in front of the wood stove, propping each other up. I do not know, now what I wrote on student papers; or what we ate, or read, or wrote checks for during that long month. (823)

I start with the most obvious pieces of missing information. Did Laird recover? How do you know? How old was he when the accident occurred? How do you know that? Who was the driver? Did Laird go back to school while he was recuperating? What were my emotions as his mother at the time of the accident? During its aftermath? Then examine the motives: Why did Laird say "I'm fine" at the scene of the accident? Why did we lie, "You're going to be all right"? Why did the doctor behave like a buffoon? And myself like an automaton? How do you know these things? Why didn't I use the word "accident" in the opening dialogue? What enables you to understand the answers? Can you tell what caused the accident? Or make a reasonable guess? Why can I as a writer trust that in fact, you do understand all these things, and more, without further explanation? What elements of this story pack enough power to compel you to remember it?

Then I tell them some of the things they couldn't know, that were in the long version I had to write for myself before I could begin to compress their essence into the more powerful, elliptical story. The phone call announcing the accident. Our hushed conversations in the hospital lobby with the unstrung parents of another victim, still unconscious; their older son had died six years earlier in a crash at the same spot. Our terse exchange with the ophthalmologist we took Laird to when his enlarged pupils wouldn't undilate, ten days later: "If this happens again you must take him immediately to the major trauma center in Richmond. Yes, even if he's in school at the time. You can't wait." "Why the rush?" we had asked. "This could mean a blood clot in his brain. It's rare, but if you don't get immediate help"—the doctor paused—"your son could die." The phone call from the teenage driver's mother, wanting reassurance that our son would be all right (her son was just fine, thank you, not a scratch)—which we could not give her. All of this and more could have made a dramatic story, but it would have diverted attention from the larger narrative (My Big Tenure Fight) in which it was embedded.

I could use any segment of any of my own creative nonfiction essays for this purpose, for nearly every detail, every portion of every story embeds a nest of other tales. I alone know this complex weave of stories and can address these and the rationale for the omissions, the compression, in class. This authorial understanding enables me to override my reservations about sharing my writing with my students. Since I can't talk about anyone else's writing with this kind of insider knowledge, I have chosen to use my own, though more reticent teachers could analyze other published work—creative nonfiction, fiction, poetry— asking these questions: What do readers know about this piece that is not made explicit in the text? What does the author trust her readers to understand? How do you, as readers, know these things?

The next logical step is for the students to analyze examples of compression from their own writing in workshop, using the model just presented. The following serve as operative principles:

1) Where's the heart of the story/illustration?
2) What key words, images, actions, details address/illuminate that?
3) What else have I put in just because it happened and because that's in my mind as I write? Does this fulfill the functions of 1 and 2? Is it diverting, distracting?
4) How much can I trust my readers to figure out, understand from what I've already said?
5) What can I leave out without losing the meaning?
6) Once compressed, is there anything that needs to be included, added back to reinforce or illuminate what's on the page?

With these precepts in mind, students who have been wrestling with the contradictory concepts of expansion and compression can understand the dynamics of both, in dialogue with their audience. By asking "Did you get it?" "What's missing?" "What's redundant?" they learn how to put their writing on a diet of the essentials. They gain power and authority from using their insider's knowledge to analyze their own work and to realize new perspectives on the work of their peers; sharing that knowledge reinforces their sense of belonging to a community of real writers.

One caveat. I've found the undergraduates' oral analysis much more compelling—particularly in class discussion—than their attempts to address in writing material they've already deleted. Thus, in the course's next incarnation, I'll ask them to highlight in an intermediate draft the passages they intend to delete but to leave them on the page for possible reinstatement, thereby allowing a graphic view of the options for expansion as well as compression. With hearts and minds, student writers of creative nonfiction can come to understand what poets know, as well—the truth of Strunk and White's "Omit needless words," of Iser's views on dynamic suggestion, how less really can become more.

Part II

Teaching Writing in—and Out of—Troubled Times

5 Writing Textbooks in/ for Times of Trauma

About suffering they were never wrong.
The Old Masters: how well they understood
Its human position; how it takes place
While someone else is eating or opening a window or just walking dully along. . . .

—W. H. Auden, "Museé des Beaux Arts"

Anything can happen, the tallest things

Be overturned, those in high places daunted,
Those overlooked esteemed. Hooked-beak Fortune
Swoops, making the air gasp, tearing off
Crests for sport, letting them drop wherever.

Ground gives. The heaven's weight
Lifts up off Atlas like a kettle lid,
Capstones shift, nothing resettles right.
Telluric ash and fire-spores darken day.

—Seamus Heaney, "Horace and the Thunder"
(After Horace, Odes, 1, 34)

September 11, 2001: Where Were You, Where Were We?

September 11, 2001 dawned, indeed like most of this most unusual autumn in New England, postcard perfect; a bright blue sky, with just a hint of briskness in the air. And there we were, dawdling over breakfast, windows open to the herb garden, savoring the day and the promise of a new year. For early September is always New Year's for academics, with the year to come shimmering on a bright canvas that we paint full of resolutions, plans, lists, and schedules—just an ordinary day when, as on every day, we were trying to impose order on our unruly corner of the universe. Yet, as on every other day, this was a day to savor—just because it was there, and we were there to share it, and because it was my husband's birthday.

Then we heard the news. Then we heard the news again. And again, and again, for days that stretched into weeks and into months, that day of days transformed in the twinkling of an eye to an unwitting watershed. The world was one way before September 11 and changed utterly thereafter. Only after the fact do I realize that the impressionistic watercolor of the Manhattan waterfront facing our bed, which I have looked at every morning for the past twenty years on first opening my eyes, is curiously up-to-date, though painted in 1955. Tall buildings, bright sugar cubes of reds and blues and whites provide a cityscape of blocks firm, but curiously fragile—as if you could pull out one from the bottom of the stack and they would all fall down. No twin towers. It is only as I write this chapter that the publication date of "Musée des Beaux Arts" strikes home: 1940, during the bombing of Britain, by a poet who had written passionate witness to the Spanish Civil War and the beginnings of World War II in the Far East. Auden was no stranger to the suffering that takes place on an ordinary day, and now, neither were we—nor anyone else in the world. These personal reactions to "Where were you when . . ." "What did you think at the time?" "What do you understand now?" invite dialogue, reflection, writing for oneself or an audience—as Heaney's "Horace and Thunder" reflects both. But whether private or public, these are in no way the last word. For 2001 was a year like no other, and though several years have passed, that year is not over, and may never be over. At this writing there is no termination, no closure.

We tell ourselves stories of cataclysmic events such as these to make sense of things that don't make sense, to bring order from chaos. As Joan Didion says, "We tell ourselves stories in order to live." As time passes, we are still trying to figure out what stories to tell, for the narratives of this fateful day and its anthrax-laced aftermath remain stories-in-progress, stories with complicated beginnings, muddled middles, and ambiguous trails that are not really endings seen through a glass dark with the rain of smoke and ash from the towers aflame in our imaginations, or smoldering still. These stories and the stories behind—and ahead—of them are the stories that I soon realized *The Essay Connection*—my textbook-in-progress—would have to invite readers to tell, understand, and interpret, even as new stories continue to emerge and undergo continual revision, their meanings in flux.

Transforming a Textbook for a Transformed World

On that fateful morning, I had been revising a textbook, seventh edition of *The Essay Connection*. "Shorten it a little," said my editor at Houghton Mifflin, in a desire to return the book, which had bulked up over time, to its earlier svelte shape. So I eliminated three chapters, and thought I was about through. That was before the towers collapsed. Within the week, I realized that in a changed world, a collection of readings intended to stimulate students' reasoned discussion and critical thinking and writing had to respond to this cataclysmic event. As Elie Wiesel explains in "Why I Write" (included in all editions of *The Essay Connection* since its publication in 1988), his reasons for witnessing the Holocaust in everything he writes, "Not to transmit an experience is to betray it." "I write," he says, "to remain faithful," "to help the dead vanquish death" (39–42). I could ask the student readers of *The Essay Connection* to do no less—not because of morbid reasons, or a sentimental desire to memorialize a past that will never come again, but as an ethical response to a world they did not ask for, but will nevertheless have to live in.

Although I knew I would be including readings on international terrorism suitable for use as a brief argumentative casebook, I realized it would be too soon to prepare the new chapter. I didn't want to assemble an instant-book of knee-jerk reactions, written in the white heat of personal assault and national injury. It would take time for thoughtful commentary to appear, grounded in profound knowledge of Middle Eastern history, Islamic culture and religion, international politics. Fortunately, I'd begun the revision a year in advance, and had time to let the fallout settle—national as well as personal.

(Lack of) Knowledge. I also had time to learn more about what I was getting into—and to get scared, both by the subject and the extent of my ignorance. I was born, raised, and educated in the U.S.A., where I have worked all my adult life as an English professor and writer, specializing in American literature and composition studies, focusing on American higher education. Although my research in creative nonfiction, essays, and American autobiography includes works by many ethnic groups from a range of cultural backgrounds, little of it is Islamic. When I write and teach in these genres, I am comfortable, with the cushion of forty years' professional experience buttressed by a native's intimate lifetime knowledge of the language and cultural experience. I know what I know, and when I don't know something I know where to look for it and how to evaluate its intrinsic worth, integrity, and intellectual resonance. I know, almost intuitively by now, the canon, literary conventions, the range of possibilities for breaking the mold in ways creative rather than simply weird.

Very little of this knowledge applies in direct ways to my new attempts to understand the world of Islam. I cannot claim expertise as a political scientist. My heritage is Christian; my husband's, Jewish. Although we have traveled extensively—including trips to Asia and the Middle East—and have friends from all over the world who have emigrated to the U.S., my knowledge of the Islamic world's culture, religion(s), history, politics is—at its most euphemistic—superficial. How, then, could I even contemplate compiling a set of well-informed, accurate, up-to-date representative readings on the subject? How, as a textbook editor, could I know—or learn—enough to make the difficult, intelligent choices of materials and aids to reading and writing about them that would be crucial to such a chapter?

Ethical and Intellectual Responsibilities. In the moral universe of the academy, however, having had the right—and good—idea to devote significant space in the new *Essay Connection* to a discussion of the implications of world terrorism how could I *not* include this? No one expects moral issues to be easy, or understanding to be either immediate or complete. If we taught only what we know for sure, taking no risks and making no intellectual leaps or creative reaching for the stars, our classes would be static and stifling. Taking heart from Emerson's observation that "Knowledge is the knowing that we cannot know," I had no choice but to soldier on. My operative motto would be Thurber's observation that "It is better to ask some of the questions than to know all the answers"—and I would not mean it ironically, as he did in *Fables for Our Time*. Isn't this the attitude that enables all experienced teachers—and writers and textbook editors—to get through every bit of new work we do? It isn't chutzpah, it's hope that leads us to tackle totally unfamiliar subjects, I reasoned (well, maybe a little chutzpah)—but in a world so totally changed by cataclysm we have no choice but to plunge in and aim to keep our heads above water.

Nevertheless, I knew that to find suitable materials on international terrorism to use as a significant portion of a textbook I'd have to learn a lot, and fast. I'd have to admit—first to myself—the vast lacunae in my understanding of the subject, then figure out what I most needed to know, find reliable sources—expert, up-to-date, reinforced by a depth of background information. Because all sources emanate from the author's particular perspective on a particular culture, I'd also have to find representative authors whose biases offset one another. To do this, I'd have to depend on the research skills I'd learned and relearned over the years, especially since the advent of the information explosion over the Internet. I'd also need some sense of where my prospective readers were coming from. What did the teachers and their first-year composition students know, think, and care about international terrorism? And in what ways did I want my readings to influence these readers? In the absence of material, which was probably not yet written, these specific questions were not easy to answer.

Generic Criteria for Selecting Material. However, because the generic considerations of selecting material remained consonant over any number of editions, I could use the following general guidelines in choosing the readings. The book's format dictated that I include four published essays by experts, preferably written with distinction, and a student essay, ditto. So vast and complicated was the topic, however, that I decided to expand the number. The material had to be teachable—that is, each piece had to be short enough to be discussed in one or two class sessions. It had to be self-contained, with sufficient information and background material to be understood by American teachers and students who, I assumed, would not be experts on the subject any more than I was. The fact that I was approaching the subject in relative innocence would enable me to see it as new students might, and serve as a reminder to address their concerns: what would they need to know, and when would they need to know it?

Would there be students in class, or teachers, perhaps of Islamic background, whose background knowledge could be drawn on to help the others? Even though the topic was current, its contours changing with every day's developing news, the essays could not be so time-bound that they would become quickly out of date. How well would these essays lend themselves to the book's rhetorical concerns of critical thinking and thoughtful argumentation? Together, if not individually, would they contribute to a balanced argument, reflect and refract upon one another with illumination and intellectual integrity rather than with fusillades and fulminations? Or should these even be expected to provide a cultural balance, given the Western values and culture of myself and most of my readers?

Controversy in Context: Implications of World Terrorism and World Peace

An Argument Casebook

Thematic Criteria for Selecting Material. I also knew even before the flood of materials on international terrorism reached the publications from which I draw most of the essays for *The Essay Connection*—such as *Atlantic Monthly, Harper's, The New York Times Magazine,* and the *The New Yorker*—some of the themes and values I wanted the discussion to incorporate. These included:

- *Definitions of war.* The unconventional nature of the terroristic activities—the use of passenger planes as guided missiles—and the identification of these with a leader and a political-religious movement rather than with a country require rethinking—and redefining—the conventional concepts of war. (*The 9/11 Commission Report,* published in July 2004 addressed these issues in time for inclusion in the 8th edition.) By inference, new definitions of war would also entail new definitions of peace.
- *New language for new concepts.* If the current political situation as the book went to press wasn't war, what was it? What should we call it? Whom—or what, in a continually turbulent situation—do we call "the enemy"? "Allies?" Is it appropriate to use such vague and general terms as "the forces of evil" to represent our antagonists? All antagonists?
- *Avoidance of polarizing language and attitudes.* I did not want to encourage an "us vs them" orientation to the subject, even for a largely American readership. Nor did I want to encourage racial profiling or other forms of racial, cultural, or ethnic stereotyping.

- *Consideration of ethical issues.* All of the above concepts embed an ethical stance toward the issues embedded in the conflict, and the recognition that not all teachers or students would share these values. I wanted student readers to balance patriotism with humanitarianism, to balance the need for national security with respect for individuals' civil liberties, to weigh issues of security against issues of freedom. Even if their conclusions differed from the idealistic stance I hoped they'd take, these issues could not be ignored—proof positive that intellectual risk and controversy are possible in a free society.
- *Concerns for the future.* I hoped the readings on terrorism would provide an abundance of issues and perspectives for students to discuss, argue over, write about, and rethink and rewrite. I wanted them to emerge wiser but not sadder, thoughtful but not angry, and—rather than to expect to live forever under terrorist threats—and to be full of hope for a peaceful future. But would hopes for peace emerge from the literature on terrorism? Who could know?

Readings on International Terrorism[2]

In contrast to the rest of the book, which consists entirely of essays, I decided to introduce the chapter with a poem written explicitly to commemorate the events of that fateful day—musing, meditative, inconclusive, Seamus Heaney's "Horace and the Thunder"—a portion of which serves as an epigraph to this essay. From a complex sea of print that included books on terrorism; Middle Eastern history, culture, and politics; editorial and op-ed pieces; and magazine and on-line articles, long and short, highly specialized and somewhat simpler, surfaced three essays and a book chapter that have survived into the *Essay Connection's* eighth edition, as well. I explain here the rationale for including them, as the beginning of a dialogue which students and teachers are invited to join, bringing to this colloquy other voices, from sources printed, on-line, and from other media that continue the conversation and debate beyond the boundaries of the textbook.

It would be tempting, as many writers and media commentators have done, to divide the world into "us"—the innocent, beleaguered victims of a horrific attack, and "them," the vile denizens of an evil empire who hate us all and will stop at nothing to destroy our free society, as Don DeLillo does in "In the Ruins of the Future," *Harper's*

(Dec. 2001).[3] This is not a good way to conduct any argument, although as we have seen, this kind of thinking is often the basis for initiating and conducting a war, emanating from the Oval Office, the halls of Congress, and branches of the military, with reverberations world wide throughout the press, television, and the Internet.

Because the *us vs. them* view is so popular, it cannot be overlooked. Yet, as the immediate impact of the events is mitigated by time, we realize that this is not the only perspective and war is not the only alternative. Even if we can't change the past, or prevent the World Trade Center's destruction, we can interpret the present in ways that we hope will prepare for the future. Thus, the chapter opens with reflections by a New Yorker. In "History Overcomes Stories," an eyewitness commentary on her experience of living ten blocks from "what used to be the World Trade Center towers," Laurie Fendrich, a painter and fine arts professor, writes a counter narrative to combat media overkill, to interpret stories that "are polluted and demeaned by having been reduced to fodder for television, movie, and slick magazine entertainment." She looks, as people do in times of trauma, for guidance "to see if we can now act the way we ought to have been acting all along," and finds focus and stability in a reaffirmation of the core values of Western culture, which trendy postmodern theory has undervalued: "individual liberty, coupled with obligations to virtue, democracy coupled with responsibility, the requirement of courage, an acknowledgment—always tempered by reason—of duty, and an assertion of basic, not jingoistic, patriotism" (529–32).

Those who examine the causes of international terrorism, as does Bernard Lewis ("What Went Wrong?" *Atlantic Monthly* Jan. 2002), are aware that there is no single interpretation and that all explanations—those of Christians, Muslims and Jews; Arabs, Turks, Persians; are controversial. Because "Who did this to us?" leads only to "neurotic fantasies and conspiracy theories," concludes Lewis, the question "What did we do wrong?" leads naturally to the search for a solution. This is difficult because the condition of liberty in the Middle East is fragile and full of complications. Lewis's answer, that the peoples of the Middle East should establish a society where people have the freedom "to question and inquire and speak; freedom of the economy from corrupt and pervasive mismanagement; freedom of women from male oppression; freedom of citizens from tyranny," makes explicit the beliefs and values that undergird Fendrich's interpretation of the subject, as well (533–38).

However, "Why can't our antagonists be more like us?" is not the only way to look at the issue; critics such as the late Palestinian scholar Edward Said (not in *The Essay Connection*) strongly object to such solutions, which they interpret as the efforts of Westerners attempting to dominate an Eastern culture. In "Theater of Terror" and "America as Enemy," excerpts from *Terror in the Mind of God,* Mark Juregensmeyer analyzes the "exaggerated violence" of terrorist attacks such as the 1993 World Trade Center bombing, eerily prescient of its 2001 successor. He explains them as "constructed events: they are mind-numbing, mesmerizing theater. At center stage are the acts themselves—stunning, abnormal, and outrageous murders carried out in a way that graphically displays the awful power of violence—set within grand scenarios of conflict and proclamation." Such horrifically violent acts, "surpassing the wounds inflicted during warfare" because of their demonstrative "secondary impact . . . [,]elicit feelings of revulsion and anger in those who witness them." Indeed, claims Juergensmeyer, "terrorism is always part of a political strategy," performed not only to "fulfill political ends" but to "have a direct impact on public policy" (538–50).

"Thoughts in the Presence of Fear," by poet, essayist, and farmer Wendell Berry, offers twenty-seven reflections on the aftermath of "the horrors of September 11," critically addressing the implications of the end of "the unquestioning technological and economic optimism that ended on that day." In one stroke, he says, these terroristic activities should cause the "developed" nations to question and revise their policies that "had given to the 'free market' the status of a god," and sacrificed to it "their farmers, farmlands, and communities, their forests, wetlands, and prairies, their ecosystems and watersheds. They had accepted universal pollution and global warming as normal costs of doing business." In his commentary, each paragraph of which could be the basis for a policy statement, an argument, an essay, even a book, he thoughtfully explains why these values are wrong and makes the case for a peaceable, self-sufficient economy, based on "thrift and care, on saving and conserving, not on excess and waste" (551–55). Though Berry's tone and language are moderate, his agrarian, pacifistic, Christian views are bound to anger those who prefer swords to ploughshares as a means of settling international conflicts.

Readings on World Peace: Nobel Prize Speeches

The Need for Peace—A Necessary Conclusion. My textbooks reflect my philosophy of life; I want students to be inspired by what they read, and not depressed or discouraged. I did not want students to regard the future with a mixture of terror, hopelessness, or resignation to a future of fear. Moreover, given the pro-Western bias of the terrorism materials, I had to locate writings that would reflect a world view. In an uncertain future, what could realistically ensure that *The Essay Connection* would end on a positive note?

As I pondered whether to include in the terrorism chapter an excerpt from Nelson Mandela's autobiography, *Long Walk to Freedom,* an inspiring account of his twenty-five years in harsh South African prisons as anti-apartheid head of the African National Congress, and the enormous changes his moral example wrought, Kofi Annan was awarded the 2001 Nobel Peace Prize. He shared it jointly with the United Nations, on whose behalf he accepted the award, three months after the terrorist attacks on the World Trade Center and the Pentagon. As I read the stirring words of his acceptance speech, the solution became clear: I would include a chapter of Nobel Peace Prize speeches. Here is the way Annan began:

> Today, in Afghanistan, a girl will be born. Her mother will hold her and feed her, comfort her and care for her—just as any mother would anywhere in the world. In these most basic acts of human nature, humanity knows no divisions. But to be born a girl in today's Afghanistan is to begin life centuries away from the prosperity that one small part of humanity has achieved. It is to live under conditions that many of us in this hall would consider inhuman.
>
> . . . I might equally well have mentioned a baby boy or girl in Sierra Leone. No one today is unaware of this divide between the world's rich and poor. No one today can claim ignorance of the cost that this divide imposes on the poor and dispossessed who are no less deserving of human dignity, fundamental freedoms, security, food and education than any of us. The cost, however, is not borne by them alone. Ultimately, it is

borne by all of us—North and South, rich and poor, men and women of all races and religions.

Today's real borders are not between nations, but between powerful and powerless, free and fettered, privileged and humiliated. Today, no walls can separate humanitarian or human rights crises in one part of the world from national security crises in another. (Annan 2001)

While the manuscript was being copyedited, Jimmy Carter was awarded the 2002 Nobel Peace Prize. On December 10, he delivered the address; on December 11, we received the text from the Nobel website and added this to the book, just as it went to the printer.[4]

Indeed, the Nobel website, www.nobel.se/peace/laureates, had the texts of all the acceptance speeches I needed. Speech after speech reflected the fact that goodness, selflessness, adherence to high moral principles, as the lives and works of the Nobel Prize winners reveal, can emerge even in times of trauma—often, in responses to the challenges of trauma itself. Their talks, like their works, offered beacons of faith, hope, and good will. If, as Franklin Roosevelt said, "the only thing we have to fear is fear itself," a chapter of Nobel Peace Prize speeches would reinforce a value system that would help the audience to lead lives governed by principles and values that brought out the best rather than the worst of our common humanity. This was the message, implied and stated overtly, by every one of the Nobel Prize winners I decided to include.

As I said, "These Nobel winners formed an international spectrum of the brave, the bold, the morally beautiful. Some are people of high visibility and power"—United Nations Secretary General Kofi Annan (Ghana); and national leaders Jimmy Carter, Yitzak Rabin (Israel), and Frederik Willem de Klerk (South Africa). Others are religious and political leaders who have suffered extensive privations for living their beliefs: the 14th Dalai Lama (Tibet), sentenced by the Chinese to lifetime exile as the embodiment of the Tibetan Buddhists; Nelson Mandela (South Africa); and Aung San Suu Kyi (Myanmar), who continues to serve as an international symbol of resistance to tyranny even throughout years of house arrest. Still others are people of humble origins whose advocacy of human rights and reconciliation catapulted them into international prominence—housewife turned peace activist Betty Williams (Northern Ireland); and Guatemalan champion of

Mayan rights and culture, Rigoberta MenchúTum. Activist humanitarian organizations are represented by Doctors Without Borders (Médecins Sans Frontières), whose members risk their own lives to travel to embattled parts of the world, providing medical aid to victims of genocide, massacre, rape, and other war crimes. "Ours is an ethic of refusal," explains James Orbinski. 'It will not allow any moral political failure or injustice to be sanitized or cleansed of its meaning'" ("Humanitarianism"). All of these Nobel recipients, and others, like Martin Luther King, Jr. (whose "Letter from Birmingham Jail" is a canonical staple of *The Essay Connection*), are "'witnesses to the truth of injustice,' as Orbinski says, willing to lay their lives on the line—and to lose them, as Rabin and Dr. King have done—for a moral cause. Like their lives, their words in these inspiring speeches, can guide us to some answers. How we as individuals, family members, friends, and citizens can do our best not only to lead the good life but to make that life better for humankind is one of the aims of a liberal education and of this book" (*Essay Connection* 7th ed. 568).

In Conclusion, the Inconclusive. . . .

I ended *The Essay Connection* with the following admonition, inevitable but necessary. Each of the issues embedded in this topic "is complicated, for matters of war and peace are never simple, never static, particularly when negotiated in an international arena. Most can be seen not just from two points of view, but from many perspectives embedded in the political, economic, religious, ethical, and cultural values of a great variety of individuals, cultures, and countries." So readers will need to consult additional, current sources in order to "avoid blanket generalizations and simplistic conclusions" (607).

To provide teaching material on the shifting sands of international politics involves, as we have seen, a leap of faith, a commitment to open-mindedness, and an abundance of good will—not just from the editor, but from the teachers who decide to teach the chapters on international terrorism and world peace, and from their students. I don't worry about the pieces becoming dated. These subjects, as our elected officials and the media remind us daily, are always with us. Even if the specific details change—and they will—the topics themselves are perennial; a publisher's website can point to supplements. I do worry that these chapters might be overlooked, as new material often is (see Chapter 2, "The Essay Canon"). Nevertheless, as a teacher and as a textbook editor, in addition presenting these new chapters from sound intellectual, ethical, and pedagogical reasons, I have to proffer them as my form of witness to the events of September 11, 2001. For all of us affected by issues of international terrorism and peace, as Annan reminds us, are interconnected in concern, remembrance, and suffering—general and personal. No one in this world is immune.

"About suffering they were never wrong,/The Old Masters"

"About suffering they were never wrong,/The Old Masters." While others were "eating or opening a window or just walking dully along," at 8:30 on that fateful morning, our daughter-in-law, Vicki, was aboard a United flight destined for Los Angeles but stuck on the runway at JFK. As the plane finally began a slow taxiing out, around 9, it was ordered to stop, and five passengers in first class, growing ever more agitated, exploded at the flight attendant, "We must take off! We can tolerate no more delay!" They continued their clamor, and when the plane finally returned to the gate, this quintet—yes, terrorists, said the F.B.I. in the investigation that followed—fled as soon as the doors were opened. "Anything," indeed, could "happen, the tallest things/Be overturned . . . Capstones [could] shift, nothing resettle right." That it took Vicki two days to return home through traumatized roadways to our son, Bard, in Westchester is a happy anticlimax. Yet, her experience is a vivid reminder that there are no guarantees that the rest of the lives of any of us, anywhere in the world, will be happily anticlimactic; our stories continue, under incessant revision. The perspectives offered in the chapters on terrorism, and peace, can help guard against personal solipsism, national narcissism, as we tell, revise, and continue to reinterpret the stories not only of those fateful days but also of the days passing and to come.

6 The Great Process Paradigm and Its Legacy for the Twenty-First Century

Most post-process theorists hold three assumptions about the act of writing: (1) writing is public; (2) writing is interpretive; and (3) writing is situated . . . and therefore cannot be reduced to a generalizable process.

—Thomas Kent, *Post Process Theory: Beyond the Writing Process Paradigm* (1999)

My lessons cover ways to compose with computers . . . to manage the time that completing a beautiful text requires, to collaborate practically with others, and to revise and evaluate one's own writing. Without these lessons in composition, typically called a 'process' but lately identified by 'post-process' theorists as an activity comprising too many distinct tasks and minute-by-minute choices to be a teachable algorithm, my students retain their awe of . . . printed texts and their writers. But demystifying lessons in the acts and habits of confident writers . . . focuses students' learning.

—Susan Miller, "How I Teach Writing," *Pedagogy* (2001)

The Great Paradigm Shift, from the "traditional prescriptive and product-centered paradigm" (Hairston 80) to "teaching writing as process, not product" (Murray, "Teach Writing") remains a significant influence in composition studies because process philosophy and research-based pedagogy continue to retain their power in textbooks and in the classroom. With modifications and contemporary upgrades, they will do so as long as one of the major aims—and responsibilities—of the profession is to continually improve our teaching of writing. Meanwhile, theory and research in the current "post process" era and in the as-yet-to-be-labeled future enable the profession to move beyond the limitations of process theory and models to address a host of other issues from diverse social, multicultural, ethical, and other perspectives. Because process remains the default mode in much of our thinking about writing, I will divide this chapter into three parts: Where We've Been—The Process Paradigm; Paradigm Drift—Post-Process Definitions and Implications, which includes a re-reading of *Lives on the Boundary;* and a look at composition studies of the future in Process, Post-Process, and Beyond.

Where We've Been—The Process Paradigm

Let's begin with a brief, nostalgic look at the good old days of the process era—when process theory, process research, and process teaching were in harmony. What we think we know we forget, as familiarity neutralizes and blurs distinctive features of even the most vital entity. In another decade or two the term *process,* once as cataclysmic as the explosion of the atom bomb, may become as bland and unremarkable as *current-traditional rhetoric* is to the entire profession at present. And though still viable, just as vague.[1] In "Stepping Yet Again into the Same Current," George Pullman offers an insightful, relativistic contemporary definition of current-traditional rhetoric, which differs significantly from the implied definition of fifty years earlier: "The expression refers to how traditional rhetoric influences our current understanding of composition, which means that current traditional rhetoric is today concerned with understanding how the tradition is written, with the work of people such as Richard Enos, and Jarrat and Schiappa, while the current traditional rhetoric [fifty years ago] was concerned with how to apply Aristotle's insights to Freshman Composition" (22–23).

So first, a definition.

Process Definition: "What's the magic word?" asked my interviewer in 1977, looking for a co-director of a National Writing Project affiliate. "Process," I shot back, in the spirit of "plastics" as the mantra of the future in *The Graduate.* We grinned conspiratorially, for we had the keys to the kingdom undiscovered by our indifferent literary counterparts. "You're hired," he said.

Here's what turned us on. In "Toward a Post-Process Composition," Gary A. Olson provides a contemporary interpretation of ten essential characteristics of the thirty-year-old process paradigm that remain significant in the new millennium:

1. Writing is an "activity," an act composed of a variety of activities.
2. The activities in writing are typically recursive rather than linear.
3. Writing is, first and foremost, a social activity.
4. The act of writing can be a means of learning and discovery.
5. Experienced writers are often aware of audience, purpose, and context.
6. Experienced writers spend considerable time on invention and revision.
7. Effective writing instruction allows students to practice these activities.
8. Such instruction includes ample opportunities for peer review.
9. Effective instructors grade student work not only on the finished product but also on the efforts involved in the writing process.
10. Successful composition instruction entails finding appropriate occasions to intervene in each student's writing process. (7)

Although these writing process principles have been interrogated, expanded, adapted, and modified from the time Hairston articulated them in the classic "The Winds of Change,"[2] they remain today a beacon for classroom teachers, glowing through turbulent post-process skies.

The Joys of Process

There are many reasons why the process paradigm won the hearts and minds of English teachers and researchers. In contrast to the current-traditional paradigm, which it either replaced (Murray, "Teach Writing As Process, Not Product") or supplemented (Crowley, "Around 1971"), the process paradigm was dynamic, not static. Coming of age in a revolutionary era that gave power to the people, especially to women and minorities, this paradigm was empowering to teachers and students alike. It was reality based, focusing on actual writers—from the most sophisticated to the most naive—in the act(s) of writing. It was obvious—to the converted, anyway, and accessible in principle and in practice. As John Clifford and Elizabeth Ervin explain, "Like New Criticism a generation earlier, process gave writing professional credibility. It could generate theory" and, I would add, research—"while allowing for an accessible pedagogy" (180). Arriving at the same time as deconstruction and other critical theories that were armored in thick abstractions and expressed in darksome jargon, process was a welcome alternative that—in research and in practice—could be discussed in understandable concepts and everyday language.[3]

Because process seemed so clear and straightforward, teachers could quickly understand its concepts and put them into effect without much (if any) training, though the National Writing Project and its affiliates were created to help translate theory and research into classroom application.[4] Particularly if teachers were writers themselves, they could recognize how the general process framework—prewrite, write, rewrite, and variations—could accommodate their own practices and those of their students. This is true, despite the fact that some teachers and whole school systems voided both theory and practice by reducing the writing process to a formula: "Prewrite on Mondays, Write on Wednesdays, Revise on Fridays" (Couture 30). Nevertheless, when employed as intended, the process paradigm allowed for considerable individuality, particularly when readers were regarded as part of the transaction, as in the 1984 revival of Louise Rosenblatt's *Literature as Exploration,* first published in 1938. Process research of scholars as diverse as Janet Emig, Donald Graves, Sharon Pianko, Nancy Sommers, Sondra Perl, and Mike Rose focused on a variety of students in school settings. The elasticity of the process paradigm was demonstrated in research by Carol Berkenkotter, Lee Odell and Dixie Goswami, and Linda Flower and John Hayes, among others,[5] whose studies expanded to include people of differing ages, abilities, jobs, and status performing varying tasks in diverse settings. It is axiomatic that process research was cutting edge in the 1970s and 1980s, and established the reputations of these scholars

In its days of youthful exuberance—the 1970s and early 1980s—the process paradigm was exhilarating. Inherently democratic, it was calculated—through accommodating a wide variety of writers and writing processes—to produce a nation of good writers committed to their own process and invested in their own writing. Its promulgators, such as Donald Murray (A *Writer Teaches Writing* and *Write to Learn*), Peter Elbow (*Writing Without Teachers*), and Mike Rose (*Lives on the Boundary*), themselves epitomized the four *Cs*—compositionists of competence, confidence, and collegiality—and thus became instant gurus with large followings of teachers who to this day remain loyal to the pedagogical philosophy embodied in their works.[6] Examining "the process of writing as followed by most professionals" (xi), in *A Writer Teaches Writing,* Murray showed teachers how to help their students discover a subject, sense an audience, search for specifics ("to show instead of tell") (5), create a design, write, rethink, rewrite (2–13). By de-centering the classroom, encouraging teachers to "come out from behind the big desk," as Nancie Atwell put it (4), the process paradigm was compatible with Paolo Freire's liberatory pedagogy, and a fitting response to the turbulent 60s, "the years of Kennedy, King, Vietnam, urban riots, student protests, and Watergate" (Joseph Harris 26).

Paradigm Drift: Post-Process Definitions

American academics are a dissatisfied lot; the academy seems to function most happily in an adversarial mode. Popular paradigms can't be all good, popular research can't be always right. The critical tradition of literary scholarship, whose antagonistic character Frey labels "literary Darwinism," has obliged composition students to "invent the university" by adopting its argumentative stance (Bartholomae, "Inventing"). Thus, it is inevitable that even the most widely adopted paradigm and the most respected process research have drawn fire. Time and knowledge move on.

Process research and its resultant pedagogy were initially centered on the individual writer, and the writer's private views of the world. Teachers worked with individual students to enable them to discover an effective process to liberate these nascent ideas struggling to breathe free. Critics equated such process orientation with expressivism—self-indulgent writing in contrast to real-world demands for meaningful, goal-directed communication; their hostility to personal-sounding writing persists to this day. Yet, the process paradigm—and virtually all of the process-oriented textbooks after the 1970s—allowed for many different kinds of writing, especially narratives, expositions, and arguments. Scholars in the early 1980s sought to open up these conceptions. In well-received articles, Lester Faigley ("Competing Theories of Process") and Patricia Bizzell ("Composing Processes") identified three principal strands of process thinking as expressive, cognitive, and social. James A. Berlin in "Contemporary Composition" labeled the "Major Pedagogical Theories" as "classicist, positivist, expressionist, and new rhetorical" (see Joseph Harris, *A Teaching Subject* 54–55). The seeds of post-process were planted in these critiques, particularly the social constructionist view that understands writing to be "culturally and socially mediated behavior" (Petraglia 54).

While the process paradigm today remains paramount in teaching writing (to which I shall return later), its survival as a subject for research has been superseded by a host of other issues and methodologies. Although some scholars label the times we live in *post-process, post-process* is a term that, like its counterpart, *postmodern,* seems vague in comparison with its referent. A poll of teachers-on-the-street might elicit a post-process acknowledgment that writing is a social action in a variety of social contexts. But even among those who use the term with confidence, there is no readily identifiable configuration of commonly agreed-on assumptions, concepts, values, and practices that would comprise a paradigm. In fact, in *Situating Composition,* Lisa Ede examines "The Writing Process Movement and the Professionalization of Composition," concluding—among other things, that process never really disappeared, because "arguments for writing as a social process rely upon the same strategies used to establish the writing process. Just as scholars arguing for writing as a process reified and essentialized a diverse group of scholarly and pedagogical projects into current-traditional rhetoric, so too did scholars arguing for writing as a social process reify and essentialize a diverse group of process-based products" (outline, chapter 2). (In Chapter 3, "Paradigms Lost," Ede amplifies on these remarks from her original book outline.)

In its minimalist sense, post-process may simply be a chronological marker to indicate the passage of time, with various topics of current concern grafted onto an essentially process-oriented view of composition studies. This seems to be the perspective of Libby Allison, Lizbeth Bryant, and Maureen Hourigan's *Grading in the Post-Process Classroom,* one of the few books with post-process in the title, whose editors claim that "lettered grades demanded at semester's end are at odds with post-process composition theory" (back cover). Yet, the contributors concentrate on the phenomenon of grading—in student-centered classrooms, the heart of the writing process.[7] Villanueva's "Afterword" reiterates the pervasive theme: "Writing is a process. Ultimately, first-year composition emphasizes awareness of writing as a process—from a process of jotting meaningful marks on a page . . . to a process of discovery, to a potential process of change (of the self and others)" (178).

Nevertheless, post-process scholars themselves do agree on the following. Process theory is too big, too encompassing, say the post-process critics, who begin where the 1980s critiques leave off. Process theory proposes a common writing process, about which generalizations can be made. In contrast, post-process theorists accept as a fundamental truth, proclaims Thomas Kent in his industrial-strength definition that introduces *Post-Process Theory: Beyond the Writing Process Paradigm*, that "no codifiable or generalizable writing process exists or could exist," and thus there is no Big Theory that can capture what writers do (1). Kent explains why, in three major assumptions about the act of writing.

1. *Writing is a public act*—a public interchange between the writer and "other language users" to whom the writing must be accessible. In fact, we "could not write at all if it were not for other language users and the world we share with others." Thus there can be nò possibility for "private" writing. Because any given act of writing is specific to individuals at specific moments in time, and because these individuals and relations are always changing, no single process or account of a process can capture what writers actually do. (1–2)

2. *Writing is "a thoroughly interpretive act"*—making sense of what is going on in both the "reception and the production of discourse." Writing means more than translation, paraphrase, or moving from one code to another, which process pedagogy encourages. Writing is always context-specific: too much of the 1970s and 1980s process research decontextualized writers, or created arbitrary, unreal laboratory settings. Post-process theory, says Kent, is sensitive to the fact that "When we read we interpret specific texts or utterances; when we write, we interpret our readers, our situations, our and other people's motivations, the appropriate genres to employ in specific circumstances. . . . Writing requires interpretation, and interpretation cannot be reduced to a process. (2–3)

3. *Writing is situated.* That "writers always write from some position or some place; writers are never nowhere" is a tenet both process and post-process theorists share. The latter suggest that to communicate we need "a cohesive set of beliefs about what other language users know" and about how they will "understand, accept, integrate, and react" to our communication. This constitutes a "prior theory." Indeed, the advice given in process textbooks (meaning, all textbooks today) rests on this assumption. According to post-process theorists, however, "no two people ever hold precisely the same prior theories"; we actually use a "passing theory" to communicate, and this shifts depending on the context. What matters is how we employ our "beliefs, desires, hopes, and fears about the world" to formulate passing theories "in our attempts to interpret one another's utterances and to make sense of the world." Because passing theory never "stops" to let us "capture some sort of unitary, complete, or determinate meaning," it "passes" away. It "never endures, never works twice in quite the same way." Thus, our acts of writing, always dependent on a situated, improvisatory "hermeneutic dance," can "never be reduced to a predictable or generalizable process." (4–5)

Kent's definition of post-process theory is to composition studies what deconstruction is to literary criticism. Its extreme situational specificity precludes the "model-making," derived from a coalescence of "law, theory, application, and instrumentation," that Thomas S. Kuhn defines as a paradigm (222). Post-process theory, strictly applied, would make a composition class an oxymoron—as well as an unteachable algorithm, to paraphrase Susan Miller's definition in the epigraph. Only individual tutoring, adapted to the specific paper of the individual student or a collaborative writing group at a particular time in a particular context would be possible.

Joseph Petraglia is not as arbitrarily dismissive of the process paradigm as is Kent. In "Is There Life After Process?", he analyzes the influence of "social scientism" to explicate the connections between process and post-process. His explanation of their relations is analogous to the phenomenon of *pentimento* in painting, where an underlying image in an older painting shows through in the newer paint that has been applied on top of it. For Petraglia says that "the fundamental observation that an individual produces text by means of a writing process has not been discarded. Instead, it has dissolved and shifted from figure to ground." The process paradigm "infuses our awareness of writing, it tinctures our thoughts about writing instruction, and trace elements of it can be found in practically every professional conversation" (53).

While to some this would indicate that the composition culture is steeped in the process paradigm, to Petraglia this signals that we are *past* process, for we "now have the theoretical and empirical sophistication to consider the mantra 'writing is a process' as the right answer to a really boring question. We have better questions now." In the late 1980s and throughout the 1990s, the conception of how writing works has been animated by three complementary sets of questions and observations, he says: (1) "Writing genres, audiences, and writers themselves are socially and culturally constructed"; (2) "The ways in which writing gets produced are characterized by an almost impenetrable web of cultural practices, social interactions, power differentials, and discursive conventions governing the production of a text, making writing more of a phenomenon than a behavior"; and (3) The notion that the writing process is a predictable and regular system has been critiqued from "political, social, philosophical, linguistic, and socio-cognitive perspectives." As with many other movements and theoretical schemes, the label is applied ex post facto to the phenomena it encompasses. As the new millennium approached, *post-process* could be attached to what Petraglia calls "not a paradigm at all, but a shorthand for an eclectic assortment of frameworks devised for the study of human activity" (53–55).

Rose's *Lives on the Boundary*: Process and Post-Process Fused

Lives on the Boundary may be read as a work embodying the fusion[8] of process and post-process theory and practice. That this is not a contradiction may be one major reason for the book's enduring popularity and iconic status.

Mike Rose didn't start out that way, but then, nobody did in the 1980s. His early work, epitomized in *Writer's Block: The Cognitive Dimension,* is traditional though ingenious process research, derived from his doctoral dissertation. He interprets laboratory case studies of students with writer's block, "a composing process dysfunction" (3) manifested, for instance, in an absence of "planning strategies," premature editing, or rigidly misapplied rules: "Writing has to be logical. . . . Writing is not good if it's not clear, vibrant prose" (49). *Writer's Block* epitomizes in theory and method what Petraglia calls the "old social scientism" that sees "writing as a compendium of discrete general skills used by individuals. Rose's research seeks to discover "the processes by which effective writing can be produced [and] taught"; he offers "heuristics to assist teachers and students of composition"; the book is "practice and pedagogy centered" (Petraglia 55).

By 1989, Rose had rediscovered his roots, literally and figuratively, in the brilliantly innovative *Lives on the Boundary*, the blockbuster book that had more influence on composition studies in the first half of the 1990s than any other work. At first glance, it looks like a process book, a literacy autobiography embedded in a characteristic American bootstraps narrative. In Rose's version, a poor but bright youth awakens to the possibilities and the promise of higher learning and "enter[s] the conversation" as a Loyola undergraduate (69). John Trimbur summarizes the plot:

"We follow Rose on a kind of pilgrim's progress, from his struggles as a high-school student who arises, miraculously, from the slough of Voc-Ed despond, through college and the temptations of literary studies in graduate school to his redemptive work as a teacher of the neglected and underprepared" ("Articulation Theory" 238). This progress is full of vignettes that serve as case studies and group ethnographies of the students' "struggles and achievements" in the arduous path toward literacy and the engagement with ideas that is "the essence of humane liberal education" (Rose, *Lives* 48).

Rose's scenarios are scenes from the theater of guerrilla teaching, rather than a scripted series of stages through which all writers must pass to arrive at the promised land. Rose does not have to spell out step-by-step the process approach that he uses to writing—as a way to learn, as a means of self-expression and self-fulfillment, as the antithesis to a rule-bound orientation. His readers already understand the process that emerges in fragments throughout Rose's discussions of classroom practice. Thus, he considers his returning Vietnam veterans at UCLA "strangers in a strange land" who want to "change their lives" through education. Rose's "careful sequencing" of reading and writing assignments, moving "slowly" from summarizing "through classifying and comparing to analyzing" assumes that the veterans will "pick up the details of grammar and usage" as they go along, without formal instruction (137–43).

Although process underlies Rose's pedagogical method, post-process dominates his philosophy. For Rose, as for Kent, learning—as manifested in thinking, reading, writing—is public act, situated, and "thoroughly interpretive" (Kent 1–3). As a post-process work, *Lives on the Boundary* incorporates—in humanistic terms, without later post-process jargon—the principles that Petraglia attributes to the "new social scientism" that undergirds post-process views of writing. From this perspective "writing is a socio-cognitive phenomenon dependent upon historical and cultural context" (Petraglia 55). Rose is acutely aware of issues of "background and social circumstance . . . intersections of class, race, and gender" (*Lives* 177). Thus, he presents every group of students he teaches—as a member of the Teacher Corps in El Monte, as a tutor for Veterans and other underprepared (often minority) students at UCLA—in multiple contexts, reinforced by his own comparable experiences. A decade ago the veterans, for instance, might have been "a high school teacher's bad dream: detached or lippy or assaultive," Rose's Voc.Ed. "comrades reincarnated" and out of reach because of "the poverty and violence of the neighborhoods," family dynamics, peer culture. But "different life experiences" bring "different perspectives on learning." The "sullen high schoolers" metamorphose into mature believers in the American dream, "bringing with them an almost magical vision of what learning could do for them"—"'I'm givin' it a hundred percent this time'" (137). Through such "'thick' description" of "writing [and learning] behavior and patterns of writing behavior," Rose seeks to provide a "deeper and more complex understanding" of the contexts of learning and of writing (Petraglia 55). However, although post-process is in general theory-centered, *Lives on the Boundary* is all about teaching and learning and how to do both better. Theory can be extrapolated from this compendium of best practices.[9]

Process, Post-Process, and Beyond

It is hazardous to predict the future of theories and the evolution of paradigms, even though the reckoning lies on the indefinite horizon. I will offer here one true thing about teaching writing in the foreseeable future, and a number of speculations.

The one true thing. The process paradigm—once radical—is now the dominant, default rubric for teaching writing. It will continue to prevail in textbooks, and presumably in the classrooms where these books are used.[10] Teachers entering the profession in the past two decades have taken process for granted, as DeJoy confesses in "I Was a Process-Model Baby."[11] The textbooks following Peter Elbow's liberating, liberatory *Writing Without Teachers* (1973), including Elbow's own *Writing With Power* (1981), have been process oriented. Yet, as Sharon Crowley ("Around 1971," 1996), Faigley (*Fragments,* 1991), Robert J. Connors (*Composition-Rhetoric,* 1997) and others have observed, most if not all of the most widely adopted books have grafted process terminology onto the pre-existing current-traditional paradigm. Among these are such staples as James McCrimmon's *Writing With a Purpose* and Connors and Lunsford's own *St. Martin's Guide.* In creating an amalgam of the two paradigms, these researchers say, the textbook authors made no significant changes; it was current-traditional business as usual—a critique that Joseph Harris levels against the textbook that Linda Flower derived from her process protocol research, *Problem Solving Strategies for Writing* (see *Teaching Subject* 67–68, 129 n.6). This paradigmatic blend continues to dominate rhetorics and many readers today.

Yet, even Harris's perceptive analysis does not raise the most potentially damning question of all, which is dauntingly difficult to investigate: Do students actually write better—however one defines the term—in a process curriculum than under other competing models? Success stories from master teachers notwithstanding,[12] I can find no compelling research on the subject—large scale, long term, or otherwise—to demonstrate the clear-cut efficacy of process teaching.[13] Since this subject does not appear to be a compelling issue in contemporary research, as long as process continues to feel good teachers will continue to use it.

Now for some speculations.

1. *The current split between theoretically sophisticated research and process-model composition classrooms will continue, and will probably widen.* Petraglia's hypothetical worst-case scenario, that

   > "the writing field hunkers down into the general writing-skills trenches and reverts to the purely service status it has struggled to overcome" is unlikely. The large numbers of composition studies specialists trained in the past twenty-five years can be counted on for

a militant defense of their hard-won turf. Nevertheless, the current orientation of post process theory, that sees writing "as another site of cultural studies lending itself to theorizations of power, ideology, and the construction of identity" will continue, at least for awhile, unconcerned with "validation from empirical research." (Petraglia 60–61)

2. *Radical changes are occurring in the ways we think about genre.* Couture explains that "textual theory has deconstructed the foundational belief that truthful writing corresponds to a single concrete reality and that facts are disassociated from beliefs." Cultural studies, for instance, has "led us to rethink assumptions about the neutrality of certain discourse forms favored in the academy or in the business world." Discourse modes and styles—such as the model of the scientific method—"establish power relationships, exclude some groups, and mask underlying ideologies and assumptions." Moreover, some researchers (Berkenkotter and Huckin, *Genre Knowledge in Disciplinary Communication;* John Swales, *Genre Analysis*) now see genre not as the static designation of a rhetorical mode, but as the entire, dynamic "context of textual production and reception" (Couture 41–42).

3. *We will continue to rethink and revise what it means to write and to teach writing in and beyond the composition classroom.* The following list illustrates some of those areas currently under (re)consideration.

* *New conceptions of literacy*—visual, technological, auditory and combinations of multimedia (some interactive) made possible through the Internet, with and without written texts—including but not limited to blogs, zines, web sites, and other forms of evolving technology. These (along with concepts related to intellectual property) are addressed in Vicinus and Eisner's theoretical, analytic *Originality, Imitation, and Plagiarism,* as well as in textbooks such as McQuade and McQuade, *Seeing and Writing;* Odell and Katz, *Writing in a Visual Age;* and Faigley, George, Palchik, and Selfe, *Picturing Texts.*

* *New conceptions of what it means to write.* These include developing "rhetorical sensitivity" in students—awareness of the rhetorical possibilities in particular social situations, and considering "verbal alternatives," attempting to "process and to choose among all possible verbal strategies *before* giving utterance to an idea" (Hart and Burks qtd. in Petraglia 62). This can be translated into "knowledge design," in which students, through analyzing others' "situated rhetorical performances" can apply the same "reflective sensitivities" to their own texts (Kaufer and Dunmire 230). In *Reflection in the Writing Classroom,* Kathleen Blake Yancey expands on the analogous concepts of *reflection in action, constructive reflection,* and *reflection in presentation* (13–14). And there is the by-now familiar concept of *Writing as Social Action* articulated by Marilyn M. Cooper and Michael Holzman.
* *New types of students.* As the culture becomes truly global, its concerns are reflected in the changing campus that models the world. The now-familiar perspectives of race, class, and gender are now being supplemented by concerns with sexual preference, disability, age (Malinowitz, *Textual Orientations;* Brueggemann, *Lend Me Your Ear;* Rinaldi, "Journeys Through Illness"; Lewiecki-Wilson and Brueggemann, *Disability and the Teaching of Writing*).
* *New areas of the curriculum.* The well-established conceptual underpinning of writing in the disciplines, in law and business schools, in and with ever higher technology, grows increasingly sophisticated (Russell, "Activity Theory").
* *New places in the extracurriculum.* Reading and writing in community settings—youth centers, inner city communities, book clubs, sites of service learning, hospitals, nursing homes, homeless shelters, prisons, governmental offices, and granting agencies (Flower, *Construction of Negotiated Meaning;* Cushman, *The Struggle and the Tools;* Gere, *Intimate Practices;* Deans, *Writing Partnerships;* Ray, *Beyond Nostalgia;* Winslow, "Poetry, Community, and the Vision of Hospitality"*).*
* *New emphasis on qualitative issues.* Lore, values, ethics, emotions, intuition, inspiration, power and powerlessness, therapy and healing (see Mortensen and Kirsch, *Ethics and Representation;* Fontaine and Hunter; *Foregrounding Ethical Awareness;* Brand

and Graves, *Presence of Mind;* Foehr and Schiller, *Spiritual Side of Writing*).
* *New conception of relations between the academy and the world beyond.* David Russell observes that "Although there has been important research in the writing processes (genre systems) of nonacademic settings, there has been comparatively little research into the relation between writing processes in activity systems of academic disciplines, professions, families, neighborhoods and activity systems of formal schooling." In "Activity Theory and Process Approaches" he shows how this can change (89). See also Anne Beaufort, *Writing in the Real World.*

4. *Most dramatically, the nature of the entire relationship of humanities teacher to student to subject may be completely transformed.* As Kurt Spellmeyer asserts in *The Arts of Living: Reinventing the Humanities for the Twenty-First Century,* ever since Matthew Arnold, we have given higher priority to criticism—a reactive, consumerist mentality—than to creation. This needs to change, for learning should once again become an active process with creation rather than criticism as its aim. Rather than believing "that in every age only a few special people manage to see matters clearly," the academy—in all disciplines, but particularly the humanities—needs to "recognize in ordinary people the creative powers long accorded to the makers of high culture." We must develop "an understanding of cultural life that supports our ideals of democracy," a world in which everyone participates in art and feels entitled to be an artist (201).

A paradigm, whether the process paradigm or any other, may be seen as a model that enables those who adopt it to tell a story, or a nest of stories, about what it means and how those meanings may be used. Newcomers become initiated into the community of paradigm-users through the stories they hear. They become members of the same community through the stories they tell—of new applications of the paradigm, variations on it, extensions of it, always pushing the boundaries, as is true of post-process developments and projections. We hear throughout professional literature and in the classroom the stories, familiar and comforting, new and exciting that our colleagues past and present are telling and will embellish in the future. As long as the fundamental narrative retains its usefulness, elegance, and beauty—and the process paradigm does so to this day—it will not perish from the composition studies universe.

7 The Ineluctable Elitism of Essays and Why They Prevail in First-Year Composition Courses

Class is academe's dirty little secret, its last taboo, that about which we dare not speak.

—Patricia A. Sullivan, "Passing"

The introductory composition course is crucially implicated in the process of cultural reproduction.

—Alan W. France, "Assigning Places"

Overview: Freshman composition is a middle class enterprise often based on elitist reading matter, the belletristic essays that constitute the essay canon, actual or prospective. Such essays, the staple of freshman composition, are an elusive, elitist genre difficult to write and nearly impossible to imitate. Nevertheless, their classroom use replicates the normative practice in college literature courses, which also focus on elite literature. Academic discussions, even when written by authors themselves from the working class or addressing working class issues are invariably conducted in Standard English, often academic jargon, and are addressed to fellow academics and other educated readers. They model the middle class attributes of the normative language in which composition classes are conducted and students are taught to write. Given the conservatism of many curricula, this pervasive split-level practice, using elitist material to teach middle class writing and style, seems likely to remain normative in American college composition courses for the foreseeable future. There is no viable alternative in an academic culture that reinforces the upwardly mobile aspirations and values of students and faculty alike.

Essays as an Elitist, Elusive Genre

Belletristic essays are an elitist genre. They are not utilitarian. They do not get to the point with speed and efficiency. Despite radical changes in subject and form in recent times, and increasing democratization, the term *essay* still "conjures up the image of a middle-aged man in a worn tweed jacket in an armchair smoking a pipe by a fire in his private library in a country house somewhere in southern England, in about 1910, maundering on about the delights of idleness, country walks, tobacco, old wine, and old books" (Good vii). Nevertheless, the up-to-the-minute *Encyclopedia of the Essay* (ed. Chevalier), which has the latest word (in fact, 973 very large pages of latest words) on the subject observes that "'even if it lives in disguise'" or what Elizabeth Hardwick calls "a condition of unexpressed hyphenation: the critical essay, the autobiographical essay, the travel essay, the political" (xiii), "the essay seems more alive than ever. . . . Whether it is labeled New Journalism, creative nonfiction, or just nature writing, the American essay has . . . been moving inexorably toward subjects that are at once more intimate and more public than the safe and chatty reveries of the genteel essayists of the late Victorian era. Today, the most respected American essayists write uninhibitedly and skillfully about issues as personal as their own addictions . . . and as public as women's liberation and environmental awareness" ("American Essay" 22).

As I have demonstrated in "The Essay Canon" (Chapter 2), the essay canon—the only game in town as an index of an essay's popularity—consists of works by today's most respected essayists that are reprinted time and again in freshman composition Readers, and used as exemplary models for student writers. These canonical Readers contain approximately 21,000 reprintings of some 8,000 different essay titles by 4,246 authors. I've used viability—rather than, say, supreme quality—as the major criterion for determining who the canonical essayists are, those whose works have been reprinted one hundred or more times during this fifty-year span. That only 175 authors have emerged as canonical may seem a surprisingly small number, but it's on par with the theoretical explanation of canon formation in, for example, poetry (see Rasula; Bloom, "Once More," 21–22). The hands-down favorites are George Orwell, E. B. White, Joan Didion, Lewis Thomas, Henry

David Thoreau, Virginia Woolf, Jonathan Swift, Martin Luther King, Jr., James Thurber, Mark Twain, Annie Dillard, and Thomas Jefferson. Lest these authors strike contemporary readers as a quaint, slightly anachronistic, assemblage, all are alive and well and living in *The Norton Reader,* 11th edition (2004), the major canon-making textbook, and in many of the *Norton*'s numerous rivals. The endurance of these authors over time does not mean that the essay canon (or any other literary canon) is a rigid, unchanging assemblage, just that change at the canon's central core is glacial, while the peripheral authors who comprise the "nonce" canon spin in and out with much greater rapidity (W. Harris, "Canonicity," 113).

Even when the essay canon is expanded to include distinguished journalistic pieces by authors such as Russell Baker and H. L. Mencken, and excerpts of illustrious autobiographies by Richard Rodriguez, Maxine Hong Kingston, Maya Angelou, James Baldwin, and Mike Rose—all of whom came from working class origins—the essay canon itself remains upper to upper-middle class in form, language, and authorial panache, if not always in substance. These canonical authors, like most belletristic (and academic) essayists, are writing for an audience of their intellectual and educational peers, and take their sophistication for granted. Consequently, ideal essay readers are expected to match the authors' wide range of reading, however eclectic and quirky; their world travels (even if by armchair) that provide understanding of diverse cultures, histories, and philosophies. Readers are also expected to appreciate the essayists' wit, allusiveness, odd angles of vision, engagement of sensory stimuli of all sorts, and the enjoyment of going along for the pleasure of the ride itself as the essay meanders into engaging byways and scenic overlooks rather than sticking to the superhighway to the main idea. Thus, the authors' and anticipated readers' common cultural repertoire, rather than intrinsic difficulty of the ideas or relevance of the topics, serves as the barrier between middle- and working-class readers.

Whether belletristic, journalistic, or more academic, essays are transplanted into Readers (the capital R indicates the textbook genure) for a variety of purposes. They can to be perused as exemplary models of both form and substance. They can be read as sources of insight or inspiration or philosophies of living; as social, political, or aesthetic analyses; as jumping off points for argument, for reading against one another or against the grain; as vicarious autobiography, immersing readers in realms or problems far beyond their immediate experience. It would be hard for many students—freshmen or more advanced (even graduate students in English) to successfully imitate these elitist models or even to use their rambling and protean shapes as vehicles for more conventional content. For confident essayists break all the rules and provide inimitably human faces and human voices. As Chapter 3, "The Essayist . . .," illustrates, essayists re-create themselves as a variety of personae; they write in the first person, using contractions as well as metaphorical language. Athletes of style and substance, they leap about in time, place and topic instead of marching through Georgia in straight lines, as Adorno says, "co-ordinating elements rather than subordinating them" as argumentative academic writing usually does (169–70). Essayists write, as Rachel Blau DuPlessis says, "on the side, through the interstices, between the pages, on top of the text, constructing gestures of suspicion, writing . . . over the top" (18). Essayists are gamesome and allusive, with whole cultures and world libraries, via print and the Internet, at their disposal—for reading, reference, quotation, allusion. The belletristic essay, says William H. Gass, "browses among books; it enjoys an idea like a fine wine; it thumbs through things. . . proposing possibilities, reciting opinions" (25). Essayists roam the world—literally and of the imagination, traveling to locations exotic or familiar—the lake, once more. Mundane matters such as whether the essayists will make money (they probably won't) or schedules (such essays take a long time to jell and are often written according to the essayist's elastic timetable rather than the publisher's firm deadline) are irrelevant to the writers' quest for the novel perspective that tames the exotic and makes familiar strange. Scott Russell Sanders, himself an exemplary practitioner of this elusive art form, summarizes the essay's modus operandi in "The Singular First Person": the essay "is an arrogant and foolhardy form, this one-man or one-woman circus, which relies on the tricks of anecdote, memory, conjecture, and wit to hold our attention" (31).

Thus, belletristic essays are often an alien genre for first-year composition students to read, in substance and in style. Given their wide range of allusions, most of the canonical essays (let alone the more esoteric works that are seldom if ever included in freshman Readers) would require a thicket of footnotes to be readily comprehensible to twenty-first century undergraduates. Consider, for instance, the following references in the first two paragraphs of "Shooting an Elephant" by George Orwell, the most widely reprinted canonical essayist: Moulmein, Lower Burma; a sub-divisional police officer; betel juice; baiting; football field [in Burma]; young Buddhist priests; British colonial imperialism; flogging with bamboos; "the utter silence that is imposed on every Englishman in the East," the dying British Empire; "the younger empires that are going to supplant it"; "the evil-spirited little beasts who tried to make my job impossible"; the British Raj; Anglo-Indian (42–43). Orwell himself, writing in 1936 for an educated British audience, would have considered this writing the embodiment of the clarity, brevity, simplicity that he advocates in "Politics and the English Language," as would his readers. But times and culture, politics and the English language change, and today's students require explanations—not just of essays written with Orwellian clarity, but of many more complex works as well.

In the works of many essayists, these aspects of style and allusiveness restrict to well-educated readers the accessibility of the genre that Cristina Kirklighter lauds as highly democratic in her compelling study, *Traversing the Democratic Borders of the Essay*. Therein, she reads the academic writings of Latin American and Latio/a essayists Paulo Freire, Victor Villanueva, and Ruth Behar alongside canonical essayists Montaigne, Bacon, Emerson, and Thoreau to demonstrate how "the essay's elements of self-reflexivity, accessibility, spontaneity, and sincerity . . . offer hope for democratizing academia through the personal essay" (124). Yet, these essayists, like their canonical counterparts, are adult professionals writing for an audience of their peers, not students—again, using sophisticated language and a wide range of allusions, as this single sentence from Behar's *Vulnerable Observer* indicates:

> At the same time, I began to understand that I had been drawn to anthropology because I had grown up within three cultures—Jewish (both Ashkenazi and Sephardic), Cuban, and American—and I needed to better connect my own profound sense of displacement with the professional rituals of displacement that are at the heart of anthropology. (21)

Behar takes for granted that readers, presumably well-trained and thoughtful anthropologists, will have some sense of what it means to grow up in Cuban, American, and Jewish cultures; that they will be aware of salient differences between Ashkenazi and Sephardic Judaism; and that, in addition to whatever these cultures may have in common, readers will understand the disparities and points of cultural conflict that contribute to the writer's "profound sense of displacement." Moreover, Behar's readers are also expected to understand the "professional rituals of displacement that are at the heart of anthropology," and be able to compare and contrast these with the causes of the author's sense of cultural displacement.

For all of these reasons, belletristic essays are an elusive genre for first year college students to attempt, as readers and writers, for neither their life experiences nor education before they enter college prepare them with the freedom, fluidity of style, wide-ranging cultural background, and personal ease with the essay form necessary to read or write with authority in this belletristic genre. Belletristic essays are not part of the customary writing repertoire in American high schools, particularly in curricula dominated by five-paragraph themes and driven by the "teach to the test" nationwide impetus of mandated mastery tests under the "No Child Left Behind" legislation. Belletristic essays are very hard to write, as anyone knows who's ever tried it, for they are not amenable to rules, formulas, prescribed formats; the drum they march to is the distinctive beat of the essayist's heart. These difficulties, present for readers and writers alike, don't mean students shouldn't have to deal with belletristic or more conventional academic essays—just that they'll have to work to move easily in and among them, whether reading with or against the texts; using them as stimuli for debates, projects in or out of class or in the larger community; imitating their form or style; or debating their subjects.

The Elitism of Discussions of Class in the Academy

Discussions of class in the academy are elitist in form and language, if not in substance. As recently as 1998, Patricia A. Sullivan observed in "Passing," reaffirming Paul Fussell's 1982 social analysis in "Notes on Class," that class "is America's dirty little secret. Sex has nothing on class in America: We are far less squeamish talking and hearing about 'the act' than we are about class," in the academy as throughout the culture. "Class," she continues, "almost never appears in the disciplined, sanctioned discourses of the academy but as that category of social analysis 'studied' by sociologists. When class is spoken of at all, it hitches itself to gender and race, [and] is subdivided into the familiar triumvirate of income, education and occupation . . ." (239).

In the past decade, the taboo identified by Fussell has largely been overcome. Discussions of working class faculty origins and working class students have bourgeoned recently, most of these written in Standard English (if not in academese) by academics for other academics. Reinforcing Sullivan's observations, most exhibit great sensitivity to and understanding of their working class subjects, and often anger at the economic inequities fundamental to class distinctions. For instance, in "Stupid Rich Bastards," Laurel Johnson Black recounts the masterplot, "a very simple one: a young woman goes from poverty to the middle class using education to move closer and closer to the stupid rich bastards she has heard about all her life. She finds ever larger contexts into which she can place everything, can get perspective. . . . Until someone says 'Fuck you!' and it all collapses" (14). As the family member designated to go to college and earn the money that would be her family's salvation, she would thereby be empowered to give "the stupid rich bastards what they had coming to them." She would "speak like them but wouldn't be one of them" (17).

Black eloquently expresses the conflict inherent in the lives and loyalties of working class faculty, whose positions as college teachers and researchers remove them from the working-class origins that are often the subjects of their academic work: "I cannot move among the rich, the condescending, the ones who can turn me into an object of study with a glance or word, cannot speak like them, live in a house like them, learn their ways, and share them with my family without being disloyal to someone. I thought learning would make it easier for me to protect and defend my family, myself, but the more I learn the harder it is to passionately defend anything" (25). Black's stance, attitude—and adherence to the conventions of Standard English—are representative of the twenty-four essays in *This Fine Place So Far From Home* (1995), though some substitute academic jargon for Black's elegant eloquence (see Pelz, Piper). The twenty-one more-or-less personal essays in Shepard, McMillan, and Tate's *Coming to Class: Pedagogy and the Social Class of Teachers* (1998), while focusing on pedagogy as much as on class, do so in conventional academic language and article formats. Although Kirklighter, in *Traversing the Democratic Borders of the Essay* (2002), argues for more democratic, essayistic writing in the academy rather than the "detached form of academic mimicry"

(129) that prevails and stultifies minority students in particular, her argument—derived from her 1999 dissertation—perforce follows academic form, language, and conventions.

Likewise, even Patricia Shelley Fox's "Women in Mind: The Culture of First-Year English and the Nontraditional Returning Woman Student" is written in conventional academic form and language, though she is defending, with nontraditional students' autobiographical writings (all depicting working-class experiences), the obligation of first-year English courses to allow students to "work within and among the competing discourses in their lives to offer us an oppositional world view" (202). In fact, Fox is also mounting an argument for the efficacy of personal writing in academia. She intends to solve the problems Gerald Graff identifies in "The Academic Language Gap" when he argues,

> Some . . . current educational progressives go so far as to maintain that the primacy of argumentation in composition classes is a form of repression, from which students are to be liberated so they can discover their own authentic voices. This attack on argumentation—which does not hesitate to avail itself of aggressive argumentation to make its points—has led some "expressivist" composition theorists to try to shift the emphasis in writing instruction from exposition, analysis, and the thesis-driven essay to creative self-expression and personal narrative. . . . Though these views often present themselves as "highly transgressive," their effect ultimately reinforces the old genteel assumption that advanced literacy is for the few—as it can only continue to be if students are deprived of the argumentative skills needed to succeed. (27)

Even though some authors (such as Fox) advocate that their students write personal essays, only one of the works about pedagogues and pedagogy identified here recommends particular essays, working class or otherwise, for classroom use. The exception is Kirklighter's article on "The Relevance of Paulo Freire on Liberatory Dialogue and Writing in the Classroom." There, she recounts teaching successes with essays by Patrick Welsh (from *Tales Out of School*) and chapters of Patricia Williams's *The Alchemy of Race and Rights* (221–34), which are often reprinted in textbooks as free-standing essays. Sections of other autobiographical works written with a class orientation, such as Richard Wright's *Black Boy* and Mike Rose's *Lives on the Boundary*, are also reprinted as essays (viz Wright's "The Library Card," alternatively titled "The Power of Books,"and Rose's "'I Just Wanna Be Average,'" all titles supplied by the textbook editors). In general, pedagogical articles addressing class never mention essays in the same breath. When referring to student writing—either composing processes or products—they generally emphasize the topics and perhaps attitudes engendered by the readings, but seldom identify the written forms in which the students are expected to respond to them.

Freshman Composition: A Middle Class Enterprise Built on Elitist Readings

The academy has, and perpetuates, highbrow taste in music, cinema, and literature, including drama (no soaps), poetry (no verse or jingles—and limericks only sub rosa), quality fiction[1] and other classics—actual or potential—of all sorts. Thus it is not surprising that a preponderance of freshman English programs continue to use elitist essays, many of which constitute the essay canon, as they have done for some 125 years (see Brereton, *Origins, passim;* and Connors, "Invention and Assignments"). Despite the acknowledged difficulties in teaching students to write belletristic essays, these materials retain vigor as models for student discussion, if not emulation. Indeed, personal essays and excerpts of autobiographies treated as essays provide expert witness for many of the political agendas and theoretical orientations that underlie the first-year curriculum. Thus, these readings support agendas oriented to issues feminist (Mary Wollstonecraft, Elizabeth Cady Stanton, Gloria Steinem); multicultural (James Baldwin, Linda Hogan, Gary Soto, Judith Ortiz Cofer); gay (David Sedaris, Kate Millett); post-colonial (Edward Said, Jamaica Kincaid, Paule Marshall); or disability (Brenda Brueggemann, Georgina Kleege, Andre Dubus); as well as to matters of class (Richard Rodriguez, Mike Rose, Esmerelda Santiago), with which they often overlap. Those working class authors who never left the working class as a consequence of their education and/or writing (most major authors, such as James Baldwin and Maxine Hong Kingston, changed class though not necessarily class loyalty) and who nevertheless become canonical are few. Other canonical representatives of non-traditional backgrounds, such as Sojourner Truth ("Ain't

I a Woman?") and Chief Joseph ("We Will Fight No More Forever"), were actually illiterate. The pieces attributed to them were composed by journalists, and are not included in textbooks to serve as pedagogical models, but as token items to raise the readers' awareness of issues of gender, ethnicity, and social and cultural marginality, rather than class.

As explained earlier, the contents of virtually all textbook collections of essays, including discussions of class written by canonical authors, such as George Orwell or Barbara Ehrenreich, are composed in Standard English. All of these essays in their original context are intended for a middle class or academic audience, the people who read *The Atlantic, The New Yorker,* and little magazines—intellectually cultivated, widely read, with sufficient leisure time to read, and enough disposable income to buy books and magazines. If working class readers encounter essays actually or potentially canonical it is likely to be in college textbooks, rather than in their publication of origin.

Moreover, the pressure to teach the essays, from the writing programs that adopt the textbooks, and from the textbook publishers who respond to the demands of their potential adopters, is to ensure that the essays, however elitist in form, may be understood in terms of middle class values and experiences, even those that discuss working class life. Thus, both the *Norton Reader* and the *Bedford Reader* include "Aria," the chapter from Richard Rodriguez's *Hunger of Memory* that uses his own childhood experience as a native speaker of Spanish, the "private language" of home, to argue against bilingual education: "What I needed to learn in school was that I had the right—and the obligation—to speak the public language of *los gringos*" (Peterson, Norton 572). Both Readers ask students to comment on public and private language ("Was there a language in your home that was similarly private? Did you and your family speak a language [or dialect] other than the dominant one . . . (X. J. Kennedy, *Bedford* 582), and to assess his arguments against bilingual education ("Is he claiming that other non-English speakers would have the same gains and losses as he did? What evidence does he base his case on?" *Norton* 578). The *Bedford Reader* also asks for a commentary on childrearing practices: "Rodriguez's mother and father seem to have had a definite idea of their parental obligations to their children. . . . What, for example, is the connection between good parenting and teaching one's child to conform?" (582). While questions such as these are designed to accommodate a range of responses drawn from the spectrum of the students' class experiences, it is understood that they will be writing in the lingua franca of the academy, as *The Bedford Reader* implies in asking for an essay "defining the distinctive quality of the language spoken in your home when you were a child. . . . Do you revert to this private language when you are with your family?" (582).

Most textbooks are commissioned by the editors of major textbook publishing houses. The authors, usually nationally known for their innovative composition studies research (think Connors, Ede, Lunsford), propose radical books, innovative readings, imaginative pedagogy. Yet their textbooks—and I speak from repeated personal experience (see Bloom, "Making Essay Connections")—are invariably pushed toward traditional middle class pedagogy, with relatively modest innovations. The publishers' perceptions of the market, buttressed by surveys of prospective adopters of the books (freshman composition teachers), tend toward cloning of successful books already on the market, which are usually centrist in content, as Kuhn argues in "The Structure of Scientific Revolutions." They contain 50–75 percent canonical or pre-canonical essays (Bloom, "Making" 141), and are middle class in pedagogy. The textbook author or editor is thus caught in a double bind: to insist on dramatic innovation is to greatly diminish sales; yet to succumb to cloning is to further glut the market already saturated with middle class values.[2]

For the teaching and writing of essays in the academy is by and large a middle-class endeavor, as I've argued elsewhere, particularly in "Freshman Composition as a Middle Class Enterprise." The academy—buttressed by handbooks, grammars, style manuals, and computer checkers of spelling, grammar, style, and other types of errors—is virtually uniform in its insistence on clean, respectable, orderly, well-documented, thesis-driven, author-effacing prose. And these are some of the stylistic features that the apparatus (consisting of those special textbooky features, the "headnotes" and "study questions" designed to provide easy access to each "selection," as well as to determine how each essay is read) addresses in calling attention to vocabulary, usage, and conventions of writing. Indeed, in fairness to the students, virtually all of whom are aiming for middle and upper middle class employment and its accompanying life style upon graduation, there is no viable alternative. The view of the authors of the 1974 College Conference on Composition and Communication position paper on "Students' Rights to Their Own Language" (see next section), that all dialects are created equal, accompanied by exhortations to "avoid judging students' dialects in social or economic terms" (16), has received virtually no reinforcement either inside or outside the academy since its inception (see Parks, passim.)[3] This is not likely to change as long as Standard English remains the dominant and normative dialect of the members of society with status, power, mobility, authority, and esteemed jobs—qualities students and the academic culture (and beyond) expect to be embedded in a college degree. Yet, the students' cultural horizons are broadened by virtually all Readers on the market today, through the cultural and ethnic diversity of their authors—all writing in Standard English—that replace the hegemonic collections by upper middle class white males that dominated the Readers of fifty years ago.

Freshman Composition, Conservator of Middle Class Values—Ever and Always?

In substance, as in style, says France, "the introductory composition course is crucially implicated in the process of cultural reproduction. Its content is the set of discursive rules that assign students to their proper place in the institutional hierarchies of corporate capitalism. . . . [W]riting assignments should be seen not only as work that the instructor is empowered to impose on students, but as a temporary grant of the instructor's power to 'speak,'" and thereby to determine the students' "'proper' place in the social distribution of power" (593). The gray sameness of many freshman textbooks makes it clear that instructors don't expect their students to speak out of turn. Despite the prevalence of elitist essays as textbook models, teachers don't expect students to produce elitist essays but a variety of non-literary forms, ranging from five-paragraph themes to analytic arguments. As a rule, these turn out to be fairly formulaic pieces of prose, a form that Scholes labels in *Textual Power* "pseudo-non-literature," produced in "an appalling volume" in freshman courses. "We call the production of this stuff 'composition,'" he laments. And nobody writes "compositions" out of school. For "compositions" are not works of literature but academic exercises, pedagogical products designed for heuristic purposes—either to enhance students' understanding of the subject at hand or to provide practice in how to write an academic essay (Chapter 1). Despite Scholes's searing critique—now over twenty years old—

and the publication of three editions of Scholes, Comley, and Ulmer's *Text Book,* a clear and readable application of an antidote—"writing through literature rather than writing about it, and on learning literary theory by emulating literary practice" (3rd ed. iv-v), New Critical writing assignments asking students to "unlock the text" continue to prevail as composition teachers replicate the culture in which they were taught.

To the extent that the academy remains middle class—in reality and in the prevailing cultural expectations of academic writing—there will be little incentive to re-orient composition pedagogy to challenge these middle class values and aims. Creative writing students may be encouraged to aspire to literary elitism, even if their characters are proletarians. But most other students are not concerned with working class readers; they are trained to write serviceable prose aimed, in accord with the goals of their college education, toward academic goals and an academic audience.

Although academia has never been otherwise, in 1972, responsive to the Civil Rights movement of the 1960s, the Executive Committee of the CCCC took issue with acceptance of Standard English as the normative language for college level work, passing the following resolution: "We affirm the students' right to their own patterns and varieties of language—the dialects of their nurture or . . . their own identity and style. . . . We affirm strongly that teachers must have the experiences and training that will enable them to respect diversity and uphold the right of students to their own language" ("Students' Right" 2-3). An amplified version was published two years later as a special issue of *CCC Students' Right to Their Own Language* (Fall 1974); it is still in print and may be purchased from National Council of Teachers of English. The policy remains on the books—but, as Stephen Parks's *Class Politics,* a comprehensive analysis of the history of the "Students' Right" advocacy demonstrates—it is not *in* the books. The books—handbooks, rhetorics, Readers—all reinforce Standard English in all academic situations, as they have always done. Thus, despite this call for democratizing the language of and in the academy, echoed in a variety of CCCC committees for a dozen years, by 1983 discussion was tabled, no action was taken, the "Students' Right" proposal "became history" (236). Thus, France's revisionist suggestions to make freshman composition readings more proletarian and thus Marxist, and therefore more sensitive to the working class (593), remain essentially ignored. By whatever means students develop a social or political consciousness, they will do so in Standard English.

It is the rare composition program, or course, that incorporates what Henry Giroux calls critical pedagogy, "in which the knowledge, habits, and skills of critical citizenship, not simply good citizenship, are taught and practiced. This means providing students with the opportunity to develop the critical capacity to challenge and transform existing social and political forms, rather than simply adapt to them" (74). Yet, programs that have the potential to be transformative of both social values and student writing exist, primarily as alternative freshman curricula based on service learning—in which students collaborate with members of a variety of real communities to accomplish real projects, from literacy tutoring to building Habitat for Humanity houses (see Cushman, *Struggle;* Flower, *Construction*). Thomas Deans's *Writing Partnerships: Service-Learning in Composition* highlights Eyler, Giles Jr., and Braxton's comprehensive study of service-learning programs affecting 1,500 students in twenty colleges. They conclude that these programs significantly affect "students' attitudes, values, and skills, as well as . . . the way they think about social issues," and found that service learning was "'the only significant or best predictor of' . . . the capacity of students *to see problems as systemic,* and the ability *to see things from multiple perspectives*" (3, ital. Deans). Deans's analysis of four exemplary service-learning programs provides the theoretical and pedagogical rationale for the curriculum he addresses in *Writing and Community Action,* derived in part from the program he directed at Haverford. The readings and writing assignments begin with personal reflections on literacy, and writing in academic communities, before moving to "Literature, Culture, and Social Reflection" and writing about, for, and with real world communities. The writing projects thus include informational brochures, proposals to address "community problems and injustices," and oral histories (see Chs. 8 and 9).

Service-learning curricula and community involvement require strong, committed, tireless leaders and continual oversight. Thus, unless universities and their faculties—either the freshman English directors or the TAs—have a significant Marxist or service imperative (how likely in today's corporate universities?) the pervasive middle class orientation with an emphasis on elitist reading material is likely to prevail, particularly if part-time teachers are constrained by full time faculty overseers to follow a common syllabus. Textbooks may, and do, include a variety of essays that support confrontation or resistance to establishment views. Yet, only a few essays have become canonical because either their philosophical breadth or style transcends the topicality of most commentaries on current events: Swift's "A Modest Proposal," Orwell's "Politics and the English Language," Thoreau's "Civil Disobedience," The Declaration of Independence, and Martin Luther King's "Letter from Birmingham Jail." Even "The Declaration of Independence" may be generalized from and read out of or beyond its historical context.

Thus, while we may hold these truths to be self-evident, that all students are created equal, that they are endowed by their country and their culture with certain unalienable rights, these rights do not include the opportunity to exercise either working class locutions or upper class elitist literary strategies. The relatively recent acknowledgment of student and faculty obligations to the wider community, the larger world as represented in service-learning programs and other types of real world writing exemplify alternatives awaiting larger scale application. That nearly all available options for college level reading and writing are conducted in Standard English is predictable, inevitable, and most would argue, desirable.

8 Good Enough Writing

What Is Good Enough Writing, Anyway?

Good enough student writing isn't bad, but it isn't great. And although it ultimately isn't good enough, it's what many of us will settle for much of the time. While many American colleges and universities claim to strive for excellence, they'll be reasonably contented with Bs. For most have adopted a de facto standard for college-level writing: whatever is good enough to warrant (note that I do not say merit) a B in whatever course it is written for at their particular school is good enough writing. Yes, this definition is pragmatic, rather than utopian. Its contours are determined locally, rather than nationally, by individual teachers in individual classes—though more exacting teachers or "hard graders" may continue to measure against the ideal.[1]

Yet we can discuss the concept of good enough writing in general because B is the standard grade in American undergraduate education in general, and in composition courses as well.[2] It is widely based on the following characteristics. B-level writing is college level writing that exemplifies the following characteristics judged according to local standards. B-level writing is good enough to satisfy first year writing standards and to meet norms of acceptable writing in more advanced classes. It is thus good enough to serve as the lingua franca for writing throughout the writer's home institution, and presumably, to meet the standard for writing beyond that college—the larger community, and the student's future professional world. If this writing is also good enough to satisfy the student writer's own expectations, so much the better, but that's a lagniappe, not a given. Although the following definition is embedded in a discussion of first year composition, the features of good enough writing are equally discernable in academic writing required in any other college course up, down, or across the curriculum except for creative writing, which is beyond the scope of this discussion.

Good enough writing is characterized by a clutch of academic virtues. These include: Rationality; Conformity; Conventionality—which is attained by using Standard English, following the rules, and otherwise maintaining proper academic decorum; Self-Reliance, Responsibility, Honesty; Order; Modesty in form and style; Efficiency; and Economy. When accompanied by Punctuality, turning the papers in on time, according to the demands of the academic schedule, a great deal of student writing that meets these criteria—perhaps most of it—should be good enough to receive a good enough grade, a B, in most institutions.[3] (Nevertheless, any teacher—and we have all met them—can override the norm through using criteria individual or idiosyncratic, such as "Any paper with more than three spelling errors gets an F.")

Many teachers would also insist on evidence of "the ability to discuss and evaluate abstract ideas" as crucial to college-level writing (Sullivan 384). Critical thinking is more variable than the tidier academic virtues, more dependent on the individual teacher's expectations and frames of reference, and often difficult to measure. It will be addressed in the last two sections of this paper. Otherwise, my analysis assumes that although we say we value and expect critical thinking, when awarding the final grade we cave on this quality. If throughout the semester we have received a preponderance of technically and politically correct papers that reflect all the other virtues, we will deem that writing good enough for a B.

Although composition studies handbooks and rhetorics hold out the Platonic ideals of excellence, particularly when their illustrations are from professional writers, classroom teachers perforce read these through the realistic lenses of "good enough." The label, "good enough writing" is an analogue of British psychoanalyst D. W. Winnicott's concept of the "good enough mother," neither negligent nor a smother-mother, but good enough to provide adequate physical and psychological nurture that will ensure the development of a distinctive individual, healthy child (17–19). Most of us tend to teach to the class average (or slightly above, but still within B range) yet oddly enough, given the tacit acceptance throughout the country of this pervasive concept, it has never been given a label that stuck.[4] Like Moliere's bourgeois gentleman, who was delighted to finally have a label to acknowledge that he'd been speaking prose all his life, the label "good enough writing" tells us what we've been teaching our students to do all along. Now we know what to call the resulting work; if good enough writing is not the best outcome, it is certainly the normative practice that we tolerate.

The Characteristics of Good Enough Writing

Rationality. The academy purports to be nothing, if not rational—a virtue as old as Aristotle. The academic writer, from student on up to faculty researcher, is constrained to write rationally, to produce nonfiction prose usually construed as expository or argumentative writing, critical or otherwise. This must be organized according to a logical plan or "purpose" and proceed by a series of logical steps from its initial premise to a logical conclusion. In pursuing this goal—the logical consequence of the five-paragraph theme construed as a heuristic, rather than a template—the writer is expected and advised in all the handbooks [5] to be reasonable, balanced, fair-minded, and "respectful of the feelings of [the] audience," to "avoid rhetorical fallacies" and "learn from others' arguments." Thus the writer should be able to "distinguish fact from opinion," "take a position" and "make claims" derived from "supporting evidence" based on "verifiable and reliable facts." S/he should "respond to diverse views," considering "at least two sides of the issue under discussion" (*Harbrace* 178–214).

Although ethical and emotional appeals receive a nod (a paragraph apiece in this 896-page book), the emphasis throughout the *Handbook*, as in the course it sustains, is on the rational. *Emotion* and *passion*—which might signal the operation of a host of non-rational elements—are not indexed; *play* refers only to the literary genre. The dead seriousness that dominates academic discourse, allegedly the epitome of rationality, must prevail. Gass contends that the article as a genre—and by extrapolation, most academic writing—is far less rational than it purports to be, that it is in fact a "veritable Michelin of misdirection; for the article pretends that everything is clear, that its argument is unassailable, that there are no soggy patches, no illicit inferences, no illegitimate connections; it furnishes seals of approval and underwriters' guarantees" (25). In point of fact, as all researchers and writing teachers know, every piece of academic writing has a point of view and presents an argument, explicit or implicit, and evidence, to reinforce the author's bias. Just because a piece of writing sounds objective (including, say, the essay you are reading right now) doesn't mean that it is; though one can—and should, in a rational universe—be fair, one can never be objective.

Conformity, Conventionality and their consequent predictability are the necessary hallmarks of respectable academic writing. Academic readers expect academic writing to exhibit decorum and propriety appropriate in style and thought to the academic universe in general and to their discipline in particular. Teachers expect students to use Standard English, and follow the rules (see, for instance, Sullivan 385); and maintain decorum of thought as well as expression. Thus, as will be clear from the following discussion, the authors of good enough papers must color—and think—within the party lines, however loosely or tightly they are drawn at any given institution. However clearly or vaguely these are spelled out at any given school, most students are acculturated to understand them. When they don't—if, for instance, they are from another culture or their first language is not English and even if they know the words they don't understand the music—their failure to conform may land them in big trouble, as the following discussion reveals.

Adherence to Standard English and Rules. No matter how informal or slangy one's speech may be outside of class, teachers and textbooks and college standards concur on the importance of Standard English as the lingua franca for writing in the academy (again, creative writing excepted), reinforced by conventional grammar, mechanics, and spelling. Failure to follow the rules will result in papers that are not Good Enough, no matter what other virtues they exhibit. Although the CCCC manifesto on "Students' Right to Their Own Language"—a defense of nonStandard English, among other things—has been on the books since 1974, teachers detest error and devote much effort to stamping it out, as Connors and Lunsford's research in "Frequency of Formal Errors" reveals. Likewise, Mina Shaughnessy's sensitive analysis of the "stunningly unskilled," error-laden writing of thousands of open admissions students in *Errors and Expectations* leads ultimately to the expectation that sensitive, insightful teachers will assume that their students are "capable of learning" what they themselves have learned, and what they now teach—Standard English (292). Three semesters of basic writing will, if done right, give students Standard English facility with syntax, punctuation, grammar, spelling, vocabulary, "order and development," and "academic forms" (285–86). Though Mike Rose's equally sympathetic work, *Lives on the Boundary*, identifies many pitfalls that must be overcome on the road to successful academic writing, he shares Shaughnessy's vision of the ultimate goal. And, as David Bartholomae's "Inventing the University" argues, when entering students have learned to talk the talk, they can walk the walk.

So taken for granted is this normative view of language that it is manifested from kindergarten through college in workbooks, grammar and usage tests, and spelling lists. Standard usage and grammar are addressed today in college and admissions (and exit) testing and placement. But these are the end of the line that now—as a consequence of the highly problematic, very politicized "No Child Left Behind" legislation—begins with mandatory testing in the primary grades and continues as long as the child remains in school. Despite objections from individual teachers and professional educational organizations, the law of the land reinforces adherence to the rules.

Decorum. Student writing must stay within the decorous boundaries of expression, and—for many teachers—suitable (however they define it) parameters of thought and ideas, even at the risk of hypocrisy. Sarah Freedman's classic research reveals that students whose writing is seen as insubordinate—too friendly, familiar, casual, presumptive of equal status with the teacher—may be penalized with lower grades (340–42). Making academic and professional norms explicit, *Harbrace* emphasizes that "respectful writers do not use homophobic" or racist or sexist language, and are "sensitive to suitability of ability, age, class, religion, and occupation." Although the advice is couched in terms of language—avoid the "stereotyping that careless use of language can create" (658–60)—its implications are clear: if the writer's true sentiments are subversive or transgressive, they should be suppressed in the writing.

Students socialized in American high schools arrive at college with an understanding of the deep as well as surface meaning of many types of writing assignments. Most of them steer clear of the cultural undertow in which they might drown, even when to do so means evading the underlying moral issues—a potential breach of ethics far more serious than surface impropriety. The heated discussion of "Queers, Bums, and Magic," a gay-bashing paper in which the Kuwait-born student author also confesses to urinating on and beating up a homeless person in "San Fagcisco," makes it clear that students who violate the prevailing moral imperatives, whether by intention or in innocence, run the risk of incurring the teacher's wrath or even legal sanctions that could get them thrown out of school, into jail, or both (see my discussion in "The Good, the Bad, and the Ugly," the next chapter).

Self-reliance, Responsibility, Honesty. Composition teachers, ever Emersonian in spirit, stress the importance of self-reliance, despite the constraints on independent thought and language imposed in the interests of decorum. "Your work must be your *own* work," we say, even in collaborative classrooms. "*Yours* is the most important voice in a paper that has your name on it," echoes the *Harbrace* (264). Yet, paradoxically, teachers distrust the personal voice (except in narratives—and, after the controversy over James Frey's alleged memoir, A *Million Little Pieces,* fictionalized, fraudulent or both), which signals ownership of the subject. In addition, teachers emphatically discount the unsubstantiated opinion. Indeed, the most elaborate discussion of a single topic in the *Harbrace,* 18.75 percent of the total, is devoted to finding, using, and citing sources responsibly (223–390); the most responsible writing, students might well infer, is that which is most heavily and accurately cited. The emphasis on citations is also intended to nip irresponsibility in the bud. From sea to shining sea, as proscribed by decrees and honor codes throughout American colleges and universities, plagiarism and piracy, now complicated and confounded by the easy accessibility of materials on the Web, are the writer's cardinal sins. The *Harbrace* epitomizes and updates conventional wisdom, beginning with a harsh opening sally: "Taking someone's words or ideas and presenting them as your own leaves you open to criminal charges." This is followed by "In the film, video, music, and software businesses, this sort of theft is called *piracy.* [bf sic] In publishing and education, it is called *plagiarism* [bf sic] or *cheating.* [bf sic] Whatever it is called, it is illegal" (278). The ensuing discussion again typifies the paradox of requiring students to be self-reliant in finding and using sources while simultaneously distrusting them to do this accurately or, more particularly, honestly: "Although it is fairly easy to copy material from a website or even purchase a paper on the Web, it is just as easy for a teacher or employer to locate that same material on the Web and determine that it has been plagiarized" (279). Gotcha!

Order. Most arenas of the academy, except those encouraging artistic creativity, depend on order—in calendars and schedules, procedures, and written documents. The academic world runs better when the participants can know, respect, and follow a predictable, conspicuous pattern. Thus, good enough writing is reasonably well organized. Writing that looks disorganized is as disreputable as disorderly conduct, for disorder implies mental laxity, if not downright confusion, and shows disrespect for one's readers. We even like to see the organizational scaffolding; witness the popularity of PowerPoint presentations that threaten to become caricatures of order, arrangement made explicit in a series of short sentences or sentence fragments. Five paragraph themes, likewise, serve as their own caricature.

Nevertheless, Richard Marius's views on order in *A Writer's Companion* represent the academic norm. He asserts that "A Good Essay Gets to the Point Quickly" and "Stays with Its Subject." It is well-integrated and does not drift without clear purpose from item to item. Thus, says Marius, "A good essay will march step by step to its destination. Each step will be clearly marked; it will depend on what has gone before, and it will lead gracefully to what comes afterward" (47–53). Marius's advice, the antithesis of postmodernism, is proffered more categorically than, for instance, that of Strunk and White, who say "12. Choose a suitable design and hold to it" (15). Their realistic analysis accommodates both the necessity of good design and the vagaries of the procedures by which it may be attained: "A basic structural design underlies every kind of writing. Writers will in part follow this design, in part deviate from it, according to their skills, their needs, and *the unexpected events that accompany the act of composition*" [emphasis added]. Writing, they say, "to be effective, must follow closely the thoughts of the writer, but not necessarily the order in which those thoughts occur. This calls for a scheme of procedure." However, they add, "In some cases, the best design is no design, as with a love letter, which is simply an outpouring" (15). Nevertheless, academic necessity puts most teachers in Marius's camp; students write no love letters on our watch.

Modesty in Form and Style. Good enough writers are advised to keep out of sight, even while taking responsibility for their own ideas. For good enough writing is moderate and temperate, its qualities of style, form, and tone quiet, steady, and inconspicuous. This is a pragmatic response to the ethos of the academy, for academics expect papers to be written in the form, language, and style appropriate to their respective discipline. When they are reading for substance, they cannot afford to be distracted by departures from conventions of form, or language that calls attention to itself, what my agriculture colleagues object to as "flowery writing."

To violate the normative literary conventions of the discipline in which one is writing is to mark the writer as either highly naive or very unprofessional. Or so the academy believes.[6] Thus, *Harbrace* identifies the particular conventions and illustrates them with sample papers: "Writing about literature follows certain special conventions" ("Use the full name of the author of a work in your first reference and only the last name in all subsequent references."); "Reports in the social sciences follow prescribed formats to present evidence"—along the lines of Introduction, Definitions, Methods and Materials, Results, Discussion and Critique; and "Writing in the natural sciences is impartial and follows a prescribed format" to ensure that the experiments can be replicated (416–32).

The sense of style conveyed in Polonius's advice to Laertes ("rich, not gaudy"; "familiar, but by no means vulgar") is reiterated today in the rules of Strunk and White, who together constitute the American Polonius: *"Place yourself in the background"* (#1); *"Do not inject opinion"* (#17). It would be as hard for anyone educated in American schools in the past thirty-five years to escape the influence of advice embodied in *The Elements of Style* (itself a direct descendant of conventional eighteenth-century advice) or its analogues as it would for any post-World War II American baby to escape the influence of Benjamin Spock's *Baby and Child Care*. "The approach to style," say these books, "is by way of plainness, simplicity, orderliness, sincerity" (Strunk 69). This precept governs much of the normative stylistic advice to students: *"Be clear"* (#16); *"Prefer the standard to the offbeat"* (#21); *"Avoid fancy words"* (#14); *"Use figures of speech sparingly"* (#18). And be patriotic: *"Avoid foreign languages"* (#20) (70–81).

The author's individual, human voice is generally not welcome, particularly in papers written by teams of authors, as in the hard sciences, where convention dictates anonymity. Yet, when the first person is permitted, Gass observes that such writing must appear voiceless, faceless, "complete and straightforward and footnoted and useful and certain" even when it is not, its polish "like that of the scrubbed step"

(25). This suppression of the self, which might otherwise be manifested in the individual writer's voice and distinctive features of syntax and vocabulary, has the effect of making a given piece of academic writing sound like every other piece in the same field. For a single writer's voice to speak out would be to speak out of turn, and thus be regarded as immodest—calling attention to the speaker rather than where it properly belongs, on the subject.[7] The emergence of the authorial self, a necessary attribute of personal writing, may be one reason curmudgeonly diehard academic critics dislike and distrust this genre.

Efficiency, Economy. Good enough academic writers squander neither time nor words. Concepts such as George Orwell's "Never use a long word where a short one will do" and "If it is possible to cut a word out, always cut it out" ("Politics" 176) and Strunk and White's "Omit needless words"—"a sentence should contain no unnecessary words, a paragraph no unnecessary sentences" (23)—govern American textbooks and much of our red-penciling. In *A Writer's Companion,* Richard Marius reiterates, "Write Efficiently. Here is one of the fundamentals of modern English style: Use as few words as possible to say what you want to say." Efficient prose, direct, honest, and to the point enables readers to be efficient, as well, "without having to back up time and again to read it again to see what it means" (10–11). Although this advice could be interpreted as designed to produce a svelte body of prose in, say advertising or the sciences, it seems just as likely to meet good enough writers where they live-writing to fulfill the letter of the required assignment (forget about its spirit) and get on with the more engaging aspects of their lives beyond the paper at hand.

By this criterion, the writer's ideal composing process would be equally efficient. I question how often the ideal is actually met, for it is antithetical to the unruly, wasteful, disorderly means by which creation usually occurs, even in good enough writing. Thus, although Lunsford and Connors in the second edition of *The St. Martin's Handbook,* for example, accurately explain that writing process is "repetitive, erratic," recursive, "and often messy," rather than proceeding "in nice, neat steps," they hold out the hope that "writing can be a little like riding a bicycle: with practice the process becomes more and more automatic" (3–4). To the extent that process follows format, this may be true. It may be possible to write on automatic pilot if writers are working with predetermined forms of academic and professional writing, such as research reports, business memos, literature reviews, lab reports, and writing against deadlines where time is truly money. Nevertheless, by the fifth edition, Lunsford has abandoned this concept: "It is inaccurate to envision a single writing process. There are, in fact, as many different writing processes as there are writers—more if you consider that individual writers vary their writing processes each time they sit down to write!" (32).

Whereas economy and efficiency are subordinated, if not suppressed, in Lunsford's commentary, these concepts drive *Harbrace's* discussion of writing against real-world deadlines. In what is likely a reflection of the writing process of many good enough students, *Harbrace* considers the fact that "It may sometimes be necessary to abbreviate the writing process," and therefore to cut corners by narrowing "the topic to a manageable scope" and drawing on one's store of academic or experiential knowledge—"but stay away, if at all possible, from a topic that requires time-consuming research." Check the topic and approach with your instructor; do the best you can in the time allotted, emphasizing the main points and a strong conclusion; proofread. And "Submit your work on time" (118).

Punctuality. The academic and business worlds must run like clockwork in order to function well. Only selected creative writers and major thinkers—Proust and James Joyce come to mind—are expected to meet Matthew Arnold's criterion of "the best that has been known and thought in the world" (420) and allowed by the workaday world (to which they are sublimely indifferent) to take their sweet time about attaining this standard of excellence. But for the good enough student writer, this is irrelevant; a balance must be struck between procrastination and production. If the writing produced against deadlines is simply good enough to do the job, but no better, that's all right for most people, most institutions, most of the time. When the Muse must report for duty on time, at least the work gets written.

The Upshot. If student papers meet all these criteria, are they guaranteed a B? Probably yes, for teachers oriented to the universe of good enough papers. But, as I indicated at the outset, not necessarily. Teachers for whom some criteria or errors weigh more heavily than others, or who employ other local or institutional norms, may mark down or fail students who don't measure up. (As in the use of sentence fragments. Which I've now done twice in the same paragraph. So flunk me!) Teachers who value critical thinking, originality, discovery, experimentation and other attributes of creativity-striking metaphors, dazzling language, a powerful individual voice-may also downgrade papers that are unoriginal, vacuous, faceless, voiceless, or otherwise bland. Let us examine why, for these teachers, good enough writing is simply not good enough.

The Consequences of Being Good Enough: What's Missing and What's Possible

We get what we ask for, a plethora of procedural virtues. Thus, we get student writing that is rational, well-organized, decorous, modest, and efficient; that plays by the rules of Standard English and academic discourse; that follows the disciplinary conventions of form and style, and is turned in on time. Handbooks, rhetorics, dictionaries, usage directives, study guides and checklists, tests reaffirm these academic values and virtues. Student writing that meets the letter of these expectations should, in many venues, be good enough to earn the B that all involved in the transaction—students, teachers, their institutions—will settle for. By and large, these are the qualities we can teach and reinforce. If, as a consequence, student papers-at least, on the introductory level, also seem predictable, pedestrian, perhaps boring, well, maybe we're implicitly asking for this as well. Beginning students can learn the conventions before they gain the knowledge and authority that will enable them to make genuine intellectual contributions to the ongoing dialogue in their field. Whether this writing could ever become better than good enough—supply the adjective—amazing, engaging, groundbreaking, earthshaking, or exciting in a myriad of other wonderful ways may be beyond our capacity to teach. But maybe not. Students may just have to cross the Great Divide between As and Bs on their own—but we would be remiss as teachers if we didn't try to help them on the ascent.

Beyond this Great Divide are, of course, the characteristics missing from the list of those that comprise good enough writing. These include: evidence of the writer's critical thinking; grappling with multiple, perhaps contradictory, sources and ideas; questioning both authority and one's own convictions; experimentation with genre, language, and other attributes of form, style, persona, and voice. Any and all of these have the potential to transform a good enough paper into a great one. In the process, they either transform, transcend, violate, or ignore a number of the attributes of good enough writing. In this section, I address some of the possibilities for writing that could change the meaning of "good enough" from the merely acceptable to the genuinely good.

Because these attributes of genuinely good writing are much more variable, they're more difficult to categorize and to define, although we—and our students—know them when we see them. Whether these can be taught to first year student writers is also somewhat imponderable, but students can certainly be exposed to the concepts. Success depends, in part, on how automatically the students can deal with the essentials of good enough writing so they can concentrate on the more challenging and creative aspects of the assignment at hand. Success depends also on the teacher's own appreciation, understanding of, and ability herself to write with creative, confrontative, or otherwise original thinking and expression, for it's hard, if not impossible, to teach what one cannot do. All my life, I have advocated writing in the genres we teach, for ourselves and our students (see "Why Don't We Write What We Teach?"). After writing a dissertation that was a critical analysis of the methodology of literary biography ("How Literary Biographers Use Their Subjects' Works"), I wrote the biography of America's best-known living author, Benjamin Spock, to learn firsthand what I could about writing biography (see "Growing Up")—a lot. Long experience as a teacher and author of textbooks convinces me that students write best about literature when they write as insiders, creators of texts in the genre, mode, and even the sensibility of the work they're studying.

Indeed, today many Readers complement the readings with demanding assignments intended to "draw on students' creative imaginations and analytical skills to turn them from passive consumers into active producers of critical and creative texts" (Scholes, Comley, and Ulmer, v)—an application of Scholes's theory articulated in *Textual Power*. Among the more thoroughgoing are Scholes, Comley, and Ulmer's *Text Book: Writing Through Literature*, now in its third edition (2002), Bartholomae and Petrosky's *Ways of Reading*, the eighth edition scheduled for 2008, and my own books, including current editions of *The Essay Connection* and *The Arlington Reader*. It is possible for imaginative teachers to create such transformative writing assignments from nearly any contemporary textbook. Whereas outsiders read and write as aliens trying to second guess the teacher's understanding of unapproachable iconic texts, insiders are reading and writing "through literature" as Scholes et al explain, to produce original texts of their own. Chapter 10, "Insider Writing," explains how such assignments can work, from the perspectives of authors of the works studied (for example, Henry David Thoreau and Annie Dillard), and from the student's autobiographical point of view, as well. We all loved the results—varied, imaginative, on target, and—a bonus for me—virtually unplagiarizable because they are so specifically geared to the texts and context of the course. Surprisingly, none of the twenty-four chapters in Buranen and Roy's otherwise comprehensive *Perspectives on Plagiarism* addresses writing assignments.

There are other types of real-world writing assignments so thoroughly embedded in innovative course material that they require extensive original investigation and very careful writing and revising—much of it conducted in groups. Linda Flower in *The Construction of Negotiated Meaning* and Thomas Deans in *Writing Partnerships: Service-Learning in Composition* explore a variety of writing courses and projects that ask students and teachers to situate their work and their writing in disciplinary as well as wider nonacademic communities with which the classes form partnerships (Deans "Writing Partnerships" 9). The writings, thus, become reports, bulletins, brochures, operating manuals, position statements, case studies and a host of other materials described in the four programs Deans examines in detail, as well as in the appendix of courses offered in sixty-one other schools (pp. 219–44). (See also Deans's textbook, *Writing and Community Action*.) The students are described as highly invested in their work, which is perforce original and usually takes a great deal of time, because the students have to learn to understand the subject to which it pertains and the contexts in which it will be read. Much of it, intended for business, professional, or community audiences, has to be technically proficient. Whether it is intellectually innovative, as well, or essentially only good enough is beside the point of Flower's and Deans's research, though the students have considerable incentive, encouragement, and models to make their writing clear, accurate, and to the point.

TRULY GOOD ENOUGH WRITING

It should be apparent by now that in the final analysis, good enough writing may not really be good enough at all, even if, as realists, we're willing to settle for it. If we're good enough teachers, are we only good enough to help students navigate the upward (and sometimes slippery) slope, but not good enough to get them to the summit? Should we, dare we, ask more of ourselves—as teachers? As innovative writers who understand from the inside out how to break the mold? If not, can we ask more of our students? If so, if we do fulfill our escalating demands on ourselves, perhaps our students still won't want to scale the peak. But, with creative assignments and latitudinarian pedagogy, we can set that vision before them, point them in the right direction, coach them for the climb, and expect the best. When we get it, that writing will truly be good enough.

Part III

Ethical Issues of Teaching and Writing

9 The Good, the Bad, and the Ugly: Ethical Principles for Dealing with Students and Student Writing in Teachers' Publications— and in the Abyss Beyond

Prelude. The academy knows what good and bad papers are. We get them all the time, in writing classes and up, down, and across the curriculum. These form the basis of pedagogy and classroom dialogue, for we can discuss them with our students, in reasoned ways, in reasonable tones, and make suggestions for their improvement. We can and do use these papers as illustrative examples, exemplary models in the textbooks we write, the research we conduct. In "Guidelines for the Ethical Treatment of Students and Student Writing in Composition Studies," CCCC has articulated ethical principles for treating these works—a vast normative range—and their student authors. The first two-thirds of this chapter discusses issues related to this policy statement.

The final third, and the coda, "The Abyss Beyond," address ugly papers, qualitatively different in register and orientation from the norm. They send stroboscopic flashes from the stack of student writings in screaming red neon. Ugly papers transgress individual and community moral and ethical standards. They violate conventions of academic and aesthetic propriety in using language, form, and style that is wildly over the top (R. Miller 39). They may also violate the law, when advocating or confessing—with pleasure and pride—to threatened or actual rape, beating, suicide, murder. We don't know what to do with them, or the students who write them, though the Virginia Tech massacre of April 16, 2007, perpetrated by creative writing student Seung-

Hui Cho, has highlighted the issues and cries out for an ethical stance and public policy to deal with such aberrations.

ETHICAL CONSIDERATIONS

Let us focus first on interrelated sets of ethical considerations: the ethical principles for representing students and student writing in the teacher's own publications of two types—in textbooks designed for student use, and in research publications and conference presentations designed for the author's peers. In accord with the orientation of the CCCC "Guidelines for the Ethical Treatment of Students and Student Writing in Composition Studies," I initially thought there should be a single standard for all published representations of students and student work, however good or bad. Yet complications arise, engendered in part by complexities of the student writing itself, and in part by the complex nature of research, its purposes, and audience. Indeed, there is not space here to summarize or even to identify all the issues raised in the host of ethical discussions abounding in the current literature, though these—identified in such publications as Peter Mortensen and Gesa E. Kirsch's *Ethics and Representation in Qualitative Studies of Literacy,* Sheryl I. Fontaine and Susan M. Hunter's *Foregrounding Ethical Awareness in Composition and English Studies,* and Richard Miller's "Fault Lines in the Contact Zone"—were available to the CCCC committee that promulgated the Ethical "Guidelines" that form the basis of the following discussion.

On the whole, it appears that authors of writing textbooks and composition researchers, irrespective of their "variety of theoretical frameworks and research methodologies . . . share a commitment"— as articulated in the CCC *Ethical* "Guidelines"—to "protecting the rights, privacy, dignity, and well-being of the students who are involved in their studies" and to representing students and their work with sensitivity and respect. Yet, in the course of exploring the implications of the single standard of these *Ethical Guidelines,* it has become clear to me that as determined by the context, researchers and teachers alike in fact use a triple standard for dealing with student papers and students themselves. Two of these standards depart considerably from criteria covered in the *Ethical Guidelines.*

According to the concepts of moral philosophy, which provide meta-ethical criteria for distinguishing morally right and wrong actions, the *Ethical Guidelines* promulgate a *deontological* perspective (i.e., they claim that certain actions are inherently right or wrong, as a matter of principle). The *Guidelines,* thus, provide the single ethical standard applicable to dealing with most papers that teachers would conventionally label *good* and *bad,* in teaching situations, textbooks, and in small scale research. The criteria for conducting large scale naturalistic research studies of bad papers, such as those that emerge in large-scale placement tests, are of necessity based on a competing view, the *consequentialist* or *utilitarian* perspective. This view, not addressed in the *Ethical Guidelines,* contends that "the rightness of an action is determined by the goodness of its consequences . . . and promotes actions that result in the greatest good" (Reamer 899)—such as, in composition research, using student placement essays for error analysis research without informing the test takers of this alternative employment of their papers. Together, these two categories probably include over 99 percent of all students and their writing. Yet, the troublesome minority of highly problematic, *ugly* papers and the students who wrote them, those that raise serious moral and legal issues, invoke the possibility not only of ethical judgments but also of social and legal action as the writing escapes from the academy and into the tumultuous and conflicted society that engendered it. Without a double standard, some of the most significant research issues could neither be raised nor explored honestly in the literature; without a triple standard writing teachers could not function as responsible citizens in society at large.

The Good

It's fitting to begin with the good. Composition students are often represented as writers-in-process, with their behavior depicted and writings quoted to illustrate whatever points the teacher-researcher wishes to make (see discussion of Mike Rose, pp. 100-102). Thus, I'd like you to meet Amrita and Mohammed, actual advanced composition students. In the context also rendered below, they served as my Introduction to *Composition Studies as a Creative Art.*

> This semester my undergraduate writing class meets in a slightly dilapidated 150 year old farmhouse, a Designated Historic Site, across the road from the central campus's swath of lush lawns and venerable oaks. . . . There we hang out on Tuesday and Thursday mornings, drinking tea and talking about writing. . . .

Today, for instance, begins with Amrita reading an early draft of her paper on a place, about her return "home" to India for a visit with her "huge family" nine years after her parents had emigrated to New York when she was seven. At debarkation, amidst the heat, the odors, and the crowds, she encountered the passport inspector, "looking at me as if I came from a different planet, commented on my incredibly long nails. . . . He asked me my age, and I replied with a big smile, 'I am 16.' He said to me, 'Why does such a young girl like you have such horrible long nails? You should be involved in your education more than in your appearance.'" Although the family dwelling needed "some new tiles," "a new paint job," and Amrita was sitting on "the ugliest printed couch I have ever seen" (a lime-and-orange paisley clone, she said, of one in our classroom), the welcome never stopped throughout the long, lazy summer, punctuated by forays to the fruit and vegetable market, and evening rides by rickshaw ("a bike attached to a carriage") to the ice cream parlor, along teeming streets where orderly traffic "is a joke," without "lanes or turn signals."

Amrita finishes reading, visibly nervous but pleased at the impact of her paper on the class. After a round of congratulatory observations ("At your run-in with the customs official, the paper took off"), the dialogue begins, with Mohammed and the paper he wrote about his visit to "the gang of cousins, uncles, and aunts" who always met him at the Karachi airport serving as a satiric counterpoint to Amrita's return to Dehli: "If deaths due to political terrorism were down to one or two persons a day, things were looking *good*. If blackouts, also known as "load shedding," were down to one or two nights a week, things were looking *good*. If tap water wasn't as cloudy as it usually is, things were looking *good*." Then the questions begin, about bureaucrats, family size and ambience, delivery and interruption of electricity, women's status, sanitation and disease, inoculations, density of population—and of traffic. Amrita answers, Mohammed corroborates that what she says about India applies to Pakistan as well. "Are there any animals on the streets?" someone asks. "It's a farm out there!" Amrita explodes. "Imagine being followed by an elephant!" When the laughter subsides, she adds, "and walking where all of them have"—she pauses—"walked."

What Amrita has presented as a paper with considerable closure has opened up, not black holes but a universe of possibilities. "I could write a book," she exclaims. "I want to deal with being part of two cultures and not losing one while I'm living in the other. And being able to move back and forth between them. I want to explain my understanding to myself—and to people who haven't been there." As class ends, she leaves in an exhilaration of opportunity. In the next class, after I read this section of the Introduction aloud—"Did I get it right?" "Yes," said the students, "yes," Amrita volunteered—amidst a chorus of suggestions of what else to put in the paper ("pedestrians and shopkeepers," "street scenes," "animals"), "I'm willing to rewrite this paper as many times as necessary to get across the spirit of my country and my people." Exactly. (*Composition Studies*, 1–3)

Ethical Principles for Representing Student Writings in Teachers' Publications

In "The Students In This Book," Amrita and Mohammed are reading from their papers—a more dramatic, interactive presentation of student writing in teacher publications than the usual quotation of student writing, whether excerpts or whole papers. These are actual students; I have used their names and quotations from their papers—works in progress; my philosophy and style of teaching are depicted in the interactive classroom dialogue and dynamics. *Composition Studies as a Creative Art* is a research work intended for other teachers. Nevertheless, the same principles hold true as well for a "best practices" representation of students and their work as exemplary models in textbooks, whether Readers or Rhetorics.

The following ethical principles govern (or should govern) such representations. Some are derived explicitly from the CCCC Ethical "Guidelines," predicated on the assumption that whatever the "theoretical frameworks and research methodologies," composition specialists "share a commitment to protecting the rights, privacy, dignity, and well-being of the students who are involved in their studies"—and, I would add, whose works (and lives) are represented in textbooks intended for student use. Thus, these *Guidelines* are intended to apply across the board, whether to formal studies carefully planned in advance or informal investigations that arise "when teaching classes, conducting student conferences, directing academic programs," or working in literacy centers (485).

In brief, the *Guidelines* identify principles for translating this commitment into action. The teacher's Hippocratic Oath, to represent students and to quote students' statements "in ways that are fair and serious and cause no harm," is particularly crucial when using student writing for illustrative or analytic purposes, either in textbooks or in research papers. Thus, the following information should be made clear to students at the outset of the research project or writing course:

1. Their work may be used in the teachers' publications, but only with their written consent (which publishers now require routinely).
2. Their work will be used for specific purpose(s), as identified.
3. Their permission is voluntary.

    They may renegotiate this at any time, for any or all work; granting or withholding permission will not affect their grades.

    Additional ethical principles arise in "naturalistic research," when analyzing or otherwise writing about what would go on in one's classes—either in progress or after the fact—whether or not the teacher wrote about it. These extensions of good classroom practice are particularly important in instructional materials, textbooks or other pedagogical aids, for which I propose the following principles. Although these are not in the *Guidelines*, they reflect their ethos.
4. Never hold student writing—or students—up to ridicule or satire.

5. Avoid bad examples of student writing in textbooks. These undermine the necessary trust between student and teacher, particularly if one's philosophy encourages students to acknowledge their authorship and to present their work to peers. Textbook authors can find abundant examples of bad writing in published sources and all over the Internet; or they can make up their own. (As will be discussed under "The Bad," I make the distinction on this point between instructional materials and research publication, for much classic research is devoted to analyses of highly problematic student writing.)
6. Avoid using potentially damaging or embarrassing student writings in instructional materials. Such writing can be used in class, with the student author's permission, for this is a context with a restricted audience of peers who know (and presumably respect) the writer and who understand the assignment that generated the writing. A corollary to this is to avoid giving assignments that engender such writing. For instance, instead of assigning a paper on "My Most Embarrassing Moment," a teacher could frame the assignment to explain the significance of "An Experience or Event in Which I Made an Important Discovery/Learned Something Important."

   Because the student writing is entirely represented by good examples in the textbooks I'm familiar with, I would also honor the text and the author according to the following rules of conduct, which supplement the above ethical principles.
7. In quotations, don't tamper with the text of student writing, except for editorial corrections of spelling and mechanics. (To leave surface errors in otherwise admirable illustrations is to signal that these are acceptable, which undercuts the utility of the example.) In many instances, ellipses can be used to remove sections of the paper that are wide of the mark, and thus permit exact quotation. Using cosmetic surgery to enhance a paper's best features for illustrative purposes does not strike me as an ethical issue.
8. If whole student papers are used, for instance, as exemplary models in revenue-producing works, the authors should be paid appropriately, and should receive a free copy of the book in which their work appears. The authors, nevertheless, retain the rights to their work.

9. Student authors should be identified by name, unless they have requested anonymity. As adult college students, they are capable of making the decision to become published authors; my students consistently experience great pride of authorship—an ownership that anonymity would deny. Because only good papers are used, there should be no need to "protect" the students by concealing or otherwise masking their identity; writing is, after all, a performing art, and the performance is public.
10. If part of the text is used rather than the whole, the student author should be allowed to see it in the context in which it will appear. As an autobiographer, I would not allow this power of censorship over my text to people I know in other roles—relatives, friends, antagonists, for example, as I explain in "Living to Tell the Tale: The Complicated Ethics of Creative Nonfiction." The world, in general, is grist for the writer's mill. But students are a special case. In many instances, their relationship to the course, subject, and teachers is involuntary; teachers, who have more power, have an ethical obligation not to take advantage of their students, in print as in person. In practice, this often means obtaining student permission to publish accounts in which they appear—not beforehand, as one would do in a controlled research project, but after the writing is done, before the work is submitted for publication. Here's why.

   The example presented above reveals that my writing classes are a combination of guerilla theater and writing workshops. Thus, the improvisatory elements and the need to accommodate the dynamics of a class engaged in finding their own ways to become writers make it difficult for me to anticipate—at the beginning of the semester and even in any given class period—exactly what will happen. I begin each course resolved to learn something significant enough to write about—new ideas, new ways to teach better, problems to solve—but until these swim into focus, I don't know what they will be. Nor do I know at the outset what the dynamics of a particular class will be, or what students will contribute to the problems, or the solutions. As the class evolves, or sometimes, after the semester is over, the issues snap into focus, and when they do I can begin to study the research literature that undergirds the subject. As the topic sharpens, how to write about it becomes clearer, including which students, writing processes, and papers best illustrate the point at hand, and what stories to tell to emphasize these.

In these instances, the students selected sometimes become characters in creative nonfiction stories or analyses of teaching, which I write without consulting them—often, after the semester is over. But once they're written, I try them out on the students—even if it means reconvening a former class (see "Finding a Family")—to find out whether I got everything right: the classroom ambience; the characterizations of individual students, their work, and their interaction; my relation to the students and classroom presence; and everyone's relation to the course material and the task(s) at hand. If they recommend changes (graduate students sometimes do, undergraduates rarely), I make them, and it is at this point that I obtain students' permission to represent them in my work.

The Bad

It was great to learn Staniflovsky's method which I know I just spelled his name wrong. As Marlon Brando always uses the method and many other professional actors and actresses. All he talked about was actors and actresses which he wished he was a professional actor. He loved the theater so all he talked about was actors, actresses, movies, plays. Which after a while became interesting to me because that's all he ever knew and I had him for 5 days a week.

—Randomly selected student writing from
Mina Shaughnessy, *Errors and Expectations* (63)

In contrast to exemplary textbook models of student writing, good research in composition studies abounds in bad examples. (I am referring to normative writing problems in this section; papers with highly charged ethical issues—the "ugly"—will be discussed in the final section.) Just as it would be impossible for medicine to advance treatment of illness and disease by examining only healthy patients, so it is impossible to enhance the teacher's understanding of student writing problems by looking only at good papers. Teachers need to see samples of actual student writing, in order to understand the problems, the research method, the researcher's analysis, and the potential applications to their own students' work. Thus, despite encouragement from many sources (see David Bleich, "Ethnography"; Ellen Cushman, "Activist Methodology"; Gesa Kirsch, "Ethics") to conduct "socially generous research" that will provide immediate benefit to the participants, much composition studies research operates from a consequentialist frame of reference, analyzing problematic student writing for the immediate benefit of teachers, with implications for subsequent generations of students rather than the participants themselves.

Institutional review boards and informed consent measures usually mandate some version of the following informed consent procedure, addressed in the CCCC Ethical "Guidelines" for students participating in such research, whether as a freestanding study or part of a class. "Obtaining informed consent" requires the researcher to explain the study so that potential participants can understand the following:

a. The purpose and possible benefits of the research.
b. What student volunteers will be asked to do and how much time this will take.
c. What the researcher plans to do with the information or data obtained.
d. Any "potential discomforts or harms the students might incur" from participating.
e. Whether or not the researcher will include identifying information—noting that the researcher will always honor student requests to conceal identifying information (486–87). Other safeguards applicable to all uses of student writing are identified in principles 1–4 above.

These safeguards can be employed with relative ease for controlled research projects planned in advance; with modifications they can be incorporated even in more naturalistic projects that evolve over the course of a class-in-progress. In either case, if students don't want their papers to be used, they can elect not to participate. Moreover, if they volunteer the participants can be assured, if they wish, that identifying features of their work will be eliminated.

It is not clear from most composition studies research that the students whose problematic writing is quoted and analyzed actually see the report of the study in which they participated. In fact, nowhere in the *Ethical Guidelines* is this possibility raised, for good reasons. Major factors inhibit this: once the research project or class has ended, it's hard to track students down; in a large-scale study to do so could take years and delay the data analysis or publication beyond the point of utility. Moreover, even when former students can be located, they often don't respond to communications, especially if to do so would result in more work on their part. If they did read the research report, and objected to the treatment of their work—now anonymous and amalgamated, perhaps, into a data set—could they force the researcher to eliminate their papers and thus re-do the numbers or rewrite the research? That is a fate most researchers entertain at the peril of their work. As Devan Cook asks in "Secrets and Ethics in Ethnographic Writing Research," "[D]oes the researcher own the data (and the student's stories) once a permission form is signed? Is it more ethical to be more observant of a student's or a researcher's readings of the data, remembering that both parties may be far from disinterested in this question?" (117). By and large, safeguards put into place in advance of the research conducted remain, realistically, the only way to ensure that the publication of bad student writing—in whole or in part—will not embarrass or otherwise harm its author.

There is one common type of large scale research that escapes this safety net. And, for the research to be useful, I can envision no way around this. Placement testing yields a great body of writing samples ideal for research analysis; nowadays these are particularly valuable because these may be the only school writings unaffected by computer-generated grammar and spelling checks. To obtain "informed consent" from students taking the placement test could compromise the nature of the placement procedure; it would certainly imply that a bait-and-switch tactic was in operation. Moreover, as research such as Mina Shaughnessy's groundbreaking *Errors and Expectations* reveals, even when the research question is identifiable at the outset, neither its implications nor its evolution may be known at the time the placement test is conducted. From 4,000 placement essays written by incoming CUNY freshmen, 1970 to 1974, many "severely underprepared," Shaughnessy drew a wealth of examples to show that basic writing students "write the way they do, not because they are slow or non-verbal, indifferent to or incapable of academic excellence, but because they are beginners and must, like all beginners, learn by making mistakes." Scrutinizing the apparent "chaos and error," Shaughnessy discerned that there was "very little that is random or 'illogical' in what they have written," concluding that "the keys to their development as writers often lie hidden in the very features of their writing that English teachers have been trained to brush aside with a marginal code letter or a scribbled injunction to 'Proofread!'" (5). Nevertheless, because Shaughnessy's research depended on an inductive examination of these writing samples to determine the problems as well as the solutions, there was no way—or need—to contrive the placement test to yield a particular sort of results.

Shaughnessy's respect for the students and her sensitivity to their learning problems meet the ethical considerations explicit in the CCCC's Ethical "Guidelines," articulated some thirty years after the fact. Yet the other criteria for informed consent could not have been satisfied, even if such "Guidelines" had been operative at the time, without co-mingling the purposes of placement testing with a very different research agenda. Placement testing is not necessarily voluntary; thus, among its virtues as a data collection device is the fact that it casts a wide net, with the potential of including the writing of an entire incoming class. If students have the option of withholding their writing samples from a research project, the study's evidence may be skewed in ways that the researcher can neither anticipate nor control. What evidence would a study yield, for instance, if all the students who thought they performed badly removed their papers? It is easy to imagine how the research questions—and their answers—might be compromised by a atypical writing samples.

Bad writing samples gained from a large population of changing students whose writing is largely unidentifiable by the researcher or the readers would seem to present no ethical problems, for either researchers or the teachers who read their work. Smaller samples or single case studies, where it is easier to identify either the student or the researcher's institution, need the protections given in the Ethical "Guidelines." And traditionally, most studies of students with learning problems, ranging from mild to more formidable, treat their subjects in ethical ways that, as the "Guidelines" say, "are fair and serious and cause no harm." Among the better known are Mike Rose's case studies of the precious, precarious student *Lives on the Boundary,* from voc-ed to veterans to a host of baffled under and over-achievers. Indeed, Rose established the gold standard, transforming the conventional subjects of teacher research and classroom narratives from stick figures with first names (real or fake) and labels ("middle-aged," "veteran") into human beings who are (or appear to be) actual students in actual classes or other contexts of learning. These dimensional figures operate as characters in a variety of academic stories, often memorable in their own right, and as illustrations of whatever theory, philosophy, pedagogy, and scholarship the author is discussing. Through these human narratives, full of "thick description" of people we quickly learn to love even though we don't know them, Rose, as a teacher-researcher, helps us to understand why the students' learning difficulties exist, and how they can be overcome. In *Works and Lives* Clifford Geertz demonstrates how noted anthropologists Lévi-Straus, Evans-Pritchard, Malinowski, and Benedict, create highly situated, "author-saturated" narratives to validate their interpretation of the cultures they study. Rose, functioning as an ethnologist of writing, uses comparable techniques to present his translation of classroom culture to an audience of teachers.

Equally well known, though without the individualizing features of Rose's *Lives on the Boundary* are Bartholomae's extended analyses (inspired by Shaughnessy) of problematic student writing in "The Study of Error" (in which "John" writes, "first of all what happen was that I got suspense from school," 99) and "Inventing the University" (in which the anonymous author of "white shoes"—"wearing my white shoes instead of black and to cover up the team socks with a pair of my own white ones"—is judged lacking in creativity (on a placement essay, scarcely the locus for ad hoc creativity) for locating his "narrative in an unconnected rehearsal of commonplaces about creativity" (150, 158). These landmark studies by both Rose and Bartholomae, like legions of others, were conducted before student consent was deemed mandatory in institutional research, and its absence has not presented problems. Given the retrospective nature of *Lives on the Boundary*, with evidence arriving unbidden throughout the first thirty years, say, of Rose's life, it would be impossible to obtain ex post facto consent anyway. The consequentialist ethical stance prevails. Yet, Richard Straub and Ronald F. Lunsford's *Twelve Readers Reading: Responding to Student Writing*, published in 1995, well after most institutions and publishers had adopted student consent guidelines, makes virtually no mention of how the fifteen student papers were selected for analysis by twelve expert composition researchers; the focus is strictly on the researchers and their analyses. Yet, one of these papers is, in my opinion, not just bad and problematic for the usual rhetorical reasons, but ugly—and its ugliness, too, is largely ignored.

The Ugly

Truly ugly student papers don't show up often in the professional literature, though they do show up in the headlines when a student goes on a shooting rampage, such as Seung-Hui Cho's massacre at Virginia Tech in April 2007, which I address in "The Abyss Beyond" that concludes this chapter, though it scarcely resolves the issues. As Richard Miller explains in "Fault Lines in the Contact Zone," English teachers, like the universities where they work, don't know they are ill prepared "to read and respond to the kinds of parodic, critical, oppositional, dismissive, resistant, transgressive, and regressive writing" produced by students writing in what Mary Louise Pratt has labeled "the contact zone of the classroom" (39). When such inflammatory writing does materialize, the researchers who discuss it do not appear to have obtained consent to publish or otherwise circulate or comment on the work at, for instance, professional meetings, where it inevitably sets off an uproar. (Moreover, given the fact that the students in these studies are usually identifiable by their teacher and institution, if not by name, they could probably be pinpointed if readers wanted to seek them out, especially with the easy availability of news reports via the Internet.) The absence of consent does not seem to be an issue, at least not overtly in the literature. But why, indeed, would a student author agree to have a paper published if it contained a confession of assault, rape, attempted or actual murder—even if the confession was a hoax? Why would a student author subject himself—as well as the work—to teachers' representations that at times seem dictated more by the legal code than a code of ethics?

One of the ugliest and most problematic papers is the student essay Scott Lankford discusses in "'Queers, Bums, and Magic': How Would You Grade a Gay-Bashing?" presented at CCCC March 19, 1992, and discussed—as I can testify from personal experience—during incendiary sessions at various professional meetings. In "Fault Lines in the Contact Zone" Miller characterizes the still-unpublished essay:

> Queers, Bums, and Magic" was written in Lankford's pre-college-level composition class at Foothill College "in response to an assignment taken from *The Bed-*

ford Guide for College Writers that asked students to write a report on group behavior." One student detailed "a drunken trip he and some friends made to 'San Fagcisco' to study 'the lowest class . . . the queers and the bums.' The essay recounts how the students stopped a man on Polk Street, informed him that they were doing a survey and needed to know if he was 'a fag.' From here, the narrative follows the students into a dark alleyway where they discover, as they relieve themselves drunkenly against the wall, that they have been urinating on a homeless person. In a frenzy, the students begin to kick the homeless person, stopping after '30 seconds of non-stop blows to the body,' at which point the writer says he 'thought the guy was dead.' Terrified, the students make a run for their car and eventually escape the city. (392)

Miller's analysis of the issues that arise when the audiences. each "with a range of competing commitments," in Pratt's terms "'meet, clash, and grapple'" with one another, is insightful. "Part of what makes 'Queers, Bums, and Magic' so powerful," he says, "is that it disables the most familiar kinds of . . . teacher responses. Here is writing that cannot easily be recuperated as somehow praiseworthy despite its numerous surface flaws, writing that instead offers direct access to a voice from the margins that seems to belong there." How should teachers deal with it? And with the student who wrote it? The reactions "fell into one of three categories: read the essay as factual and respond accordingly; read the essay as fictional and respond accordingly; momentarily suspend the question of the essay's factual or fictional status and respond accordingly" (392).

For our purposes here, the third option can be dealt with briefly. A teacher could "pull the paper out of the private corridor running between the student writer and the teacher and move it into the public arena," turning the essay into a "teachable object." In this case, the entire class would study "Queers, Bums and Magic" in conjunction with legal definitions of hate speech, moving from the focus on a single text and author into the contact zone where, as Pratt says, "No one [is] excluded and no one [is] safe" (Pratt 39, Miller 393–95). This does not preclude dealing with the moral and legal aspects of the abusive actions; in fact, such a discussion might well focus on them.

The second category of teacher response is represented by Lankford himself, openly gay. He elected "'to respond to the essay exactly as if it were a fictional short story,'" commenting favorably on the student's word choice, "'straightforward depictions of nightmarish 'mega-violence' and surrealistic detail,'" and imagined audience. Yet, other teachers who had read the paper disagreed with Lankford's favorable evaluation, recommending a variety of textual changes. This strategy, says Miller, "asks teachers to look away from what the student's writing is attempting to do—at the havoc it is trying to wreak in the contact zone—and restrict their comments to the essay's surface features and formal qualities. . . . Such a strategy itself invites parody: . . . Would such changes help inch it towards being, say, an excellent gay-bashing essay, one worthy of an A?" (393–94).

The second, text-based type of response strikes me, as it did Miller, as morally evasive, hampered rather than enhanced by implicit adherence to the moral stance of the CCCC "Guidelines." It is also of limited pedagogical value because of the surface and counter-intuitive responses it mandates in a moral universe that (in accord with reporting policies mandatory at many institutions) argues "that the student be removed from the classroom and turned over either to a professional counselor or to the police" (Miller 392). Yet, this type of bland response to the text, and nothing but the text, is the one generally exhibited by the researchers quoted in *Twelve Readers Reading* to an anonymous student paper titled "Street Gangs: One Point of View," in which the writer asserts his authority to discuss the subject "because I was once part of one." He claims that most of the actions of his gang, "THE CRIPPS," such as "beating someone up or vandalizing someone [sic] property" were for revenge, with the exception of one time at "the pool," where we singled out "one person at a time" as a "target" to be "sucker punched." The only teacher who addresses the sadistic, bullying nature of this violence at all is Peter Elbow, who says mildly, "you give the example of picking on people at the pool. You tell it in a kind of deadpan way, but it's kind of horrifying for me. I think I was the kind of person who was picked on. . . ." Although Glynda Hull writes in the margin, "Oh, my—were you ever the one to do the punching?" the general nature of her commentary, like that of the other evaluators, including Elbow, Anne Gere, and Jane Peterson, is to ask for greater development, and some reorganization (101–104, 221–38). Richard Larson's recommendations are characteristic: "Your goal here is to enlarge the reader's knowledge of a subject that the reader might find important and might genuinely want to know more about. I think you've got such a subject (I surely would be glad to learn more about gangs . . . ." (97). Ignoring the ugliness, or reacting to it with messages so mild that even a genteel audience of other teachers would miss any interrogation of the status quo (if in fact any interrogation is going on), sends the message to the student that the activity, as well as the writing, is a worthy endeavor. Such comments, like Lankford's responses to the "Gay Bashing" paper, would seem to be the logical extension of the profession's collective decision to represent students in a positive light at all costs—in the instances of ugly papers, to "protect the rights . . . dignity, and well being of the students" ("Guidelines" 485), even when the students represent themselves as denying comparable rights to other people.

A exception to this stance is William E. Smith's "Blurring the Boundaries of Academic Intimacy and Moral Neutrality." Here, Smith treats with forthright complexity the alternatives of the ethical and pedagogical dilemma Miller raises, whether "to read the essay as factual and respond accordingly; [or] read the essay as fictional and respond accordingly." Smith provides a respectful and careful discussion of a writing director's "ethical dilemmas" in advising a TA who brought him a freshman paper—completely beyond the parameters of class discussion—in which "the writer recounts his own gang initiation, three years prior, when he held down a fourteen-year-old while his two friends stabbed the boy to death." "'We killed him executionary [sic] style. I held his arm while he died." The writer "names his accomplices, dates, and addresses," all of which (except the murder) the police later verify as real. "He ends his essay with a statement of remorse, describing how this incident tortures his sleep" (71).

Smith offers his analysis as "a template for dealing with individual and programmatic responses to pseudo-confessions, dishonesty, and criminal acts." During the complicated discussion that ensues, weaving among university counselors and lawyers, the TA, Smith as writing director, the NCTE Code of Ethics Committee and Deputy Director, the campus police, and the city police, the student—known only by institution and the quarter when took the course—virtually disappears from Smith's paper. In fact, he had disappeared from class for four days, raising further suspicions, only to surface to learn from the TA that his paper is in the hands of the campus police. As the

TA "advises the student to seek professional help" (legal? psychological?) "the student becomes agitated, admits he fictionalized the event, basing it on newspaper articles and one popular book on gangs. His anger increases, and he leaves," returning a half hour later to report that "he has called home to tell his mother . . . [who] rebukes him, saying"—in the liveliest exchange of the entire article, "'What did you expect when you wrote what you did. I'm surprised they don't kick you out of school.'" After two days' more discussion among the principals and a call from the city police reporting that "there were no unsolved murders for the entire month in question anywhere near the location mentioned in the student's essay," the student talks with Smith, who explains why "we read the paper as a confession, a cry for help," even a desire to be arrested. Smith offers suggestions for responsible and accurate writing in the future, and how to obtain legal help if necessary. The case closes when "the student asks [Smith] to call the police for him and to explain that the experience was fictional, and that he had written the paper to impress his teacher" and Smith complies (71–75).

In this case, understanding of the context in which the paper was written and in which it was read can help to transform the ugly and unmanageable work into the misguided product of the writer's bad judgment—again, an ethical dimension not covered by the CCCC "Guidelines." Thus, Smith's explanation reveals how important a knowledge of multiple contexts—the writing class, the writer's relation to the teacher and the class, the writer's prior and current standing outside the school, and information from the community and police records—helps to explain the student's misjudgment. Nevertheless, if the paper had not proven to be fiction, Smith and his university would have had no choice but to obey the law of the land, the prevailing standard that overrides the professional code of ethics, as Gothard explains in "Legal Issues: Confidentiality and Privileged Communication." Teacher-student communications are not considered "privileged communication" under the law, and are thus not "protected by law from compelled disclosure." Academic institutions may extrapolate from a variety of legal decisions, one of the most notable being the landmark *Tarasoff v. The Regents of the University of California* (Supreme Court of California, 1976). The teacher is analogous to the therapist in Tarasoff case,[1] which led to the promulgation of a number of new state laws addressing the issue of whether recipients of a communication concerning impending danger have a duty to warn the prospective victim. The general criteria that must be met "for a *Tarasoff* duty to exist are: (1) There must be a serious threat of severe bodily harm, (2) the person making the threat must have the ability to carry it out, and (3) there must be an identifiable victim" (1582). There is an equal urgency to report a crime after the fact, as in the numerous state statutes requiring teachers (and physicians and others) to report cases of abuse—including those that surface in student writing—to the law, for the protection of the victim. That in colleges this duty often falls to the teacher of the first year writing class, where most of the ugly papers are likely to appear, and thus puts the burden on the most vulnerable faculty, does not exempt the university from assuming this responsibility. Under most reporting protocols, the TA can bring the matter to her supervisor, who then assumes the responsibility for pursuing it, in the manner that Smith recounts.

By supplying additional information about comparable factors that influenced the writing of "Queers, Bums, and Magic," Miller interprets the paper more as a manifestation of cultural and academic naiveté, rather than as willful transgression. The student writer "grew up in Kuwait; English is his second language; he was writing during the onset of the Persian Gulf War." A cultural outsider, he did not understand the essence of the *Bedford Guide's* assignment, to "Station yourself in a nearby place where you can mingle with a group of people gathered for some reason or occasion." After observing the behavior—such as a bar mitzvah or an emergency room—"report on it" and "offer some insight" (Kennedy, *Bedford Guide* 2nd ed., 41). Students more familiar with common American educational practices would grasp the assignment's subtext—"when you write this essay, report only on a group from which you are safely detached and on behavior unlikely to disturb others"—and select "a less explosive topic." Missing these cues in cultural ignorance, the Kuwaiti student's "hyperconformity" to the assignment led him to manifest "the mixture of anger, rage, ignorance, and confusion" that so distressed his teacher and made him the butt of professional opprobrium. Miller suggests that the choice of a more benign topic would have left the "surface calm of the educational community undisturbed"—not necessarily a good thing in a class that encourages the "unsolicited oppositional discourse" that Pratt advocates (397–99). But that is another story. And even Lankford, the teacher, and consequently Miller, do not know whether the student's story is true.

If this story were to be confirmed—and Lankford had an obligation to follow the procedure Smith articulates in order to ascertain the truth—then I contend that the initial—and emphatic majority—response of audiences who in discussing "Queers, Bums, and Magic" urge "that the student be removed from the classroom and turned over either to a professional counselor or to the police" (R. Miller, 392) is ethically and legally correct. The social and legal code has no choice but to trump the principles articulated in the CCCC "Guidelines"; as Robert L. Barker and Douglas M. Branson explain in "When Laws and Ethics Collide," when "a law and a professional's ethics are in conflict, it is always the ethical position that succumbs" (qtd. in Gothard 1583). Smith offers a judicious conclusion whose principles a revision of the CCCC "Guidelines" would do well to accommodate: "Unless we [writing program administrators] train ourselves and our writing faculties to view our own actions and choices against larger historical, social and cultural frameworks, we will not be able to make difficult ethical decisions that often affect our students' lives. Underlying our ethical choices is a sense of community and a sense of differences that coexist within that community. We can show our students how institutions and ideologies limit their freedom, how they create and are created by forces that shape their identities and roles in their community," a position that reinforces the implication of Miller's "contact zone" response. Like our students, we, too, says Smith, "live in a society of competing discourses, where pragmatics and idealism collide, and where, ultimately, none of us can remain comfortable as a passive, neutral audience" (80). Ultimately, we live in a society where, as one strand of this discourse makes clear, inside as well as outside the academy, nobody is above the law.

The Abyss Beyond

There is not world enough and time to examine here all of the complicated issues in the ugliest contemporary case of all, the ethical, psychological, medical, legal, philosophical, political dimensions raised by student Seung-Hui Cho's massacre of thirty-two students and faculty at Virginia Tech on April 16, 2007. Space barely allows me to address some of the salient pedagogical and administrative aspects.

Judging from the thorough reports released after the massacre, university faculty and administrators did all they were humanly, institutionally, and legally authorized to do in dealing with Cho, as a student and obviously troubled human being. Cho, a creative writing major, from all reports maintained a menacing silence in every class. By October 2005, he had begun turning in writing that was "'like something out of a nightmare'" (Bartlett et al, A7).[2] At that time, distinguished poet Nikki Giovanni "refused to let him stay in her class because his writing was 'intimidating,' and he frightened other students." To accommodate Cho, creative writing director Lucinda Roy tutored him privately, one-on-one, after he left Giovanni's class; and Lisa Norris, who placed him off to the side in her own creative writing seminar, contacted the associate dean of students about his troubling writing. Faculty members were sympathetic, worried, and "proactive," said Carolyn Rude, department head "attending seminars on how to help students in distress," a particularly relevant skill for English professors whose students' creative writing presents a window for intimate viewing of their "troubles and temperaments" (Dewan and Santora A1, 18).

Later that fall, two different female students complained to the campus police that Cho, who had been suspected of photographing female students under the classroom table, was stalking them. An acquaintance of Cho's "notified the police that he might be suicidal," and he was referred to off-campus mental health counseling. "A counselor recommended involuntary commitment, and a judge signed an order saying that he 'presents an imminent danger to self or others,'" and sent him to a psychiatric hospital. There, the examining doctor determined that though Cho was mentally ill, he was "not an imminent danger" to others, assessing "his insight and judgment" as "sound." As a consequence, the judge released him and ordered outpatient treatment, but Virginia Tech officials don't know whether or not he obtained it (Dewan and Santora A 1, 18).

During Cho's senior year, his "increasingly bizarre and frightening" writings continued to disturb his creative writing professors and classmates alike. It has been my experience over many years that college classrooms are de facto civil communities; nearly all college students understand acceptable boundaries of behavior without having to have these spelled out or even overtly enforced.[3] Unless they are employing an alternative cultural or psychological frame of reference (see

Richard Miller's discussion above), even the most imaginative and experimental pushers of the envelope accommodate these limits in their writing. That the truly psychologically disturbed do not acknowledge or respect such boundaries is the hallmark of truly ugly papers.[4]

Students in Professor Edward Falco's playwriting class found Cho's work so full of violence and profane rants that they refused to read and analyze it (Dewan and Santora A 1, 8). Ian McFarlane, a typical classmate, observed, "The plays had really twisted, macabre violence that used weapons I wouldn't have even thought of [including shoes, plates, wrenches, pipes, a half-eaten cereal bar—and a chainsaw, shades of the *Texas Chainsaw Massacre*]. Before Cho got to class [we worried . . .] about whether he could be a school shooter. I was even thinking of scenarios of what I would do in case he did come in with a gun, I was that freaked out about him." Adds McFarlane, that when commenting on Cho's work, "we were very careful with our words in case he decided to snap" ("Virginia Killer's").

Yet, even with incendiary warning signals flashing to signal violation of moral and aesthetic codes, Cho had broken no statutes. He had not, at that point, committed violent acts or made direct threats to anyone, menacing though his behavior seemed to others. His violent writing, though even more amateurish than many undergraduate works, is in the (porno)graphic, obscene, misogynistic, highly sexualized, drug laden, over-the-top mode of many contemporary media in which American youth are continually immersed: films (think *Reservior Dogs,* snuff films), gangsta rap, and video games such as *Manhunt,* or *Halo,* with their business-as-usual acceptance of bludgeoning, burning, mass murders, and spread of massive infections. As if in corroboration of this influence, after committing the first two murders, Cho mailed a package to NBC before the final conflagration and suicide. Accompanying the self-justifying rants and diatribes are eleven photographs which show him aiming "one or two handguns at the camera, posing as if in an action movie" (Dewan and Santora A 18).

Falco emailed his students after the massacre, hoping to allay their sense of guilt "'at not having done something or said something that might have prevented this horror.'" As he emailed Jonathan Mandell of CNN, "'Cho's behavior was disturbing to all of us—and the English department tried, with the best of intentions, to both get him help and to make the appropriate authorities aware of his disturbing behavior. We did all that we thought it was reasonable to do.'" Falco continued, "'There was violence in Cho's writing—but there is a huge difference between writing about violence and behaving violently. We could not have known what he would do. We treated him like a fellow student, which is what he was. I believe the English department behaved responsibly in response to him'" (Jonathan Mandell).

There is no last word on this troubling subject, at least not at this writing. Perhaps there cannot be, as long as we live in a land that protects both civil liberties—including free, vile, and violent expression—and the ownership of private arsenals. Katherine S. Newman, Princeton sociologist and co author of *Rampage: The Social Roots of School Shootings,* characterizes the rampage shooters at Columbine High (1999), Westside Middle School (1998), and Virginia Tech as youths "trying to turn the reputations they live with as [inept] losers into something more glamorous, more notorious." They (all males) try to "reverse their social identities" by "becoming violent, going out in a blaze of glory, and ending it all by taking other people with them." This is "one script that plays out in popular culture and provides a road map for notoriety." Newman concludes her analysis with praise for "those at Virginia Tech who did exactly what we would want them to do. They alerted the counseling staff to the scary writing submitted by the shooter; they tried to cajole him into treatment; and they warned the police." Nevertheless, in an academic context that mandates respect for student privacy, and in a society unwilling "to lock up people who have committed no illegal acts"—for "it is not a crime to be depressed or even scary"—they failed. This is the heavy burden a free society, and a free university environment, must bear (Newman B 20; See also Lipka).

As a creative writer and a teacher of creative writing students, I would not curtail the extraordinary benefits of free expression, which *Writers Without Borders* addresses throughout. Given the risks attendant on other aspects of life—driving, flying, marriage, childbirth—the risks of freedom of speech and of writing far outweigh the alternatives of *1984*-esque censorship and ultimately, mind control. Nevertheless, as an ethical being and responsible teacher, I want to have it both ways, for I can't condone student writing or behavior whose most extreme consequences would put the lives of my students, colleagues, or myself at risk. So I establish boundaries at the beginning of every writing class designed to ensure that student authors will not supplant the Golden Rule with the law of the jungle; I confer privately with troubled students (with my office door open); I keep in touch with the counseling staff—not only concerning violent students, but the silent, the sad, and the sullen. I hold my breath—and keep on writing.

10 Insider Writing: Plagiarism-Proof Assignments

Whose words these are, I think I know. . . .

It was the best of assignments. . . . Newcomers to St. Louis in 1974, we had chosen to live in Clayton because of its excellent public schools. So my heart leapt up when I beheld the instructions for our sixth grade son's very first English assignment, "Write a poem in the manner of Robert Frost." This Laird did, refusing—as usual—to let us even see his work until he brought it home with the teacher's comments. I do not remember the poem, alas, but I do remember how all changed, changed utterly when at the bottom of the quatrains appeared, in impeccable copperplate, the teacher's only observation: "This is a very good poem—if YOU wrote it." Maintaining my customary decorum—I had yet (nor have I still) to punch any rogue and peasant slave in the nose—I suppressed my outrage and asked Laird, "May I complain to your teacher?" "Over my dead body," quoth the innocent (not his exact words), so I forbore.

This cynical skepticism reveals how even good assignments can go bad if a teacher doesn't trust her convictions, or her students. Today, she'd have gone straight to the Internet, where a Google search would reveal some 19,100 hits for the combination of "Robert Frost" and "Whose woods" in English alone. What a waste of time, and what a displacement of intellectual energy! Laird's teacher was, in fact, on the right track and should have had confidence in the integrity of her assignment, recognizing that it was, if not plagiarism-proof, then plagiarism-resistant. For hers was a classic "insider writing" assignment.

As teachers, we need to exploit the broad spectrum of possibilities for insider writing assignments—those that inspire originality *because* they are plagiarism-proof. To do so, we need to examine how we ourselves understand our own discipline as insiders. Whatever we take for granted as disciplinary assumptions and knowledge, norms and values, how and why we do our work, what we consider big issues and ongoing problems, can become the basis for writing assignments that will invite students to look inside, to understand, to remember.

Why the Current Concern with Plagiarism-Proof Writing Assignments?

It is far easier, more intellectually interesting, and more ethically satisfying to prevent plagiarism than to track it down. It's far more productive, and a lot more fun for teachers and students alike to work in the atmosphere of trust that insider assignments engender, with their implications of collegial creativity, rather than with the suspicion adhering to more conventional assignments. Innovative assignments resistant to plagiarism are particularly important in an era when student culture implicitly condones copying software and downloading MP3 files, is dependent on Internet search engines, and believes that information is there for the taking, copyrighted or not. These *insider writing* assignments are original in conception; they encourage student writers to be original, thoughtful, and engaged; they can be revised and refined anew for every student in every class. Implicit is the expectation that students actively participate as insiders in investigating the topic at hand, and in creating some of the issues and materials to be studied, rather than approaching topics from the outside as passive consumers of ancillary sources.

Insider Writing vs. Outsider Writing

Outsider writing. Scholes claims that in writing conventional critical papers students are put in the position of trying to second guess the teacher's interpretation of unassailable iconic texts. They too often feel forced to read and write as aliens, bowing in reverence before the sacred texts of the literary canon, "'the best that has been thought and said,'" offered up by teachers serving as "priests and priestesses in the service of a secular scripture" (12–13 ff). The same obsequiousness prevails when students, novices to the subject at hand, rely heavily on experts on any topic, in any field. Students, writing of necessity as outsiders, see themselves as pressured to consult the experts, to patch together others' ideas and words (see Howard) in hopes of coming closer to understanding the subject than they would if they depended on their own ideas. Yet, as outsiders suppressing their own judgments, student writers serving as ventriloquists of published scholars are not positioned to own the primary material or to trust their opinions of it. With so little of themselves in their writing, they have little incentive to care very much about their work.

Insider writing. In contrast, when students write from *inside* the problem, issue, or literary or historical work at hand, they operate as engaged participants rather than as alien outsiders whose understanding comes through what others—sometimes centuries of others—have had to say on the subject. As I explain below, through the examples of my own literature course and those in other disciplines, teachers in all fields can construct assignments that compel their students to understand its perspectives, values, beliefs, norms, customs as insiders. By creating dialogues, dramatizations, primary documents, or position papers in the process, students are directed to produce meaning, rather than to reproduce received opinion.

With such assignments, student authors perforce have to accept and assume some authority for knowing and understanding the problem/issue at hand. Admittedly, this authority is limited by the students' actual experience with or understanding of the situation they're writing about, as it would be in most undergraduate papers. Yet, these assignments have considerable integrity, and consequently, so do the students. Teachers whose courses are described below (and others—see Adler-Kassner, Crooks, and Watters; Downing, Hurlbert, and Mathieu; Flower, *Construction;* Grobman) claim that because as a rule the students are heavily invested in the lively dialogues or events in which they're participating, they work harder, learn more (they generally have to buttress their insider understanding with outside sources), and write far more convincingly than with the usual routine academic exercises. Because these writing assignments are highly specific to both the courses and to the individual student's participation in them, they're more varied, more interesting, and nearly impossible to plagiarize. As the context changes every semester, so do the assignments; students have to construct their specifically nuanced topic from the ground up, every time.

How Insider Writing Works: Model Courses

"Coming of Age in American Autobiography." This course, which I've taught over the years to honors freshmen and a variety of upper division undergraduates, took on new vitality when I changed the writing assignments from conventional papers of literary criticism to imaginative scenarios in which the students create or re-conceive the autobiographers and significant moments in these lives. My students examine autobiographies, including those of Benjamin Franklin, Frederick Douglass (the 1845 version), Harriet Jacobs, Henry David Thoreau, Annie Dillard, Richard Wright, and Maxine Hong Kingston, in their human, historical, and literary contexts in order to understand as readers, critics, and writers the significant issues and problems of the autobiographer's art.

The students analyze the ways autobiographers shape their self-presentations in a variety of roles: as members of a particular gender, ethnicity, or social class; as individuals in family, occupational, and other group contexts; and as people fulfilling particular destinies or roles in a specific historical context. To accomplish these aims, the students "become" the characters they are writing about through employing a variety of literary forms, including monologues, dialogues, dramas, philosophical presentations, letters of job application or professional vitas, and imaginary journal entries.

Among the many possibilities for writing is an assignment that asks pairs of students to "Write a dialogue between Franklin and Douglass in which they discuss, debate, and ultimately define the meaning(s) of one of the following concepts as it pertains to either coming of age as an individual or as a nation (or both): independence, self-reliance, defiance of authority, citizenship, maturity, contributions to/engagement in the larger society." Another asks student duos to "Design a 21st century house for Thoreau (will it be static or mobile, rigid or free form?), in an appropriate setting (will it remain at Walden Pond? Or will you relocate it? Why?). One of you (as Annie Dillard) acts as the decorator, while the other is the environmental engineer and landscaper. Remembering Frank Lloyd Wright's dictum, 'Form follows function,' this dwelling and its environment should reflect and symbolize the predominant values of both Thoreau and Dillard. These characteristics are reflected in Appendix 3, *Writing in the Manner of Thoreau and Other Nature Writers*. You may include illustrations—a drawing, floor plan, sketches, photos, whatever, ad lib."

Because the papers have to be historically accurate, characters from different times must have a plausible way of communicating with one another, one that respects the era and the ethos of each; the students may choose a contemporary or future time if they wish. One memorable presentation was that of an engineering student, who delightedly filled all the whiteboards in the classroom with diagrams of an environmentally friendly geodesic dome, from various angles, employing mathematical formulas to illustrate its ecological properties. Other briefer writings involve keeping a Thoreauvian journal; telling a joke Dillard's family would appreciate; making a list imitating Richard Wright's lists of sensory encounters with objects and phenomena; and constructing a cautionary tale analogous to "No Name Woman" that opens Kingston's *Woman Warrior*.

I consider these assignments *historical rendering* because they are embedded in factual information. My students, however, call them *creative writing*, in part because they're highly unusual in freedom, form, and voice for academic writing, and they are unique in the students' experience. Students deadened by conventional expectations revive as they reanimate their subject in a process which compels independent thought and allows them to tap wells of creativity they didn't know they had. While working with partners, they learn from one another—not so much factual information, which both have to find from external sources—but perspective, pacing, the sound and sense of sentences, dialogue, organization. Many seem surprised that such enjoyable assignments require them to work harder than they expected to, even though they are sharing the work, and at how extensively they need to revise (often, by supplying additional evidence or information) once the class has heard their intermediate version.

Of course, to fully experience autobiography as a literary form, it is essential for the students to write an autobiographical essay, thereby to understand the genre as insiders once again, in this case as real time, real world autobiographers. This is, perhaps, the ultimate "insider" writing, the quintessence of a paper impossible to plagiarize. Students still have to figure out ways to make accounts of first true love/recognition of life's unfairness or random chance/experience with war or exile or divorce or death meaningful in new ways to the jaded reader. Thus, about midway through the semester, when the students felt comfortable with each other and with me, I ask them to "Tell a true story of your experience with an event, person or group, recognition or development of a belief or value system, or other phenomenon that was pivotal in your coming of age and/or understanding of the world." In the interests of full disclosure, I share with them my autobiographical "Living to Tell the Tale: The Complicated Ethics of Creative Nonfiction." Here, I use the story of discovering my twinhood, whose existence and neonatal death my parents had concealed from me (including denial, altering my birth certificate, swearing talkative relatives to secrecy) as the vehicle for exploring such fundamental issues as "Who owns the story?" "Who has the right to tell/suppress/interpret it?—for what readers?" and more. The implied message is clear: if I can do this, making myself vulnerable to readers and at the same time transforming life into art, so can they.

Although these assignments specify three to five pages, most of the students write double or triple that number, not counting revisions. They expect to be able to dash off a personal reminiscence; then artistic and philosophical and ethical issues intervene, and they revise again and again. And again. In an era when many students take writing-intensive courses simply to fill a requirement, this is surely an index of student investment.[1] And yes, of course I too invest a lot of time responding to these multiple drafts, but the results are worth our collective effort, say the students, in class and on evaluations, enthusiastic affirmations of this writing that, as one student said, "'makes me better than I am.'"

My students' class presentations stimulate lively, invested, and involved discussion. The students come alive when they read these papers, individually or in pairs, to their primary audience, the class; their discussions are energetic, enthusiastic, and engaged. When I asked the students to evaluate each assignment individually, to a person, they loved "trying new modes of writing and getting into the heads of the authors we were reading." "I was pleasantly surprised with the assignments. I liked them a great deal more than the simple, mechanical, and stereotypical critical papers I was used to." The autobiography, voted "the best paper of the year," provided further validation of insider writing: "It gave everyone a hands-on experience with the genre. While I found writing about myself exceedingly difficult, this assignment gave me a great appreciation of the subject matter of this course."

Other Sample Insider Writing Assignments

Two areas examined below, classical studies and service learning, are representative of the bourgeoning literature on writing across the curriculum, as addressed in John Bean's *Engaging Ideas* and Art Young's *Teaching Writing Across the Curriculum*. Many of their suggested writing assignments ("microthemes," peer-reviews, assessment of evidence or issues in learning) can be adapted to specific disciplines, and further refined to employ an insider's perspective.

Dramatizations of classical works. Classical studies professors Christy Friend and Mark C. Carnes created classroom experiences comparable to my own. Desperate to liven up classes full of passive, tuned-out students, each teacher devised classroom dramatizations of classical works in which students played insider roles in the cultures they were learning about. In each course, as in mine, the students, well-informed, wrote more sophisticated and longer papers analyzing the issues addressed.

Friend's students re-enacted the *controversiae* on affirmative action from Quintilian's *Institutio Oratoria,* openly "questioning assumptions about merit and equality, and examining the political, historical and cultural factors" influencing these (9–12). In Carnes's "Liminal Classroom," students enacted scenes from their reading, such as Plato's account of the trial of Socrates in *The Republic* and Confucius's resolution of disputes in *The Analects,* examining the classical works within "the contexts of the impassioned debates and dramas from which they had emerged." Because the students in both teachers' classes became so thoroughly invested in their subjects that they not only "spent countless hours outside of class meeting in factions and cajoling the undecided [,] they worked harder on papers and submitted more of them," even though the assignments "far more demanding" than they had been earlier, when students merely read the texts (Carnes B 6–7, 20).

REAL WORLD WRITING: INSIDER WRITING IN SERVICE-LEARNING COURSES

Service learning courses in all disciplines put students into real-world writing situations where it's impossible to plagiarize. The students serve as aides or interns in nonprofit organizations, public schools, hospitals, prisons, homeless shelters, and other community service endeavors (see Deans *Writing Partnerships,* Appendix B; Grobman 129; Cushman "Service Learning," "Sustainable"). From their "insider" perspective, albeit one with limited authority, they write either in, about, or for that context. Often, they cross "cultural and class boundaries by collaborating" both in writing and in "pragmatic civic action" with "community partners" who may be very different from themselves (Deans *Writing Partnerships* 9–10). Their writings are thus specific to both context and situation: reports, bulletins, brochures, operating manuals, position statements, case studies, reflections on programs and the student's participation therein are among the plethora of possibilities (see Flower, *Construction;* Deans, *Writing Partnerships;* Cushman, "Sustainable"). Service learning owes much to Freire's liberation pedagogy of "social dreaming," which assumes "that if students perform ideological analysis and critical literacy in the classroom, they will parlay that critical consciousness into concrete civic action later in their lives" (qtd. in Deans, *Writing Partnerships* 109).

Space considerations allow only a single characteristic service learning assignment to represent the philosophical and pedagogical rationale for such writing. Deans's textbook, *Writing and Community Action,* offers two alternative forms: either a "Community-Based Research Essay" that explores "A Social Concern or Local Problem," or an "Agency Profile Report." Both incorporate experience and comparable research methods, requiring students to interview agency personnel and community members and to do fieldwork through writing field notes and journal entries, evaluating sources, and synthesizing material from agency documents, library, and Web sources. The student's investigation might be a *"prelude to community service,"* helping newcomers—new tutors, for instance—"understand social issues and engage in community work." Or students could use community service to "explore complex problems, and spur critical reflection" through analyzing their field work in its social context. For instance, a student working in a homeless shelter could progress from the fairly literal "How do I make sense of what I saw today?" to the broader "What options for job training are available?" to considering the most general and most difficult, the influence of "local, national, and global economic forces" on homelessness. In addition, community-based research can be *"a form of social action in its own right,"* if students, as they work with community members can actually produce position papers or reports that "can help social change organizations do their work." In all assignments, students examine ethical issues: What is the project's purpose? Does it respect everyone's "rights and dignity"? Who might it benefit, and how? Might there be any "potentially problematic consequences"? *(Writing and Community Action* 273–76).

As this assignment illustrates, writing in service-learning courses involves so many separate components, each embedded in the students' ongoing experiences, that they would be impossible to fake. Although these writings are not without problems associated with, as Cushman points out, the "liberal do-gooder stance" of the newly socially-conscious ("Public Intellectual" 132), or the "hit it and quit it" superficiality of a single semester's involvement ("Sustainable Programs" 40), all are perforce original. Claims that exceed the authority of the students' limited experience can usually be tempered by judicious questions, to be addressed in the requisite revision, on the order of: How do you know? What's your evidence—and from what sources? Is what you say always true? Applicable in all instances?

Insider Assignments—They're Really Not About Plagiarism

In the final analysis, avoiding plagiarism is fundamentally a secondary concern for teachers, whose efforts are better spent inventing writing assignments that are original, intellectually demanding, participatory—the essence of insider writing. As we have seen, such assignments can open up new ways of responding to the student's world, to the world of ideas, to issues that are relevant to contemporary life. These writing assignments promise to be exhilarating, creative, fun. Best of all, they inspire the passion that comes from investment in one's work, pride of authorship of writing one owns, and loves.

11 Negotiating the Grading Contract: No More Lobbying, Bullying or Crying

SOME WRITERS' BEGINNINGS: THE STUDENTS BEHIND THIS PAPER

This semester, my undergraduate advanced writing class meets in a boring, generically tacky 1950s classroom whose main advantages are two: it has movable chairs, so we can keep on reconfiguring the room; and it is across the hall from my office, so students can drop in for quick conferences en route to class. Right from the start, I have set the pace of energetic briskness that governs all our meetings, of seriousness of purpose coupled with enjoyment of the work. We have a syllabus that lays out a lot of writing during the semester—about people, places, performance, science, controversy, humor—and related readings. And we adhere to the schedule; we have to, to make sure the writing never stops. I want students to own their writing, and to care so much about it they'll be willing to write and rewrite and rewrite again—concepts that seem more alien to some of the students from New England than to those in this class from Uzbekistan, Cuba, China, Morocco, the Dominican Republic, and Brazil, and to that end I shape the course. Yet, I never know exactly what's going to happen during any class, and I suspect the students don't either. Those who can't tolerate being slightly off balance have jumped ship in the first week. The rest, like their teacher, seem to value the elements of surprise, the need to accommodate to the dynamics of a class engaged in finding their own route, their own way to becoming writers, on subjects and in styles that matter to them and to their readers—not just other members of this class, but a larger community.

I also regard this course, like every course I teach, as an opportunity to experiment and tinker with ideas and teaching methods to help us all, students and teacher alike, to do a better job, and have more fun. My big—very big—experiment this semester is with a grading contract. Not only have I never used one in three previous decades of college teaching, I have actively resisted doing so. Yet, the students seemed far more nonchalant about the contract than I was when I handed it out the first day of class. After their incredulous reactions, "You mean we're guaranteed a B if we just come to class and do the work on time?" "Nope," I replied, "the catch is that you also have to think about your writing and say something that's not trivial. No 'What I Did on My Summer Vacation' papers." "You won't put grades on papers? How will we know what we're getting?. . . Oh, I get it." "If you earn an A on a paper, I'll tell you after you've turned in your final revision." As we figured it out together, they seemed content with what they heard, and we moved on. What follows is the story of why I used a grading contract in my most recent advanced composition course, what its terms and expectations were, and what happened as a consequence.

RATIONALE: HOW I LEARNED TO LOATHE LOBBYING, BULLYING AND OTHER FORMS OF GRADE AGITATION

Throughout my career, I've been firm believer in the sanctity of earned grades. I believe that students' work of high quality should receive high grades, work of acceptable but undistinguished quality should get a passing grade, unacceptable work should flunk. In writing courses, work done in the second half of the semester, when students had presumably learned a lot from their earlier work, would be weighted more heavily—even double—that of work done in the first half. A humane corollary is that students' effort, or lack of it, should be calculated in the final reckoning to push the grade higher or lower. These criteria constituted the traditional, if unspoken, grading contract that my students and I understood. Even as recently as a decade ago this method of reckoning worked reasonably well, with a minimum of pain on both sides of the desk.

Then I became aware of a major climate change, toward global grade warming. At first, I thought that my own purity of standards exempted me from what was happening not only at my own university, but at colleges throughout the country. The average grade in upper division undergraduate courses, I learned to my surprise, is a B.[1] Surely my own students' grades reflected the curve I thought they warranted. But when I scrutinized my own grade records, what to my wondering eyes should appear but a string of Bs. Semester after semester after semester my students' grades in Advanced Composition met the university average, as well as their own expectations. Really, really good writers got As; most of the rest got Bs; C was the default goof-off grade. How could this have happened? Two factors stuck out: a sea change of student attitudes, leading to major changes in their behavior, and the easy availability of papers on the Internet.

Attitudes: The students' attitude toward grades had changed over time and place. Perhaps my students in Virginia twenty years ago, mostly the first in their families to attend college, cared more about their college education than their peers in Connecticut. Perhaps the Virginia students, being courteous Southerners, had more respect for a teacher's authority than uppity Northerners. Or perhaps the temper of the 1980s was more mellow than the in-your-face 1990s.

Behaviors: Whatever the cause, colleagues around the country in the past two decades corroborate my impression that students' relationships to grades and grading practices have changed. Some treat grades as a commodity to be purchased rather than earned; they've paid their tuition, and expect an A (why settle for a B?) in return. With A as the default grade in their minds, these (hopefully, few, but don't bank on it) students feel justified in engaging in a variety of lackadaisical behaviors that would in an earlier era have automatically lowered their grades. So they cut large numbers of classes, or don't read the assigned material, including drafts of other students' papers assigned for workshop response. They turn in papers late, or later, or not at all. They avoid mandatory revision. At some schools, undergraduate tradition says that one either comes to class or reads the textbook, but to do both is overkill—as I found out in an earlier semester when one student, a transfer from such a school, vanished for the last month, only to surface on the last day bearing a sheaf of overdue papers. At my own university, the undergraduate weekend begins by tradition on Thursday night, making (in their view) attendance at Friday classes optional; I try to teach on Tuesdays and Thursdays.

It has also been my experience that when some students don't like their grades, they are prepared to argue about them, rather than to do the substantive revisions that usually warrant higher grades. Most will accept a B, but anything from a B- on down seems to be fair game for lobbying, nagging, pleading (I allow the sick or dying grandparent excuse only once per student, per semester; the Connecticut elderly appear extraordinarily susceptible to mortal perils), whining, sulking (which results in even less work on later papers), or disappearance for extended periods. Although the students are generally respectful, even amidst their adolescent behavior, I occasionally receive physical threats; one student whose weight easily doubled mine let me know that her preferred mode of negotiation was to punch out those who crossed her. She was incredulous at my suggestion, "Why don't you just talk to them?" even after I explained that discussion was the university's way. After that I made sure never to be alone with her.

Plagiarism: The other issue that has changed dramatically in the past decade is the specter as well as the actuality of plagiarism, now made incredibly easy by ubiquitous papers on innumerable web sites (88,700,000 hits as of November 17, 2007), the weeds of the Internet. I aim to give unplagiarizable assignments, we all know how to do this (see Chapter 10, "Insider Writing"). But some students—in my experience, one a semester—try to subvert the patient, stage-by-deliberate-stage approach, with its requisite rethinking and redrafting, and head straight for such web sites as Cheathouse, Research Papers on Time, SuperiorPapers, or—my favorite if only for the title—BigNerds.com. It is usually not hard for an experienced teacher to spot the result, especially if she is familiar with the alleged author's characteristic work. While I have zero tolerance for plagiarism, I also have zero tolerance for being a plagiarism sleuth. Life is too short to go on the prowl, even with the aid of programs such as EVE and Turnitin that can be used to search for those familiar paragraphs found in online term papers. Moreover, I refuse to engage in adversarial tactics. My relationship with students, illustrated in the opening paragraphs, is to help them to learn and to learn how to teach themselves, not to prosecute them.

As a parent, now also a grandparent, and always as a teacher, I have zero tolerance for bad attitudes and any of the above behavior. But how could I unobtrusively deal with these infractions of academic civility and downright dishonesty, and yet maintain my class's exuberant ambience without becoming either a martinet or calling attention to unacceptable behavior I didn't want to encourage? What to do?

How I Learned to Stop Worrying and Love the Grading Contract

Until I realized that my own grading practices were so closely in line with the university's normative B grade that I could have been a cheerleader for Bs-Across-the-Board, I shunned the possibility of a grading contract. Students' grades should reflect the quality of their work, I reasoned, and improvement, with some allowance for effort and attitude (good or bad). I still believe that. So how could I switch to a grading system that would guarantee a B in exchange for a package of good behaviors, faithfully performed? Even with the contract, any grade better than a B would be qualitative. But would I in fact end up giving good grades to masses of dull papers, turned in on time? Would students slack off mentally while fulfilling the letter of the schedule? I would find out. There has to be some intrinsic satisfaction in learning to write well; if I didn't believe this I shouldn't teach the course.

Well, I thought, if using a grading contract in my advanced composition course would eliminate the problems I've identified above, and enable all of us to concentrate on the writing at hand and enjoy it instead of fretting and hassling over grades, it would be worth the switch. The class's grade average would be a B under either system, and if a contract-based class proved to be a disaster—say, if the papers were really flaccid or the students' casual behavior continued to subvert the course aims—I could return the following semester to my qualitative ways.

But—another potential problem—I hate to keep score. Never in my life have I (well, maybe once) balanced my checkbook to the penny. Accurate scorekeeping would be essential to the fairness of this system; attendance, punctuality, and participation would require continuous monitoring and precise record keeping. Worse than sticking to a diet, I would have to change my lax, impressionistic ways and keep records day after day. So it was with some trepidation that I asked Peter Elbow to send me a copy of the grading contract he had used with success in freshman composition at the University of Massachusetts, English 112, Spring 1999. When I told him I planned to adapt his excellent idea, first to my course, then to this article he replied, "Steal away. We all steal from each other—to everyone's benefit" (Elbow, email to author, 7 March 2000). The contract I drew up is Appendix 2. The language is mine except where quotation marks indicate Peter's exact words; the concepts are a blend of Peter's and my quite compatible pedagogical styles and philosophy.

Why the Grading Contract Worked

The grading contract in place largely eliminated fretting and haggling about matters of attendance, punctuality, and other non-productive student behavior. Students could see me taking attendance, swiftly but conspicuously at the beginning of each class period, and checking off papers that were turned in on time. I never nagged, and only discussed attendance to request medical verification of absences (which I did not always receive).

Best of all, for all of us, I didn't put grades on any papers, although I kept a qualitative record in my grade book. Students knew they'd get a B or better as long as they adhered to the contract; and this knowledge let us concentrate on the writing and other work at hand. Throughout the semester, these undergraduates displayed a level of conscientiousness that in the 1990s I had come to associate primarily with graduate students. They did the assigned reading, which they discussed in class with engaged intelligence. They turned in their work on time. They revised their papers in accord with peer feedback from their writing groups on virtually every version of every paper, mini-conferences with me during the workshop sessions, and my more elaborate written commentary. Potential slackers actually worked harder than they might have done otherwise because they were accountable for every aspect of their behavior. As one student said, "It's what students can reasonably be expected to do in any course."

Moreover, the secure knowledge of a B in hand gave the students the "calm confidence" of Mark Twain's "Christian with four aces"; they felt free to experiment, innovate, and take risks. Inspired by having their writing treated seriously in class discussion, and praised, they revised their papers extensively. As a consequence, their writing improved enormously; those students whose native language was Uzbek, Chinese, or Spanish were particularly proud of being able to write well in English, colloquial yet precise. With the exception of two students, morale was high throughout the semester. They were excited by what they had accomplished, and so was I. Course evaluations were highly positive; the students were particularly enthusiastic about the writing assignments and the feedback on their writing. Everyone felt their writing had improved enormously, and except for the problem pair to be discussed later, so did I. Their writing momentum was up; it would have impelled many into a sequel, had one been available. "Can I take this course again? Or one just like it?" is the ultimate compliment.

Grades: The final grades surprised me, for they were lower under this system than they might have been if the quality of papers had been the only criterion. The grades in fact were not all Bs. The grade distribution looked like this: one A, four A-, one B+, five B, one B-, three C+, one C, all for the usual reasons students would earn these grades except for the straight C, lowered because of a string of late papers. I attribute the C+ grades primarily to lapses in attendance; there would have been more Cs if I had not allowed considerable leeway to students with undocumented extended illnesses and other hardship cases. Even so, some students seemed not to believe that my attendance policy was real, despite the contract, and I had to insist, politely but firmly, that it was. Indeed, the grading contract drove one student, a very good writer, to drop the course after three weeks; she had planned to turn in papers but not to come to class, and realized she couldn't get away with this.

For discussion during our end-of-the-semester portfolio reviews, I asked students to write me a letter telling me what grade they thought they deserved, and why. That they couched their answers in terms of the grading contract rather than on the quality of their work is perhaps an inevitability of the contract's existence—and power. A few argued for a latitudinarian interpretation of the contract, whose implications seemed to have dawned on them at the last minute, attempting to justify elastic policies on attendance and late papers. A couple of others whose writing remained, alas, undistinguished, lobbied to raise their grades above a B on the basis of punctilious behavior. Since the quality and possibilities of the writing were the focus of every class, this orientation surprised me, though since the day of reckoning was nigh, it probably shouldn't have done so.

Two other students received the grade of D-, more than I usually award. Because I consider student failure my failure, I take particular measures to prevent this. Both students routinely cut class, failed to turn in some assignments, and turned in other work very late; the contract would indeed have allowed me to give them Fs. Both were on academic probation, though I did not know this until after the semester was over. There were, however, significant differences between them. In every writing course I've ever taught, there's always one student who regards the work with cavalier indifference—in this case, Sam (not his real name). Sam had been advised to take the course by another teacher who desperately wanted him to think and write logically. He would saunter in to the class a few minutes before it ended (though his dorm was across the street from the classroom), sneer at his writing group's papers, and bear the brunt of their exasperated inability to comprehend his incoherent sentences before they finally wrote him off entirely. My frequent conferences with him were better natured, but equally frustrating, for he seldom wrote a clear sentence, despite inflated diction and an ego to match.

In many advanced writing courses, there's a misplaced student. Although Davi (not her real name either), like Sam, had passed the prerequisite freshman courses, I made the mistake of allowing her to enroll in an upper division course as a sophomore (her boyfriend was in the class) and she couldn't keep up. Despite frequent tutoring sessions with me, Davi never seemed to grasp the principle that everything obtained over the Internet was not of equal reliability or value, and she had great difficulty in assessing information and using it in her work. Her papers spiraled downward as the assignments became more complex; she cut class for a month and returned with an impeccable paper. Fortunately, the contract came to my rescue, though not hers. Her poor attendance and abundance of late and missing work provided ample justification for her D- grade (which she appealed, and lost), and I didn't have to deal with the messy possibility of plagiarism.

Could the grading contract have prevented either student's problems? Only to the extent that they might have dropped the course, sensing an impending failure, rather than staying for the denouement. However, that intimation of doom should have been apparent in any kind of college course, for it is not unreasonable to expect students, like the rest of the world, to assume major responsibility for their own actions.

What I'd Change

I would have the students sign the contract as proof that they'd read it and were willing to abide by its provisions; if they wouldn't sign, they couldn't stay in the course. I'd be more explicit at the outset about the criteria and my enforcement of them. That might eliminate the pressure at the end of the semester, unrealistic and surprising to me, for mediocre As—perhaps as a reward for showing up and doing the work. If I were using this contract for freshman composition, might set the bar a bit lower and guarantee every student a C+ grade for behavioral participation, not a B, as Elbow does.

Why I'll Use the Grading Contract Again

I've never met a writing class I didn't like. They've all been fun, and enough students make enough progress throughout the course of the semester to make it worthwhile and satisfying. When students publish their work, and some do, this is a great incentive for the rest to keep up the pace.

On the basis of this trial semester, I have used the grading contract with great satisfaction—mine and the students'—in undergraduate literature, as well as composition courses (honors courses excepted; honors students don't need a contract to mandate what they do as a matter of course). The courses with the grading contract in place have been notably different from their predecessors in three significant ways.

- *Good:* Because the students can be depended on to come to class and to have done the assignments, I can count on meaningful class discussion every day. The workshop sessions greatly benefit from the fact that everyone has read the student papers in advance, and they can offer worthwhile commentary to the author, who is also present.
- *Better:* Students are truly liberated from the yoke of grades, and emancipated from writing "safe" papers, technically correct and boring just to fulfill the assignment. They are freed to think both inside and outside the box, to experiment and innovate.
- *Best:* I don't have to scold, nag, threaten, or negotiate. We can all concentrate on the reading and writing at hand, which is, after all, the point of the course.

Appendix 1 (Ch. 2, The Essay Canon) Shortened Version of Bibliography of Canonical Readers

ANTHOLOGIES THAT PROVIDE THE DATABASE
FOR "THE ESSAY CANON"

[Due to frequent changes of editors and publishers of anthologies and space restrictions, the following citations include only titles, editions, and dates.]

75 Readings: An Anthology. 1st-5th ed. 1987–1995.
Assignments in Exposition. 1st-11th ed. 1946–1994.
Bedford Reader. 1st-5th ed. 1982–1994.
Borzoi College Reader. 1st-7th ed. 1967–1992.
Collection of Readings for Writers. 1st-6th ed. 1946–1967.
College English: The First Year. 1st-8th ed. 1952–1982.
Compact Reader. 1st-5th ed. 1984–1996.
Conscious Reader. 1st-6th ed. 1984–1996.
Contexts for Composition. 1st-5th ed. 1965–1979.
Crossing Cultures. 1st-4th ed. 1983–1994.
Current Issues and Enduring Questions. 1st-4th ed. 1987–1996.
Current Thinking and Writing. 1st-7th ed. 1946–1976.
Dolphin Reader. 1st-4th ed. 1986–1996.
Eight Modern Essayists. 1st-6th ed. 1965–1995.
Elements of Argument. 1st-4th ed. 1985–1994.
Essay Connection: Readings for Writers. 1st-4th ed. 1984–1995.
Essayist, The. 1st-5th ed. 1963–1985.
Exploring Language. 1st-7th ed. 1977–1995.
Fields of Writing. 1st-4th ed. 1984–1994.
Harbrace College Reader. 1st-6th ed. 1959–1984.

Invention and Design. 1st-4th ed. 1975–1985.
Life Studies: An Analytic Reader. 1st-5th ed. 1983–1995.
Literary Reflections. 1st-4th ed. 1967–1982.
Little, Brown Reader. 1st-7th ed. 1977–1996.
Macmillan Reader. 1st-4th ed. 1987–1996.
McGraw-Hill Reader. 1st-5th ed. 1982–1994.
Models for Writers. 1st-5th ed. 1982–1995.
Norton Reader. 1st-9th ed. 1965–1996.
Norton Reader, Shorter Ed. 1st-9th ed. 1965–1996.
Norton Sampler. 1st-4th ed. 1979–1993.
Our Times. 1st-4th ed. 1989–1995.
Outlooks and Insights. 1st-4th ed. 1983–1995.
Patterns: A Short Prose Reader. 1st-4th ed. 1983–1994.
Patterns for College Writing: A Rhetorical Reader and Guide. 1st-6th ed. 1980–1995.
Patterns of Exposition. 1st-14th ed. 1966–1995.
Patterns Plus. 1st-5th ed. 1985–1995.
Prentice Hall Reader. 1st-4th ed. 1986–1995.
Problems in Prose. 3rd-5th ed. 1950–1963.
Prose Models. 1st-10th ed. 1964–1996.
Prose Reader. 1sat-4th ed. 1987–1996.
Reading Critically, Writing Well. 1st-4th ed. 1987–1996.
Reading for Rhetoric. 1st-4th ed. 1962–1979.
Reading, Writing, and Rhetoric. 1st-5th ed. 1967–1983.
Readings for a Liberal Education. 1st-5th ed. 1948–1967.
Readings for Writers. 1st-8th ed. 1974–1995.
Rhetorical Considerations. 1st-4th ed. 1974–1984.
Riverside Reader. 1st-5th ed. 1981–1996.
Short Essays. 1st-7th ed. 1977–1995.
Short Prose Reader. 1st-7th ed. 1979–1994.
Short Takes: Model Essays for Composition. 1st-5th ed. 1983–1996.
Strategies in Prose. 1st-5th ed. 1968–1983.
Subject and Strategy: A Rhetoric Reader. 1st-7th ed. 1978–1996.
Subject and Structure: An Anthology for Writers. 1st-8th ed. 1963–1984.
Ways of Reading. 1st-4th ed. 1987–1996.
World of Ideas. 1st-4th ed. 1983–1994.
Writer's Reader. 1st-7th ed. 1976–1994.
Writing with a Thesis: A Rhetoric and Reader. 1st-6th ed. 1976–1994.
Writing and Reading Across the Curriculum. 1st-5th ed. 1982–1994.

Appendix 2 (Ch. 2)
Table 1. The Essay Canon

Name	Rept	Titles	Anth	Eds.	Beg	End
1 Orwell, George	357	19	45	221	1952	1996
Politics and the English Language	118					
Shooting An Elephant	113					
2 White, E. B.	268	37	40	177	1946	1996
Once More to the Lake	88					
3 Didion, Joan	219	30	43	151	1971	1996
On Keeping a Notebook	44					
4 Thomas, Lewis	204	50	41	141	1976	1996
Notes on Punctuation	21					
5 Thoreau, H.D.	180	29	35	139	1948	1996
Civil Disobedience	48					
6 Woolf, Virginia	177	26	37	122	1946	1996
The Death of the Moth	44					
7 Swift, Jonathan	173	7	38	163	1957	1996
A Modest Proposal	151					
8 King, Jr., Martin Luther	165	14	35	145	1967	1996
Letter From Birmingham Jail	50					
I Have a Dream	68					
9 Thurber, James	158	35	31	116	1946	1996
University Days	35					
10 Clemens, Samuel L.	143	30	32	131	1946	1996
Two Views...	25					
11 Dillard, Annie	136	39	37	109	1974	1996
Sight into Insight	21					
12 Jefferson, Thomas	132	9	28	110	1952	1996
The Declaration of Independence	96					

	Name	Rept	Titles	Anth	Eds.	Beg	End
13	Baker, Russell	126	45	37	99	1967	1996
	The Plot Against People	21					
14	Eiseley, Loren	121	31	28	108	1960	1996
	The Brown Wasps	25					
15	Forster, E.M.	118	11	22	86	1957	1996
	My Wood	47					
16	Angelou, Maya	113	16	26	105	1973	1996
	Graduation	44					
17	Goodman, Ellen	112	45	33	95	1979	1996
	The Company Man	11					
18	Baldwin, James	102	15	25	82	1962	1996
	Stranger in the Village	37					
19	Rodriguez, Richard	99	21	34	94	1977	1996
	Aria	23					
20	Plato	96	8	23	80	1948	1996
	The Allegory of the Cave	45					
21	Zinsser, William	87	14	21	78	1968	1996
	College Pressures	18					
22	Walker, Alice	86	15	30	70	1976	1996
	Beauty: When the Other Dancer Is the Self	24					
23	Gould, Stephen Jay	85	28	25	61	1980	1996
	Evolution as Fact and Theory	8					
24	Russell, Bertrand	84	27	23	67	1948	1996
	A Free Man's Worship	14					
25	Catton, Bruce	81	8	19	80	1959	1996
	Grant and Lee: A Study in Contrasts	70					
26.5	Mead, Margaret	78	29	27	68	1948	1996
	The Gift of Autonomy	7					
26.5	Hayakawa, S. I.	78	17	20	61	1946	1996
	How Dictionaries Are Made	16					
28.5	Hughes, Langston	77	3	20	74	1963	1996
	Salvation	74					
28.5	Asimov, Isaac	77	28	25	67	1965	1996
	The Eureka Phenomenon	10					
30.5	Lewis, C.S.	76	21	18	61	1948	1996
	The Efficacy of Prayer	8					
30.5	Bettelhein, Bruno	76	17	22	67	1965	1996
	A Victim	17					

Appendix

	Name	Rept	Titles	Anth	Eds.	Beg	End
32	Mencken, H.L.	75	15	22	67	1948	1996
	The Penalty of Death	14					
33	Brady, Judy [Syfers]	71	4	18	71	1972	1995
	I Want a Wife	71					
34	Cousins, Norman	67	21	24	61	1948	1996
	Who Killed Benny Paret?	17					
35	Mitford, Jessica	65	14	16	63	1972	1996
	Behind the Formaldehyde Curtain	18					
36	Mannes, Marya	64	17	17	51	1963	1996
	How Do You Know It's Good?	22					
37	Highet, Gilbert	63	15	20	55	1952	1996
	The Mystery of Zen	12					
38.5	Lawrence, D.H.	62	20	14	50	1962	1995
	Pornography	11					
38.5	Petrunkevitch, Alexander	63	1	14	63	1959	1996
	Spider and Wasp						
40	Bacon, Francis	60	10	15	50	1948	1996
	The Idols	26					
41	Wolfe, Tom	59	17	20	58	1968	1996
	O Rotten Gotham...	15					
42	Momaday, N. Scott	56	5	22	55	1972	1996
	Way to Rainy Mountain	50					
43	Krutch, Joseph Wood	55	26	19	48	1946	1996
	Killing for Sport	10					
44.5	Ciardi, John	54	12	15	48	1952	1996
	...An ulcer, gentlemen, is an unwritten poem	10					
44.5	Carson, Rachel	54	13	19	54	1952	1996
	A Fable for Tomorrow	15					
46.5	Selzer, Richard	53	17	20	49	1978	1996
	The Discus Thrower	20					
46.5	Bronowski, Jacob	53	11	17	45	1964	1996
	The Reach of Imagination	23					
48.5	Kingston, Maxine Hong	52	13	20	49	1980	1996
	No Name Woman	12					
48.5	Huxley, Thomas H.	52	5	15	49	1946	1995
	Comfort	5					

	Name	Rept	Titles	Anth	Eds.	Beg	End
50.5	Welty, Eudora	51	18	19	46	1971	1996
	One Writer's Beginnings	10					
50.5	Steinem, Gloria	51	14	22	49	1972	1996
	Why Young Women are More Conservative	10					

Appendix 3 (Ch. 10)
Writing in the Manner of Thoreau (and Other Nature Writers)

[Quotations are from Henry David Thoreau, *Walden and Other Writings*. Ed. William Howarth. New York: Modern Library, 1981.]

Thoreau set the style and pace for 150 years of American nature writers who continue to follow in his footsteps. Among the major characteristics are the following.

> *First person perspective.* "It is, after all, always the first person that is speaking" (107).
> *Unassuming authorial persona*
> *Desire for simplicity.* "My purpose in going to Walden Pond was . . . to transact some private business with the fewest obstacles" (119).
> *Self-reliant and resourceful.* "I lived alone . . . a mile from any neighbor, in a house which I had built myself. . . and earned my living by the labor of my hands only" (107).
> *Philosophical.* "To be a philosopher . . . [is] so to love wisdom as to live according to its dictates, a life of simplicity, independence, magnanimity, and trust" [e.g. a natural philosopher] (116).
> *Curious,* intellectually, philosophically, existentially about everything.
> *Love of solitude.* "I find it wholesome to be alone the greater part of the time." (See Solitude chapter.)
> *Compulsion to march to a different drummer.* "The greater part of what my neighbors call good I believe in my soul to be bad, and if I repent of any thing, it is very likely to be my good behavior" (113).

- *Sensitivity to the natural world,* all things under the sun, great and small. "For many years I was self-appointed inspector of snow storms and rain storms" (118).
- *Cosmic awareness, a vision of infinity, eternity.* Walden has become situated not only in Massachusetts but also in the heart of America and in the center of the universe.
- *A desire to live fully in the moment.* "In any weather, at any hour of the day or night, I have been anxious to improve the nick of time . . . have been anxious . . . to stand on the meeting of two eternities, the past and future, which is precisely the present moment" (117).
- *Sense of moral superiority and physical well-being.* Uses the natural setting as the basis for providing a critique of society (including the entire world), and sets up his corner of the universe as a model for the world to follow.

This is a partial list, to which we can add. (See also Lawrence Buell, *The Environmental Imagination: Thoreau, Nature Writing, and the Formation of American Culture.* Harvard UP, 1995.) Your Thoreauvian notebooks should exhibit some of these characteristics in each entry; try in some entries to imitate Thoreau's style of writing, as well. Feel free to disagree with Thoreau's opinions, as you wish.

Appendix 4 (Ch. 11)
The Grading Contract Itself

(Adapted from Peter Elbow's grading contract, Spring 1999, University of Massachusetts, Amherst. Quotations indicate Elbow's exact words.)

Grading Contract: We'll be using the grading contract this semester to create a course structure where you can have considerable freedom to think and to experiment, where I can be a supportive ally to you, but also push you to do your best work, and where we can ultimately arrive at a course grade that is fair. Here's how it will work. The B contract provides a safety net, a guaranteed grade of a B that won't be affected by my judgment of the quality of your essays, but by your behavior as a student and a writer throughout the semester. This is intended to be a fail-safe system that will allow you to take risks, be daring with your writing, enjoy your work, experiment with confidence, and land on your feet.

Throughout the semester, I'll "give you feedback on most of your writing (not all), to tell you my reactions, thoughts, and suggestions" that will help you become a better writer. Your classmates will do the same, in class discussions and (sometimes) in writing. "However, I won't be putting grades on your papers, and my comments on your papers will not be related to your course grade, up to the level of B." (Yes, you can get an A and I'm eager to help you do this; I hope lots of people hop on the A bandwagon. Read on.)

Note: If terrible weather and/or hazardous road conditions prevent you from coming to class, you will not be penalized for lateness, absence or late papers on that day. If there are no UConn weather closing announcements on the radio or Internet before you leave for school, email my secretary the morning of class, or me, to find out whether class will meet.

Conditions for a B

1. *Attend class regularly and punctually.* Therefore, you can't miss more than one week's worth of classes (two 1.5 hour sessions). If you're more than ten minutes late to any given class this will count as an absence. Illness must be verified by a doctor's (or UConn program director's if you're away on UConn-scheduled activities) excuse on official stationery. If there's a conflict between your work schedule and class schedule, class comes first!
2. *Turn in all work, in printed out hard copy, at the beginning of the class meeting on the assigned due dates.* Email attachments will not be accepted except by prior authorization. A paper will be considered late if it's turned in after 10 a.m of the assigned due date [the class began at 9:30]. Late papers will be authorized only in connection with absence policy in #1 above, or by advance negotiation with me, for extraordinary reasons. An unauthorized late paper (either original or revision) will lower your grade one letter increment each day it's late: one day=B-; two days C+; three days C, and so on.
3. *Do the assigned reading for every class meeting, bring your books to class, and participate thoughtfully in the class discussions of the works and points at hand.* One way to focus your thinking will be to be able to answer the study questions at the ends of the essays in the textbook, and to discuss the issues embedded in the checklists at the end of each chapter.
4. *Participate actively in writing groups.* This means in (and perhaps) out of class, and as the occasion arises, through e-mail or WebCT; working cooperatively in peer groups and pairs; listening carefully the writing of others and providing full, thoughtful, respectful responses, preferably with helpful suggestions for improvement, as necessary.
5. *Write thoughtful, well-developed, original papers, and submit at least one revision of each paper.* This will involve demonstrating a solid level of effort and involvement in all drafts of papers, from start to finish. This means that you have to put in serious thought and work on your writing, that will show up in the following features:
    a. *Perplexity or surprise*(!). In each draft, "show that your writing is driven by some genuine question or perplexity or wondering." For instance, if you're writing about a person,

don't just identify four obvious features that would fit on a census report (age, sex, nationality, residence). "Show how your portrait is rooted in a felt question" about this person, a problem or complexity that you're writing to try to understand. (By the way, this is a "crucial skill" to sharpen throughout college: "how to find a question that interests you," and thus that will interest your readers, "even in a boring assignment.") Some of the best writing comes from surprising yourself as you work on the subject; you'll see and hopefully, understand aspects of your subject as you write that you never thought of before.

b. *Thinking.* "Having found a perplexity," think it through and try to figure it out. "Make some conceptual gears turn." Again, surprise yourself! Your paper will need "to show a movement of thinking or a succession of points, it needs to move or to go somewhere."

c. *Originality.* Any subject may be treated in an original manner (surprise!); conversely, a boring, thoroughly conventional, completely predictable treatment can kill off even the most potentially exciting topic. Avoid: mundane treatments of mundane topics ("My Dog Spot"); papers about your high school; papers about overworked subjects on which it's hard to be original (taboo topics *du jour* to be determined). *Your work must be your own. All outside sources must be acknowledged. A plagiarized paper will result in an automatic F in the course.*

d. *Revise for substance.* When a given draft requires revising (and most early versions of papers that you turn in will require revisions), you will need to make *substantive* changes, not just tighten, correct, and clean up. The revisions may not necessarily be *better,* but they should be "substantially *different*" from the original version; often this will mean adding more information, explanation, telling details, or looking at the subject from a different, perhaps unfamiliar, angle. Revisions offer the opportunity for practice in rethinking and reshaping your writing, in trying things differently.

e. *Edit for correctness.* Your final draft needs to be "free from mistakes in spelling and grammar." Spell-check will help, to a point. Beware of homonyms and words *your computer doesn't know!*

f. *Each revision must be accompanied by a paragraph or two of commentary,* telling me what you did on your revision, and why. You may number the paragraphs of the original and revised versions and/or highlight portions of the papers to show efficiently where the changes are.

Conditions for grades of A, A-, B+

Whereas the criteria for a grade of B reflect behaviors, for higher grades, B+ and above, the criteria reflect "judgments of the quality of your writing." In an upper division course at UConn, every student is certainly capable of earning a B. Everyone can get a B if they meet the above conditions with "good time, effort," and originality, but in order to get a higher grade, your writing will have to be excellent on a predictably regular basis. "Of course, you will also have to meet all the conditions for a B."

Quality and excellence are matters of judgment, realms where people often disagree. I, as teacher, will be the one who will ultimately make these judgments, but remember that my judgments won't affect your grade up to the level of B; "you can get a grade of B even if you completely disagree with my judgments of quality," as long as your behavior meets the criteria for a B. We'll have plenty of discussions about quality, and will try to reach some agreement on criteria for excellence as indicated on rating sheets I'll give you. Again, the Checklists in Bloom, *Fact and Artifact* provide guidance.

Conditions for Grades lower than B

"I hope no one will aim for lower grades. The quickest way to slide to a C is to hold back on effort, involvement, thinking, originality. The quickest way to slide to a D or F is to miss classes," to be mentally absent (i.e. tune out or sleep in class, or show up without assignments), or to do utterly perfunctory writing. Plagiarism isn't a slide, it's an instant descent to an F. "*This much is non-negotiable: you are not eligible for a passing grade of D unless you have attended*" at least 13 of the 14 weeks of *classes, and completed 90 percent of the assignments ON TIME.* Because the writing process in this course is cumulative, you can't just turn in all the late work at the end of the semester and expect to pass the course."

Notes

Chapter 1. Academic Essays and the Vertical Pronoun

1. Indeed, today's *Times* columnists not only write in a more personal manner, they encourage others to do so. For instance, in "Ants, Better With Dose of Humanity (and Humor)," James Gorman encourages scientists to present in their books and papers written for general readers personal "interludes and asides," little first-person "stories to go along with methods, discussion, and conclusions" that would release their writing from "the stranglehold of scientific jargon" and provide "a real glimpse of what science is and how it is done by human beings, rational and irrational, grappling with technique, nature and the gathering of information" (D3).

Chapter 2. The Essay Canon

1. To the extent possible, the information in this essay has been updated as of 2006, except for the canon figures 1946–96, the period initially studied, which spans five decades from the end of World War II to the beginning of widespread Internet usage.

Chapter 3. The Essayist in, and Behind the Essay: Vested Writers, Invested Readers

1. Service-learning projects such as those discussed by Ellen Cushman (all items in Works Cited), and many of the other possibilities for *Curricular Reform in a Global Economy* (see David B. Downing et al) seem to be inspired more thoroughly by contemporary events, innovative curricular planning, and moral commitment, buttressed by the teacher's example, even when they may be undergirded by assigned reading.

Chapter 5. Writing Textbooks in/for Times of Trauma

1. See, for instance, such diverse novels as Nicholas Rinaldi's *Betweeen Two Rivers* (2004), Philip Roth's *The Plot Against America* (2004), and Jonathan Foer's *Extremely Loud and Incredibly Close* (2005), to say nothing of the enormous number and range of nonfiction commentaries, analyses, and memoirs.

2. Some of the material in this section is adapted from my Introductions to Chapters 14 and 15 of *The Essay Connection,* 7th ed.

3. "The disconnect between last Tuesday's monstrous dose of reality and the self-righteous drivel and outright deceptions being peddled by public figures and TV commentators is startling, depressing. The voices licensed to follow the event seem to have joined together in a campaign to infantilize the public. Where is the acknowledgment that this was not a 'cowardly' attack on 'civilization' or 'liberty' or 'humanity' or 'the free world' but an attack on the world's self-proclaimed superpower, undertaken as a consequence of specific American alliances and actions? How many citizens are aware of the ongoing American bombing of Iraq? And if the word 'cowardly' is to be used, it might be more aptly applied to those who kill from beyond the range of retaliation, high in the sky, than those willing to die themselves in order to kill others. In the matter of courage (a morally neutral virtue): whatever may be said of the perpetrators of Tuesday's slaughter, they were not cowards." (*The New Yorker,* 24 Sept. 2001)

4. Additions in the ninth edition (forthcoming, 2010) include excerpts from the Nobel Peace Prize lectures of Wangari Maathai (2004) and Al Gore (2007). The beat goes on.

Chapter 6. The Great Paradigm Shift and Its Legacy for the Twenty-First Century

1. Try this quiz. Q: Name at least ten features of the current-traditional paradigm, some aspects of which (especially concerns with form and style) still remain current.

A: We'd all get this one: "An emphasis on the composed product rather than the composing process" (Richard Young qtd. in Hairston 78). A corollary is the resultant emphasis on prose models, epitomized in the four modes of discourse: description, narration, exposition, and argument. But would we still remember that the emphasis is on "expository writing to the virtual exclusion of all other forms," that this paradigm "neglects invention almost entirely" (Berlin and Inkster qtd. in Hairston 78), concentrates on style and usage (Richard Young qtd. in Hairston 78), and "posits an unchanging reality which is independent of the writer and which all writers are expected to describe in the same way regardless of the rhetorical situation" (Berlin and

Inkster qtd. in Hairston 78)? Hairston supplies three additional features: "Its adherents believe that competent writers know what they are going to say before they begin to write"; thus their most important task at the outset is to find the appropriate form that will organize this content. The adherents also believe in a linear composing process, and that "teaching editing is teaching writing." Unlike the process paradigm, which is derived from the "composing processes of actual writers," research, and experimentation, the current-traditional paradigm "derives partly from the classical rhetorical model that organizes the production of discourse into invention, arrangement, and style"; and is a "prescriptive and orderly view of the creative act" (78).

2. Hairston's account shares with Olson's the holistic view that regards writing as a "recursive rather than linear process" and a "way of learning." But whereas Olson treats this paradigm "first and foremost [as] a social activity," Hairston focuses on "the writing process," teaching "strategies for instruction and discovery," considering "audience, purpose and occasion." She explains that its recursive nature involves a combination of overlapping, intertwining "pre-writing, writing, and revision" activities accomplished through rational, "intuitive and non-rational" means. Writing is a "disciplined creative activity that can be analyzed and described" by linguists and process researchers, anatomized in textbooks, and taught preferably by teachers who themselves write. The underpinning of cognitive psychology and linguistics, and the variety of writing modes, from expository to expressive (86), have faded from Olson's rendering of this paradigm (Hairston 76–88).

3. Because it can be discussed in accessible language does not mean that the process paradigm is devoid of theory, nor that theory can only be expressed in abstract, difficult concepts and language, "the smart for the smart," as Susan Miller characterizes it in "Writing Theory" (62). That this accessibility has meant that some literary critics consider composition studies as "theory lite" (in contrast to the more dense, abstruse language of critical theory) in no way diminishes the value of either the theory or the process.

4. While English and language arts teachers have a disciplinary advantage in understanding and applying writing process principles, teachers in other disciplines have more problems. Their impulse is to use the model they remember from their own high school or undergraduate schooling rather than the processes they engage in as publishing professionals. Typically, they assign specific topics, providing few if any directions on how to write the paper. They read and comment only on the final draft, using intermediate drafts (if any) to ensure against Internet plagiarism. Revision opportunities are few. Instructors in writing across the curriculum faculty development programs often have to spend considerable time convincing participants of the inadequate pedagogy of this approach; even when teachers are unhappy with the papers written in this traditional manner, they are often reluctant

to change, usually on the grounds that responding to drafts is too time consuming.

5. It would not be too great a stretch, in my view, to include among highly influential works embodying process concepts James Moffett's *Teaching the Universe of Discourse* (1968) and his *Student-Centered Language Arts Curriculum K-13* (1992); James Britton's *The Development of Writing Abilities* (11–18) (1975); Mina Shaughnessy's *Errors and Expectations* (1977); and much of the 1960s and 70s sentence combining research and pedagogy (Frank O'Hare; Morenberg, Daiker, and Kerek, et al) and pre-writing (Kytle).

6. The common sense, friendly tone, and accessible language of these authors not only ensured their popularity but also seems to have protected them from destructive negative criticism until after their work and reputations were well established. Murray and Rose, I believe, have no significant detractors except for the generic argument espoused by J. Elspeth Stuckey in *The Violence of Literacy* that school-sanctioned literacy practices deracinate the culture of those who must conform to middle class language and embedded values. Trimbur, however, defends Rose against this charge by showing that "what allows Rose to evade the class-bound limits of the self-made coming of age narrative . . . is his refusal to separate himself from the lives on the boundary and to take on the kind of distanced lucidity that Sartre finds characteristic of the genre . . . . Rose never quite leaves his neighborhood or his youth behind" ("Articulation" 248). Those who tar Elbow with the expressivist brush and dismiss all expressivism include Elbow's primary antagonist, David Bartholomae, in "Writing With Teachers: A Conversation With Peter Elbow" (*CCC* 46, 1995), which diminished neither Elbow's following, nor his reputation.

7. For example, in the lead chapter of Allison, Bryant, and Hourigan's *Grading in the Post-Process Classroom,* David Bleich asserts, "It is about time that we stop wringing our hands about grading and, instead, commit ourselves, teachers and students, to the principles of teaching without competitiveness, hierarchy, and authoritarian value, to teaching through cooperation, interaction, mutual respect, and communication" (33). These are Freire's liberatory principles articulated in the works of teachers most closely associated with process, Murray, Elbow, Rose, Atwell.

8. I use the term as physicists would, to denote "a nuclear reaction in which nuclei combine to form more massive nuclei with the simultaneous release of energy" (*American Heritage Dictionary* 714).

9. Rose, who often interprets student writings as records of struggle, "testaments of desire" (*Lives* 147), has been criticized for providing ways to help students accomplish what they themselves want to do: to learn the lingua franca, a "discourse of possibility" (79) and to learn the values of the upper middle class mainstream, rather than encouraging them to resist these (see Stuckey, *Violence of Literacy*). This narrow, elitist argument is not par-

ticularly post-process, and it ignores the pervasive message of *Lives on the Boundary:* "Philosophy, said Aristotle, begins in wonder. So does education" and that sense of wonderment and delight are within the reach of everyone on earth (M. Rose 223).

10. Lisa Ede discusses the implications of this in Chapter 4 of *Situating Composition,* "Thinking Through Practice: On the Resistance to Theory." Here, she examines how "scholarly practices of writing may (unintentionally and ironically) contribute" to the resistance of students and teachers to theory in composition, with a particular focus on her own changes over the years in directions to students on the processes of how to write papers and other considerations of context. (The quotation is from an advance copy of Ede's annotated book outline, which she thoughtfully provided.)

11. Newer teachers cannot experience the "heady sense of breakthrough" of '70s teachers who encountered Peter Elbow's *Writing Without Teachers,* the quintessential anti-textbook of its time. Smitten with "desire to operate outside oppressive institutions and avoid the errors of the past," recalls Trimbur, newly-liberated teachers embraced "freewriting," "growing," "cooking," the "teacherless writing class" and other manifestations of process pedagogy that remain serviceable today ("Taking the Social Turn" 110).

12. Elbow's *Writing without Teachers,* Murray's *Write to Learn,* Rose's *Lives on the Boundary,* Atwell's *In the Middle* exude the happiness, the euphoria, the sense of discovery and progress that energize teachers and students in the best process classrooms, and, indeed, the best classrooms of any sort, as exhibited in the works of Wendy Bishop (*Teaching Lives*), Pat Hoy (*Instinct for Survival*), Susan H. McLeod (*Notes on the Heart*), Richard J. Murphy (*The Calculus of Intimacy*), Joseph Trimmer (*Narration as Knowledge*), Victor Villanueva (*Bootstraps*), and Kathleen Blake Yancey (*Reflection in the Writing Classroom*), among others. These books are full of individual examples and anecdotal evidence that process works, but because their authors are such gifted teachers anything they do might work equally well.

13. There are a number of reasons why such research doesn't exist. Even if distinctively positive results could be demonstrated for a class of process writers, or for a process-oriented curriculum or group of teachers, it is almost impossible to conduct the research in a way that could replicate the results. Various sites of the National Writing Project have at times been under pressure to demonstrate the efficacy of process teaching in the schools of funded teachers. Why spend taxpayers' money on a major pedagogical change that has little or no measurable impact? The attitudes and knowledge of Writing Project teachers can be measured, pre-and post participation. That is often done, supplemented with information about curricular changes, in-service workshops and other in-school evidence of the exposure of teachers and students to the Writing Project's philosophy and practice. For instance, the 2001 National Writing Project evaluation, as reported by the Academy

for Educational Development, focuses on the amount of time NWP teachers spend per week in teaching writing, "an analysis of teacher assignments and corresponding student work, written surveys, and telephone interviews with NWP teachers, focusing on authentic intellectual work, the original application of knowledge and skills rather than the routine use of facts and procedures . . . and the emphasis NWP teachers place on such work in their assignments" (Bradshaw 1).

None of these phenomena, however, address the quality of student writing or how well teachers and students retain and apply process principles over time. The same sorts of illustrative examples that buttress the professional literature can shore up the general impression of success (no one wants to demonstrate failure) in a given year of a particular program, just as they can in college writing programs. But definitive, replicable data is hard to come by. (See, for instance Witte and Faigley, *Evaluating College Writing Programs*.) Large-scale longitudinal studies are plagued by high attrition rates of student participants, even from one course in a composition sequence to the next. Writing Project teachers don't necessarily have the same students before and after their project participation, so pre- and post-tests are hard to give to the same students (or groups of students). Student writing is subject to a myriad of influences, for better and worse, in addition to those they encounter in composition class. Over time, writing ability deteriorates unless it is used and reinforced continually, but according to what criteria? And more problems too numerous to identify here.

Chapter 7. The Ineluctable Elitism of Essays and Why They Prevail in First-Year Composition Courses

1. High quality fiction dominates undergraduate literary curricula, despite the occasional genre courses devoted to science fiction, mysteries, or graphic novels. As a rule, only more esoteric graduate studies (mostly dissertations) allow examination of popular, formulaic, genre, and pulp fiction.

2. The exceptions may be found in the often confrontative, oppositional readings encouraged by the editors of the widely-used *Ways of Reading*, David Bartholomae and Anthony Petrosky, who begin their Introduction with "Reading involves a fair measure of push and shove. You make your mark on a book and it makes its mark on you. . . . We think of reading as a social interaction, sometimes peaceful and polite, sometimes not so peaceful and polite" (4th ed., 1). In this chapter I am intentionally using the most recent editions of books published during the time frame of my essay canon research, 1946–1996/97.

Nevertheless, the readings of essays by the only canonical authors in the 4th edition which Bartholomae and Petrosky encourage, Richard Rodriguez, Alice Walker, and Virginia Woolf, do not seem idiosyncratic; the considerations they raise about these texts are common concerns of textbook editors (and composition teachers) nationwide. One example should suffice: "As you read her essay ["In Search of Our Mothers' Gardens"], observe Walker's methods of working. How does she build her arguments? Where does her evidence come from? her authority? To whom is she appealing? What do her methods allow her to see (and say) and not to see? And, finally, how might her conclusions be related to her methods?" (648).

3. *It's Mine and I'll Write It That Way,* by Dick Friedrich and David Kuester, the textbook that wholeheartedly embraced this philosophy, was published by Random House in 1972, the year that CCCC first addressed "Students' Right. . . ." It should be noted that the authors were colleagues of Elizabeth McPherson, promulgator of the resolution when she was president of CCCC, at St. Louis Community College, Forest Park. That the book was published in only a single edition implies that it was not widely adopted.

Chapter 8. Good Enough Writing

1. For instance, in "What Is 'College-Level' Writing?" Patrick Sullivan reports that his informal survey of community college faculty and administrators reveals their common understanding that what is " 'college-level' at one institution [is] clearly not college-level at others" (383).

2. *Evaluation and the Academy.* Rosovsky and Hartley's thoroughgoing survey of the research literature 1960-mid 1990s provides comprehensive evidence to demonstrate that large scale surveys show that "the number of As increased nearly four fold" during this time, from "7 percent in 1969 to 26 percent in 1993, and that the number of Cs declined 66 percent (from 25 percent in 1969 to 9 percent in 1993)"; that "across all institutional types GPAs rose approximately 15–20 percent from the mid-1960s through the mid-1990s," by which time "the average grade (formerly a C) resided in the B- to B range. More recent research [1995] across all types of schools shows that only between 10 percent and 20 percent of students receive grades lower than a B-" (p. 5 includes the authors' extensive citations).

3. See also my discussions of "The Seven Deadly Virtues" and "Freshman Composition as a Middle-Class Enterprise."

4. A literature search reveals only a single, fleeting use of the concept, likewise derived from Winnicott, by Peter Elbow:

> By "good enough writing," I do not mean mediocre writing with which we cannot be satisfied. But I do not mean excellent writing, either. . . . In my view, the concept is particularly appropriate for required writing courses where many students are there under duress and are more interested in satisfying the requirement acceptably than in achieving excellence. (Can we hold that against them?) Yet, in elective

writing courses, "good enough writing" is also appropriate because students there are more ready to develop their own autonomous standards. (87)

5. I am using as the source of normative advice *The Writer's Harbrace Handbook* (Glenn et al), the 2004 descendant of the ubiquitous ur-Harbrace, with thirty-nine editions from 1941 to 1998, a status warranted by its longevity and ascendancy in the market for years.

6. For example, to claim in a paper of literary criticism on Shakespeare that "Shakespeare was a great writer," though true, is considered a mark of critical naiveté, for everyone (however that is determined) knows this. Nevertheless, if a noted critic were to make that claim, the cognoscenti would attribute this apparent banality to extreme sophistication, since the critic couldn't possibly be that naïve, and try to puzzle out what arcane meaning s/he intended by making such an obvious statement.

7. Harbrace, surprisingly, says that "The first person is typically used" in literary analyses (416), though a brief survey of the industry standard, *PMLA,* reveals that of eight substantive articles in the January 2003 issue, only three (by John Carlos Rowe, Lori Ween, and Michael Berubé) used the first person, Rowe and Ween very sparingly and impersonally: "I admit there is a tendency" (Rowe 78); "I will mention only" (Rowe 83); "I extend to the marketing of novels James Twichell's observation" (Ween 92). This seemingly idiosyncratic advice is not borne out by other widely used handbooks, Lunsford's *St. Martin's Handbook,* 5th ed. (2003); Kirzner and Mandell's *Brief Handbook,* 4th ed. (2004); or Hacker's *Writer's Reference,* 5th ed. (2003).

Chapter 9. The Good, the Bad, and the Ugly: Ethical Principles for Representing Students and Student Writing in Teachers' Publications, and The Abyss Beyond

1. Gothard summarizes the Tarasoff case: "a female student broke off a brief relationship with a male student," he was upset, saw one of the University's psychological counselors, and "confided that he intended to kill his ex-girlfriend, Tarasoff. The psychologist, with the concurrence of two psychiatrists in the clinic, determined that the threats were real, notified the campus police, and intended to commit the student for observation in a mental hospital. The student was taken into custody but, satisfied that he was rational, the officers released him on his promise to stay away from Tarasoff; neither Tarasoff nor her parents (who later filed the lawsuit) were notified of the potential danger to her. After he was picked up by the police, the student

refused to seek further therapy. Shortly thereafter, he went to Tarasoff's residence and killed her" (1582).

2. Cho's short plays "Richard McBeef" and "Mr. Brownstone" are available at http://www.thesmokinggun.com/archive/years/2007/0417071vtech1.html>. In addition to being crude and violent, the characters are too underdeveloped even to be stick figures. Although the thirteen-year-old protagonist accuses his stepfather, Richard McBeef, of murdering his father a month before the play began in order to marry his mother, this youth is no Hamlet; calling him a "bisexual psycho rapist murderer" and accusing him of pedophilia says more about the youth's (and the author's) state of mind than McBeef's character. The mother's attempt to murder her new husband, and the stepfather's actual murder of the boy occur, as do the rest of the play's unconnected violent actions, like machine-gun shots randomly sprayed into a dark abyss.

3. They also, says creative writing teacher Monica Barron, "have a keen ability to recognize the age-specific experience encoded in each other's language on the page. Closeness in age and similarity of experience drive the reading of each other's work as much as or more than the words on the page. Students recognize stories of the tribe and congratulate each other for telling them so economically. Theirs are the authorized readings in class" (42–43).

4. Cho's papers were ugly both morally and aesthetically. As a creative writing teacher, it is difficult for me to imagine what the unfailingly sympathetic Virginia Tech professors told Cho about the barely literate exchanges of scurrilous language, undeveloped motivation, and consistently debased behavior that comprised the bulk of his work (references to excrement and "doggy style" sex are prominent, along with the boy's attempt to strangle his stepfather with a "half eaten banana cereal bar"). It is unlikely that better writing could redeem such a terrible play, or move an audience to Aristotelean fear and pity, unless it were for the author rather than the characters. At the risk of making light of the underlying tragedy, I am reminded of Flannery O'Connor's classic observation, "Everywhere I go, I'm asked if I think the universities stifle writers. My opinion is that they don't stifle enough of them."

Chapter 10. Insider Writing: Plagiarism-Proof Assignments

1 In addition to being strikingly original, their quality is sufficiently high to enable me to use some as exemplary models of student writing in *The Essay Connection*. See Kate Loomis's "Spiderwebs" and Megan McGuire's "Wake Up Call" in the eighth edition.

Chapter 11 Negotiating the Grading Contract: No More Lobbying, Bullying, or Crying

1. Figures 200–205 reflect pervasive grade inflation throughout American high schools and colleges, from community colleges to the Ivy League. Julie Westfall in "The Rate of (Grade) Inflation" reports in *The Daily Illini* 6 Dec. 2000 at the University of Illinois that the trend fueled in the 1960s by pressure to give students higher grades than they'd earned to help them avoid the Vietnam War draft has continued: In 1999 40 percent of the grades were As, another 40 percent were Bs; Cs (which had comprised 28 percent of the grades in 1967) totaled only 16 percent in 1999. Harvey Mansfield reports that in 2001 "one-fourth of all grades given to undergraduates are now A's, and another fourth are A-'s" ("Grade Inflation"); and Lisa Birk ("Grade Inflation") identifies comparable grade inflation among high school students. As of November, 2007, three years of efforts at Princeton, Harvard, Cornell, Penn, and other Ivies and to reduce grades have had mixed results, with Princeton claiming the greatest success (Bruno, "Princeton Leads"; News@Princeton 19 Sept. 2005).

Works Cited

Adler-Kassner, Linda, Robert Crooks, and Ann Watters, eds. *Writing the Community: Concepts and Models for Service-Learning in Composition*. Washington, DC: Amer. Assn. for Higher Education, 1997.

Adorno, Theodor. "The Essay as Form." Trans. Bob Hullott-Kentor and Frederic Will. *New German Critique* 32 (Spring-Summer 1984): 151–71.

Allison, Libby, Lizbeth Bryant, and Maureen Hourigan, eds. *Grading in the Post-Process Classroom: From Theory to Practice*. Portsmouth, NH: Heinemann, 1997.

Altieri, Charles. "An Idea and Ideal of a Literary Canon." *Canons*. Ed. Robert von Hallberg. Chicago: U of Chicago P, 1984, 41–64.

"American Essay." *Encyclopedia of the Essay*. Tracy Chevalier, ed. London: Fitzroy Dearborn, 1997. 14–23.

American Heritage Dictionary. 4th ed. Boston: Houghton, 2000.

Annan, Kofi. "Nobel Lecture." 2001. 26 March 2008 <http://nobelprize.org/peace/laureates/2001/annan-lecture.html>/

Arnold, Matthew. "The Function of Criticism at the Present Time." 1865. *The Critical Tradition: Classic Texts and Contemporary Trends*. Ed. David H. Richter. 3rd ed. Boston: Bedford/St. Martin's, 2007. 415–28.

Atwan, Robert. Preface and Introduction. *The Best American Essays, College Edition*. Ed. Robert Atwan. 2nd ed. Boston: Houghton, 1998. xv–xviii and 1–11.

—. Series Editor. Cynthia Ozick, Guest Editor. *The Best American Essays of 1998*. Boston: Houghton, 1998. (Collections for 1986–1993 published by Ticknor and Fields.)

Atwell, Nancie. *In the Middle: Writing, Reading, and Learning with Adolescents*. Portsmouth, NH: Heinemann, 1987.

Auden, W. H. "Museé des Beaux Arts." 1940. Rpt. *Norton Anthology of Poetry*. Ed. Margaret Ferguson, Mary Jo Salter, and Jon Stallworthy. New York: Norton, 2005. 1471–72.

Barker, Robert L., and Douglas M. Branson. "When Laws and Ethics Collide." *Forensic Social Work*. Ed. Carlton E. Munson. New York: Haworth, 1993. 43–53.

Barron, Monica. "Creative Writing Class as Crucible." *Academe* 93.6 (Nov.-Dec. 2007): 40–43.
Bartholomae, David. "Inventing the University." *When a Writer Can't Write: Studies in Writer's Block and Other Composition-Process Problems.* Ed. Mike Rose. New York: Guilford, 1985. 134–65.
—. "The Study of Error." *College Composition and Communication* 31 (1980): 253-69.
—. "Writing with Teachers: A Conversation with Peter Elbow." *College Composition and Communication* 46 (1955): 62–71.
Bartholomae, David, and Anthony Petrosky, eds. *Ways of Reading: An Anthology for Writers.* 4th ed. 1996. 7th ed. New York: Bedford/St. Martin's, 2004.
Bartlett, Thomas, et al. "Sounding the Alarm." *Chronicle of Higher Education.* 27 April, 2007. A 6–11.
Basset, Rachel Hile, ed. *Parenting and Professing: Balancing Family Work with an Academic Career.* Nashville: Vanderbilt UP, 2005.
Bean, John C. *Engaging Ideas: The Professor's Guide to Integrating Writing, Critical Thinking, and Active Learning in the Classroom.* San Francisco: Jossey-Bass, 1996.
Beaufort, Anne. *Writing in the Real World.: Making the Transition from School to Work.* New York: Teachers College P, 1999.
Behar, Ruth. *The Vulnerable Observer: Anthropology that Breaks Your Heart.* Boston: Beacon, 1996.
Berkenkotter, Carol, and Thomas N. Huckin. *Genre Knowledge in Disciplinary Communication: Cognition/Culture/Power.* Hillsdale, NJ: Erlbaum, 1995.
Berkenkotter, Carol, and Donald Murray. "Decisions and Revisions: The Planning Strategies of a Publishing Writer, and Response of a Laboratory Rat; or, Being Protocoled." *College Composition and Communication* 34 (1983): 156–72.
Berlin, James. "Contemporary Composition: The Major Pedagogical Theories." *College English* 44 (1982): 765–77.
Berry, Wendell. "Thoughts in the Presence of Fear." 2001. *The Essay Connection.* 7th ed. 551–55.
Bérubé, Michael. "American Studies without Exceptions." *PMLA* 118.1 (Jan. 2003): 103–13.
Birk, Lisa. "Grade Inflation: What's Really Behind All Those A's." *Harvard Education Letter: Research Online* Jan. Feb. 2002 <http://www.edletter.org/past/issues/2000-jf/grades.shtml>
Bishop, Wendy. "Places to Stand: The Reflective Writer-Teacher-Writer in Composition." *College Composition and Communication* 51.1 (Sept. 1999): 9–31.
—. *Teaching Lives: Essays and Stories.* Logan, UT: Utah State UP, 1997.

Bizzell, Patricia. "Cognition, Convention, and Certainty: What We Need to Know About Writing." *Pre/Text* 3 (1982): 213–43.

—. "Composing Processes: An Overview." *The Teaching of Writing*. Ed. Anthony Petrosky and David Bartholomae. Chicago: U of Chicago P, 1986. 49–70.

Black, Laurel Johnson. "Stupid Rich Bastards." Dews and Law 13–25.

Bleich, David. "Ethnography and the Study of Literacy: Prospects for a Socially Generous Research." Gere, *Into the Field* 99–116.

—. "What Can Be Done About Grading?" *Grading in the Post-Process Classroom: From Theory to Practice*. Ed. Libby Allison, Lizbeth Bryant, and Maureen Hourigan. Portsmouth, NH: Heinemann, 1997. 15–35.

Bloom, Harold. *The Western Canon: The Books and School of the Ages*. New York: Harcourt, 1994.

Bloom, Lynn Z. *Composition Studies as a Creative Art: Teaching, Writing, Scholarship, Administration*. Logan: Utah State UP, 1998.

—. *Doctor Spock: Biography of a Conservative Radical*. Indianapolis: Bobbs, 1972.

—. "The Essay Canon and Textbook Anthologies." *Symplok* 8.1–2 (2002): 20–35.

—, ed. *The Essay Connection: Readings for Writers*. 7th ed. 2004; 8th ed. Boston: Houghton, 2007.

—. *Fact and Artifact: Writing Nonfiction*. 2nd ed Englewood Cliffs, NJ: Prentice Hall, 1994.

—. "Finding a Family, Finding a Voice: A Writing Teacher Teaches Writing Teachers." *Journal of Basic Writing* 9.2 (1990). 3–14.

—. "Freshman Composition as a Middle Class Enterprise." *College English* 58.6 (Oct. 1996): 654–75.

—. "Growing Up with Doctor Spock: An Auto/Biography." *A/b: Auto/Biography Studies* 8.2 (1993): 271–85.

—. "Living to Tell the Tale: The Complicated Ethics of Creative Nonfiction." *College English* 65.3 (Jan. 2003): 275–89.

—. "Making Essay Connections: Editing Readers for First Year Writers." *Publishing in Rhetoric and Composition*. Ed. Gary A. Olson and Todd Taylor. Albany: SUNY P, 1997. 33–44.

—. "Once More to the Essay: The Essay Canon and Textbook Anthologies." *Symplok* 8:1–2 (2000): 20–35.

—. "The Seven Deadly Virtues." 2004–2005. *The Seven Deadly Virtues and Other Lively Essays*. Columbia, SC, 2008.

—. "Teaching College English as a Woman." *College English* 54 (Nov. 1992): 818–25.

—. "Why Don't We Write What We Teach? And Publish It?" Olson and Dobrin 143–55.

Bloom, Lynn Z., and Louise Z. Smith, eds. *The Arlington Reader: Canons and Contexts*. Boston: Bedford, 2003. 2nd ed. 2008.

Bloom, Lynn Z., Donald A. Daiker, and Edward M. White, eds. *Composition in the Twenty-First Century: Crisis and Change*. Carbondale, IL: Southern Illinois UP, 2003.

—, eds. *Composition Studies in the New Millennium: Rereading the Past, Rewriting the Future*. Carbondale, IL: Southern Illinois UP, 1996.

Bradshaw, Andy. "NWP Evaluation Continues to Show Positive Results." *The Voice: A Newsletter of the National Writing Project*. 6.4 (Sept.-Oct. 2001): 1, 20.

Brand, Alice Glarden, and Richard L. Graves, eds. *Presence of Mind: Writing and the Domain Beyond the Cognitive*. Portsmouth, NH: Heinemann, 1997.

Brereton, John, ed. *The Origins of Composition Studies in the American College, 1875–1925*. Pittsburgh: U of Pittsburgh P, 1995.

Britton, James, et al. *The Development of Writing Abilities (11–18)*. London: Macmillan, 1975.

Brueggemann, Brenda Jo. *Lend Me Your Ear: Rhetorical Constructions of Deafness*. Washington, D.C.: Gallaudet, 1999.

Bruno, Laura. "Princeton Leads in Grade Deflation." 2007. 26 March 2008 <http://www.usatoday.com/news/education/2007-03-27-princeton-grades_N.htm>.

Buell, Lawrence. *The Environmental Imagination: Thoreau, Nature Writing, and the Formation of American Culture*. Harvard UP, 1995.

Buranen, Lise, and Alice M. Roy, eds. *Perspectives on Plagiarism and Intellectual Property in a Postmodern World*. Albany: SUNY P, 1999.

Butrym, Alexander J., ed. *Essays on the Essay: Redefining the Genre*. Athens: U of Georgia P, 1989.

Carnes, Mark C. "The Liminal Classroom." *Chronicle of Higher Education*. 8 Oct. 2004: B 6–8.

CCCC Ad Hoc Committee on the Ethical Use of Students and Student Writing in Composition Studies. "Guidelines for the Ethical Treatment of Students and Student Writing in Composition Studies." *College Composition and Communication* 52.3 (Feb. 2001): 485–90. Also <http://www.ncte.org/cccc/positions/ethics.shtml>.

Chevalier, Tracy, ed. *Encyclopedia of the Essay*. London: Fitzroy Dearborn, 1997.

Cho, Seung-Hui. "Mr. Brownstone." 17 April 2007. 25 March 2008 <http://www.thesmokinggun.com/archive/years/2007/0417071vtech1.html>

—. "Richard McBeef." 17 April 2007. 25 March 2008 <http://www.thesmokinggun.com/archive/years/2007/0417071vtech1.html>

Clifford, John, and Elizabeth Ervin. "The Ethics of Process." Kent 179–97.

Connors, Robert J. *Composition-Rhetoric: Backgrounds, Theory, and Pedagogy*. Pittsburgh: U of Pittsburgh P, 1997.

—. "Invention and Assignments." Connors, *Composition-Rhetoric* 296–327.

Connors, Robert J., and Andrea Lunsford. "Frequency of Formal Errors in Current College Writing, or Ma and Pa Kettle Do Research." *College Composition and Communication* 39 (1988): 395–409.

—. The *St. Martin's Handbook*. New York: St. Martin's, 1989.

Cook, Devan. "Secrets and Ethics in Ethnographic Writing Research." Fontaine and Hunter 105–20.

Cooper, Marilyn M., and Michael Holzman. *Writing as Social Action*. Portsmouth, NH: Heinemann, 1989.

Couture, Barbara. "Modeling and Emulating: Rethinking Agency in the Writing Process." Kent 30–48.

Crews, Frederick C. *The Pooh Perplex*. New York: Dutton, 1963.

Crick, Bernard. *George Orwell: A Life*. Boston: Little, Brown, 1980.

Crowley, Sharon. "Around 1971: Current-Traditional Rhetoric and Process Models of Composing."@ Bloom, Daiker, and White, 1996, 64–74.

Cushman, Ellen. "Activist Methodology." *The Struggle and The Tools*. 21–38.

—. "The Public Intellectual, Service Learning, and Activist Research." *College English* 61 (1999): 328–36.

—. "Service Learning as the New English Studies." Downing, Hurlbert, and Mathieu, 204–18.

—. *The Struggle and the Tools: Oral and Literate Strategies in an Inner City Community*. Albany: SUNY P, 1998.

—. "Sustainable Service Learning Programs." *College Composition and Communication* 54 (Sept. 2002): 40–65.

Deans, Thomas. *Writing and Community Action: A Service-Learning Rhetoric with Readings*. New York: Longman, 2003.

—. *Writing Partnerships: Service-Learning in Composition*. Urbana, IL: NCTE, 2000.

Decker, Randall, ed. *Patterns of Exposition*. 4th ed. Boston: Little, Brown, 1974.

DeJoy, Nancy. "I Was a Process-Model Baby." Kent 163–78.

DeLillo, Don. "In the Ruins of the Future: Reflections on terror and loss in the shadow of September." *Harper's* (Dec. 2001): 33–40.

Dettmar, Kevin J. H. "Writers Who Price Themselves Out of the Canon." *Chronicle of Higher Education* Aug. 4, 2006: B 6–8.

Dewan, Shaila and Marc Santora. "Killer Showed Troubled State in Fall of 2005." *New York Times* 19 April 2007: A 1,18.

Dews, C. L. Barney, and Carolyn Leste Law, eds. *This Fine Place So Far From Home: Voices of Academics from the Working Class*. Philadelphia: Temple UP, 1995.

Didion, Joan. "Why I Write." 1976. L. Bloom, *Essay Connection*. 3rd ed. 43–50.

Dillard, Annie. "Introduction." *TheBest American Essays 1988*. Ed. Robert Atwan. New York: Ticknor, 1988.

Dixon, Kathleen. "Gendering the 'Personal.'" *College Composition and Communication* 46.2 (May 1995): 255–75.

Doctors without Borders. "About Us." 2006. 26 March 2008 <http://www.doctorswithoutborders.org/aboutus/>.

Downing, David B., Claude Mark Hurlbert, and Paula Mathieu, eds. *Beyond English, Inc.: Curricular Reform in a Global Economy*. Portsmouth, NH: Boynton, 2002.

DuPlessis, Rachel Blau. "F-words: An Essay on the Essay." *American Literature* 68.1 (March 1996): 15–45.

Eastman, Arthur, Caesar R. Blake, Hubert M. English, Jr., Alan B. Howes, Robert T. Lenaghan, Leo F. McNamara, James Rosier, eds. *The Norton Reader*. New York: Norton. 1st ed. 1965.

Ede, Lisa, ed. *On Writing Research: The Braddock Essays 1975–1998*. Boston: Bedford/St. Martin's, 1999.

—. *Situating Composition: Composition Studies and the Politics of Location*. Carbondale, IL: Southern Illinois UP, 2004.

Elbow, Peter. "Introduction: About Voice and Writing." *Landmark Essays on Voice and Writing*. Ed. Peter Elbow. Davis, CA: Hermagoras P, 1994. xi-xlvii.

—. "Writing Assessment in the 21st Century: A Utopian View." Bloom, Daiker, and White, 1996, 83–100.

—. *Writing Without Teachers*. New York: Oxford UP, 1973.

—. *Writing With Power: Techniques for Mastering the Writing Process*. New York: Oxford UP, 1981

Eliot, T[homas] S[tearns]. "Tradition and the Individual Talent." 1920. Rpt. *The Critical Tradition: Classic Texts and Contemporary Trends*. 3rd ed. Ed. David H. Richter. Boston: Bedford, 2007. 537–41.

Emig, Janet. *The Composing Processes of Twelfth Graders*. Research Report #13. Urbana, IL: NCTE, 1971.

Encyclopedia of Social Work. Ed. Richard L. Edwards and June Gary Hopps. Washington, D.C.: National Association of Social Workers. 19th ed., 1995.

Epstein, Joseph, ed. *The Norton Book of Personal Essays*. New York: Norton, 1997.

—. "Piece Work: Writing the Essay." *Plausible Prejudices*. New York: Norton, 1985. 379–411.

Estvanik, Nicole. "Babysitter: A Study in Power Relations." *Essay CONNections*. v.2. Storrs, CT: University of Connecticut English Department, 1998. 66–73.

Faigley, Lester. "Coherent Contradictions: The Conflicting Rhetoric of Writing Textbooks." *Fragments* 132–62.

—. "Competing Theories of Process: A Critique and Proposal." *College English* 48 (1986): 527–42.

—. *Fragments of Reality: Postmodernity and the Subject of Composition*. Pittsburgh: U of Pittsburgh P, 1992.

Faigley, Lester, Diana George, Anna Palchik, and Cynthia Selfe. *Picturing Texts*. New York: Norton, 2004.

Farris, Christine, and Chris M. Anson, eds. *Under Construction: Working at the Intersections of Composition Theory, Research, and Practice*. Logan, UT: Utah State UP, 1998.

Fendrich, Laurie. "History Overcomes Stories." 2001. Rpt. Lynn Z. Bloom *The Essay Connection: Readings for Writers*. 7th ed. Boston: Houghton, 2004. 529–32.

Flower, Linda. *The Construction of Negotiated Meaning: A Social Cognitive Theory of Writing*. Carbondale, IL: Southern Illinois UP, 1994.

—. *Problem-Solving Strategies for Writing*. Fort Worth: Harcourt, 1981.

Flower, Linda, and John Hayes. "Images, Plans, and Prose: The Representation of Meaning in Writing." *Written Communication*. 1 (1984): 120–60.

Foehr, Regina Paxton and Susan A. Schiller, eds. *The Spiritual Side of Writing: Releasing the Learner's Whole Potential*. Portsmouth, NH: Heinemann, 1997.

Foer, Jonathan Safran. *Extremely Loud & Incredibly Close*. Boston: Houghton, 2005.

Fontaine, Sheryl I., and Susan M. Hunter, eds. *Foregrounding Ethical Awareness in Composition and English Studies*. Portsmouth, NH: Boynton/Cook, 1988.

Fox, Patricia Shelley. "Women in Mind: The Culture of First-Year English and the Nontraditional Returning Woman Student." Yagelski and Leonard 183–203.

France, Alan W. "Assigning Places: The Function of Introductory Composition as a Cultural Discourse." *College English* 55.6 (Oct. 1993): 593–609.

Freedman, Diane, and Olivia Frey, eds. *Autobiographical Writing Across the Disciplines*. Durham, NC: Duke UP, 2003.

Freedman, Sarah Warshauer. "The Registers of Student and Professional Expository Writing: Influences on Teachers' Responses." *New Directions in Composition Research*. Ed. Richard Beach and Lillian S. Bridwell. New York: Guilford, 1984. 334–47.

Frey, James. *A Million Little Pieces*. New York: Doubleday, 2003.

Frey, Olivia. "Beyond Literary Darwinism: Women's Voices and Critical Discourse." *College English* 52.5 (Sept. 1990): 507–26.

Friedrich, Dick, and David Kuester. *It's Mine and I'll Write It That Way*. New York: Random, 1972.

Friend, Christy. "Imitations of Battle: Quintilian on the Classroom and the Public Sphere." *Composition Forum* 14.1 (2003): 1–16.

Fussell, Paul. "Notes on Class." *The Boy Scout Handbook and Other Observations*. New York: Oxford UP, 1982. 46–60.

Gass, William H. "Emerson and the Essay." *Habitations of the Word: Essays*. New York: Simon, 1985. 9–49.

Geertz, Clifford. "Blurred Genres: The Refiguration of Social Thought." *Local Knowledge Further Essays in Interpretive Anthropology*. New York: Basic Books, 1983. 19–35.

—. *Works and Lives: The Anthropologist as Author*. Stanford: Stanford UP, 1988.

Gere, Anne. *Intimate Practices: Literacy and Cultural Work in U.S. Women's Clubs, 1880–1920*. Urbana, IL: U of Illinois P, 1997.

—, ed. *Into the Field: Sites of Composition Studies*. New York: MLA, 1993.

Giroux, Henry. *Border Crossings: Cultural Workers and the Politics of Education*. New York: Routledge, 1992.

Glenn, Cheryl, Robert Keith Miller, and Suzanne Strobeck Webb. *The Writer's Harbrace Handbook*. 2nd ed. Boston: Thomson/Heinle, 2004.

Golding, Alan. *From Outlaw to Classic: Canons in American Poetry*. Madison: U of Wisconsin P, 1995.

Good, Graham. *The Observing Self: Rediscovering the Essay*. London: Routledge, 1988.

Gorman, James. "Ants, Better With Dose of Humanity (and Humor)." *New York Times* 25 April 2006: D3.

Gothard, Sol. "Legal Issues: Confidentiality and Privileged Communication." *Encyclopedia of Social Work*. Vol. 2. 1579–84.

Graff, Gerald. "The Academic Language Gap." Yagelski and Leonard 23–33.

—. "The University and the Prevention of Culture." *Criticism in the University*. Ed.. Gerald Graff and Reginald Gibbons. Evanston, IL: Northwestern UP, 1985. 62–82.

Grobman, Laurie. "Is There a Place for Service Learning in Literary Studies?" *Profession 2005*. New York: MLA, 2005. 125–40.

Gusdorf, Georges. "Conditions and Limits of Autobiography." 1956. Olney 28–48.

Hacker, Diana. *A Writer's Reference*. 5th ed. Boston: Bedford, 2003.

Hairston, Maxine. "The Winds of Change: Thomas Kuhn and the Revolution in the Teaching of Writing." *College Composition and Communication* 33 (1982): 76–88.

Hardwick, Elizabeth. "Introduction." *The Best American Essays 1986*. Ed. Elizabeth Hardwick and Robert Atwan. New York: Ticknor, 1986. xiii-xxi.

Harris, Joseph. *A Teaching Subject: Composition Since 1966*. Upper Saddle River, NJ: Prentice, 1997.

Harris, Wendell V. "Canonicity." *PMLA* 106.1 (Jan. 1991): 110–21.

—. "Reflections on the Peculiar Status of the Personal Essay." *College English* 58.8 (Dec. 1996): 934–53.

Harvey, Gordon. "Presence in the Essay." *College English* 56.6 (Oct. 1994): 642–54.

Heaney, Seamus. "Horace and the Thunder." *Times Literary Supplement* 18 Jan. 2002.

Holdstein, Deborah H., and David Bleich, eds. *Personal Effects: The Social Character of Scholarly Writing*. Logan, UT: Utah State UP, 2001.

Howard, Rebecca Moore. *Standing in the Shadow of Giants: Plagiarists, Authors, Collaborators*. Stamford, CT: Ablex, 1999.

Howarth, William L. "Some Principles of Autobiography." 1974. Olney 84–114.

Hoy, Pat. *Instinct for Survival*. Athens: U of Georgia P, 1992.

Inge, M. Thomas. Letter. *PMLA* 104.5 (Oct. 1989): 904.

Iser, Wolfgang. "The Reading Process: A Phenomenological Approach." 1974. *Reader-Response Criticism: From Formalism to Post-Structuralism*. Ed. Jane P. Tompkins. Baltimore: Johns Hopkins UP, 1980. 50–69.

Jacobus, Lee, ed. *A World of Ideas*. 4th ed. New York: St. Martin's, 1994.

Jamieson, Sandra. "Composition Readers and the Construction of Identity." *Writing in Multicultural Settings*. Ed. Carol Severino, Juan C. Guerra, and Johnnella E. Butler. New York: MLA, 1997. 150–71.

Juergensmeyer, Mark. "Theater of Terror" and "America as Enemy," excerpts *from Terror in the Mind of God*. 2000. L. Bloom *Essay Connection*. 7th ed. 538–50.

Kaufer, David, and Patricia Dunmire. "Integrating Cultural Reflection and Production in College Writing Curricula." *Reconceiving Writing, Rethinking Writing Instruction*. Ed. Joseph Petraglia. Mahwah, N.J.: Erlbaum, 1995. 217–38.

Kennedy, X. J., and Dorothy M. *The Bedford Guide for College Writers*. 2nd ed. Boston: Bedford, 1990.

Kennedy, X. J., Dorothy M. Kennedy, and Jane E. Aaron, eds. *The Bedford Reader*. 6th ed. Boston: Bedford, 1997.

Kent, Thomas, ed. *Post-Process Theory: Beyond the Writing-Process Paradigm*. Carbondale, IL: Southern Illinois UP, 1999.

Kirklighter, Cristina. "The Relevance of Paulo Freire on Liberatory Dialogue and Writing in the Classroom." Yagelski and Leonard 221–34.

—. *Traversing the Democratic Borders of the Essay*. Albany: SUNY P, 2002.

Kirsch, Gesa. "Ethics and the Future of Composition Research." Bloom, Daiker, White, 2003, 129–41.

Kirsch, Gesa, and Patricia A. Sullivan, eds. *Methods and Methodology in Composition Research.* Carbondale, IL: Southern Illinois UP, 1992.

Kirszner, Laurie G., and Stephen R. Mandell. *The Brief Handbook.* 4th ed. Boston: Thomson/Heinle, 2004.

Kuhn, Thomas S. *The Structure of Scientific Revolutions.* 2nd ed. Chicago: U of Chicago P, 1970.

Kytle, Ray. *Prewriting: Strategies for Exploration and Discovery.* New York: Random, 1972.

Lauer, Janice, and J. William Asher. *Composition Research: Empirical Designs.* New York: Oxford UP, 1988.

Lauter, Paul. *Canons and Contexts.* New York: Oxford UP, 1991.

—. "Preface to the First Edition." *The Heath Anthology of American Literature.* 2nd ed. Vol. 1. Lexington: Heath, 1994. xxx-xl.

Leggo, Carl. "Questions I Need To Ask before I Advise My Students To Write in Their Own Voices." *Rhetoric Review* 10.1 (Fall 1991): 143–52.

Leonardi, Susan J. "Recipes for Reading: Summer Pasta, Lobster à la Riseholme, and Key Lime Pie." *PMLA* 104.3 (May 1989): 340–47.

Lewiecki-Wilson, Cynthia and Brenda Jo Brueggemann, eds. *Disability and the Teaching of Writing: A Critical Sourcebook.* Boston: Bedford/St. Martin"s, 2008.

Lewis, Bernard. "What Went Wrong?" 2002. L. Bloom. *The Essay Connection.* 7th ed. 533–38.

Lipka, Sara. "Lessons from a Tragedy (Safety and risk-managements experts debate Virginia Tech's response)". *Chronicle of Higher Education* 27 April 2007: A 12–13.

Lopate, Phillip, ed. *The Anchor Essay Annual: The Best of 1997.* New York: Anchor, 1997.

—, ed. *The Art of the Personal Essay: An Anthology from the Classical Era to the Present.* New York: Doubleday, 1994.

Lunsford, Andrea. *The St. Martin's Handbook.* 5th ed. New York: St. Martin's, 2003.

Lunsford, Andrea, and Robert Connors. *The St. Martin's Handbook.* 2nd ed. New York: St. Martin's, 1992.

Lunsford, Andrea A., et al. "Foreword: Considering Research Methods in Composition and Rhetoric." Mortensen and Kirsch vii-xv.

McCrimmon, James. *Writing With a Purpose.* Boston: Houghton, 1950.

MacDonald, Susan Peck. "The Literary Argument and Its Discursive Conventions." *The Writing Scholar: Studies in Academic Discourse.* Ed. Walter Nash. *Written Communication Annual.* v.3. Newbury Park, CA: Sage, 1990. 31–62.

McLeod, Susan H. *Notes on the Heart: Affective Issues in the Writing Classroom.* Carbondale, IL: Southern Illinois UP, 1999.
McQuade, Donald M. "Composition and Literary Studies." *Redrawing the Boundaries: The Transformation of English and American Literary Studies.* Ed. Stephen Greenblatt and Giles Gunn. New York: MLA, 1992. 482–519.
McQuade, Donald, and Christine McQuade. *Seeing and Writing.* 2nd ed. Boston: Bedford, 2003.
Malinowitz, Harriet. *Textual Orientations: Lesbian and Gay Students and the Making of Discourse Communities.* Portsmouth, NH: Heinemann, 1995.
Mandell, Barret J. "Full of Life Now." Olney 49–72.
Mandell, Jonathan. "Cho's professor to classmates: Don't feel guilty." 2007. 26 March 2008 <http://www.cnn.com/2007/US/04/18/vatech.professor/>.
Mansfield, Harvey C. "Grade Inflation: It's Time to Face the Facts," *Chronicle Review: Chronicle of Higher Education.* 6 April, 2001. 26 March 2008 <http://chronicle.com/free/v47/i30/30b02401.htm>.
Marius, Richard. *A Writer's Companion.* 3rd ed. New York: McGraw, 1995. 4th ed. 1999.
Martin, Eric. "The WPA Annual Bibliography of Writing Textbooks." *Writing Program Administration* 19.3 (Spring 1996): 83–102.
Miller, Nancy K. *Bequest and Betrayal: Memoirs of a Parent's Death.* 1996. Bloomington: Indiana UP, 2000.
—. "Getting Personal: Autobiography as Cultural Criticism." *Getting Personal: Feminist Occasions and Other Autobiographical Acts.* New York: Routledge, 1991. 1–31.
—. "My Father's Penis." *Getting Personal.* 143–47.
Miller, Richard E. "Fault Lines in the Contact Zone." *College English* 56.4 (April 1994): 389–408.
Miller, Richard, and Kurt Spellmeyer, eds. *The New Humanities Reader.* 2nd ed. Boston: Houghton, 2006.
Miller, Susan. "How I Teach Writing: How to Teach Writing? To Teach Writing?" *Pedagogy.* 1.2 (Fall 2001): 479–88.
___. "Writing Theory: Theory Writing." *Methods and Methodology in Composition Research.* Ed. Gesa Kirsch and Patricia A. Sullivan. Carbondale, IL: Southern Illinois UP, 1992. 62–83.
—. "A Million Little Lies." 8 Jan. 2006. 26 March 2008 <http://www.thesmokinggun.com/archive/0104061jamesfrey1.html>.
Moffett, James. *Student-Centered Language Arts Curriculum K-13.* 1968. Portsmouth, NH: Boynton, 1992.
—. *Teaching the Universe of Discourse.* Boston: Houghton, 1968.

Montaigne, Michel de. "Of the Resemblance of Children to Fathers." *Essays, Travel Journals, Letters*. Trans. Donald M. Frame. *The Complete Works of Montaigne*. Vol. 2 Stanford: Stanford UP, 1957. 574–98.

Morenberg, Max, Donald Daiker, and Andrew Kerek. "Sentence Combining at the College Level." *Research in the Teaching of English*. 12 (1978): 245–56.

Mortensen, Peter, and Gesa E. Kirsch, eds. *Ethics and Representation in Qualitative Studies of Literacy*. Urbana, IL: NCTE, 1996.

Murphy, Jr. Richard J. *The Calculus of Intimacy: A Teaching Life*. Columbus: Ohio State UP, 1993.

Murray, Donald. "Teach Writing as Process, Not Product." 1972. Rpt. *Rhetoric and Composition*. Ed. Richard L. Graves. Rochelle Park, NJ: Hayden, 1976. 79–82.

—. *A Writer Teaches Writing*. Boston: Houghton, 1968.

—. *Write to Learn*. New York: Holt, 1984.

Myers, Kimberly R., ed. *Illness in the Academy: A Collection of Pathographies by Academics*. West Lafayette, IN: Purdue UP, 2007.

National Council of Teachers of English. NCTE Position Statement: "On the Students' Right to Their Own Language." 1974. 6 June 2006. <http://www.ncte.org/about/over/positions/category/lang/107502.htm>.

Nesteruk, Jeffrey. "Fatherhood, in Theory and Practice." *Chronicle of Higher Education* 11 Feb. 2005: B5.

Newman, Katherine S. "Before the Rampage: What Can Be Done?" *Chronicle of Higher Education* 4 May 2007: B20.

News@Princeton. "Committee issues message on grading results for 2004-05." 19 Sept. 2005. 26 March 2008 <http://www.princeton.edu/main/news/archive/S12/71/58E12/index.xml?section=nnewsreleases>.

Nobelprize.org. "All Nobel Peace Prize Laureates." 2008. 26 March 2008 < http://nobelprize.org/nobel_prizes/peace/laureates/>.

North Stephen M. *The Making of Knowledge in Composition: Portrait of an Emerging Field*. Upper Montclair, NJ: Boynton, 1987.

Odell, Lee and Dixie Goswami. "Writing in a Non-Academic Setting." *Research in the Teaching of English*. 16 (1982): 201–23.

Odell, Lee, and Susan M. Katz. *Writing in a Visual Age*. Boston: Bedford/St.Martin's, 2006.

O'Hare, Frank. *Sentence-Combining: Improving Student Writing Without Formal Grammar Instruction*. Urbana, IL: NCTE, 1973.

Olney, James, ed. *Autobiography: Essays Theoretical and Critical*. Princeton, NJ: Princeton UP, 1980.

Olson, Gary. "Toward a Post-Process Composition: Abandoning the Rhetoric of Assertion." Kent 7–15.

Olson, Gary A., and Sidney I. Dobrin, eds. *Composition Theory for the Postmodern Classroom*. Albany: SUNY P, 1994.

Orbinski, James. "Humanitarianism." 1999. 26 March 2008 <http://nobelprize.org/nobel_prizes/peace/laureates/1999/msf-lecture.html>.
Orwell, George. "Politics and the English Language." 1945. *Essays*. Sel. and Introd. John Carey. New York: Knopf, 2002. 954–67.
—. "Shooting an Elephant." 1936. *Essays*. 42–49.
—. "Why I Write." 1947. *Essays*. 1079–85.
Parks, Stephen. *Class Politics: The Movement for the Students' Right to Their Own Language*. Urbana, IL: NCTE, 2000.
Pelz, William A. "Is There a Working-Class History?" Dews and Law 277–85.
Peterson, Linda H., John C. Brereton and Joan E. Hartman, eds. *The Norton Reader*. 9th ed. New York: Norton, 1996.
Petraglia, Joseph. "Is There Life after Process? The Role of Social Scientism in a Changing Discipline." Kent 49–64.
Piper, Deborah. "Psychology's Class Blindness: Investment in the Status Quo." Dews and Law 286–97.
Pratt, Mary Louise. "Arts of the Contact Zone." *Profession 91*. New York: MLA, 1991. 33–40.
Pullman, George. "Stepping Yet Again into the Same Current." Kent 16–29.
Rasula, Jed. *The American Poetry Wax Museum: Reality Effects, 1940—1990*. Urbana, IL: NCTE, 1996.
Ray, Ruth. *Beyond Nostalgia: Aging and Life-Story Writing*. Charlottesville: U of Virginia P, 2000.
Reamer, Frederic G. "Ethics and Values." *Encyclopedia of Social Work*. Vol. 1. 893–902.
Rinaldi, Jacqueline. "Journeys Through Illness: Connecting Body and Spirit." Foehr and Schiller 118–28.
Rinaldi, Nicholas. *Between Two Rivers*. New York: HarperCollins, 2004.
Roney, Stephen K. "Postmodernist Prose and George Orwell." *Academic Questions* 15.2 (Spring 2002): 13–23.
Root, Jr., Robert L. *E. B. White: The Emergence of an Essayist*. Iowa City, IA: U of Iowa P, 1999.
—. "The Experimental Art." *JAEPL* 9 (Winter 2003–04): 12–19.
Rose, Mike. *Lives on the Boundary: The Struggles and Achievements of America's Underprepared*. New York: Free P, 1989.
—. *Writer's Block: The Cognitive Dimension*. Urbana, IL: NCTE and Carbondale, IL: Southern Illinois UP, 1984.
Rose, Phyllis. "The Coming of the French." *American Scholar* 74.1 (Winter 2005): 59–67.
Rosenblatt, Louise M. *Literature as Exploration*. 1938. 4th ed. Vol. 2. New York: MLA, 1983.

Rosovsky, Henry, and Matthew Hartley. *Evaluation and the Academy: Are We Doing the Right Thing?* Cambridge, MA: American Academy of Arts and Sciences, 2002.
Roth, Philip. *The Plot Against America.* Boston: Houghton, 2004.
Rowe, John Carlos. "Nineteenth-Century Literary Culture and Transnationality." *PMLA* 118.1 (Jan. 2003): 78–89.
Russell, David. "Activity Theory and Process Approaches: Writing (Power) in School and Society." Kent 80–95.
Sabine, Gordon A. *Memoir of a Book: The Norton Reader An Anthology of Expository Prose.* Ann Arbor: U of Michigan Library, 1993.
Sanders, Scott Russell. "The Singular First Person." *Secrets of the Universe: Scenes from the Journey Home.* Boston: Beacon, 1991. 187–204.
Schmidt, Jan Zlotnik, ed. *Women/Writing/Teaching.* Albany, New York: SUNY P, 1998.
Scholes, Robert. *Textual Power: Literary Theory and the Teaching of English.* New Haven: Yale UP, 1985.
Scholes, Robert, Nancy R. Comley, and Gregory L. Ulmer. *Text Book: Writing through Literature.* 3rd ed. Boston: Bedford, 2002.
Shaughnessy, Mina P. *Errors and Expectations: A Guide for the Teacher of Basic Writing.* New York: Oxford UP, 1977.
Shepard, Alan, John McMillan, and Gary Tate, eds. *Coming to Class: Pedagogy and the Social Class of Teachers.* Portsmouth, NH: Heinemann, 1998.
Shuman, R. Baird. Letter. *PMLA* 104.5 (Oct. 1989): 904.
Slevin, James F. "Reading and Writing in the Classroom and the Profession." *Writing Theory and Critical Theory.* Ed. John Clifford and John Schilb. New York: MLA, 1994. 53–72.
Smith, Barbara Herrnstein. *Contingencies of Value: Alternative Perspectives for Critical Theory.* Cambridge, MA: Harvard UP, 1988.
Smith, William E. "Blurring the Boundaries of Academic Intimacy and Moral Neutrality: What Is the Responsibility of the WPA?" Fontaine and Hunter 70–82.
Smitten, Paige Dayton. "Bibliography of Writing Textbooks." *WPA* 16.3 (Spring 1993): 80–99.
—. "Bibliography of Writing Textbooks." *WPA* 17.3 (Spring 1994): 75–94.
Social Science Research Council. "Critical Views of September 11." n.d. 26 March 2008 : <http://www.ssrc.org/sept11/toc11b.htm>
Sontag, Susan. [untitled]. *New Yorker.* 24 Sept. 2001. 26 March 2008 <http://www.newyorker.com/archive/2001/09/24/010924ta_talk_wtc>.
Spellmeyer, Kurt. *The Arts of Living: Reinventing the Humanities for the Twenty-First Century.* Albany: SUNY Albany P, 2003.
Spellmeyer, Kurt, and Richard Miller, eds. 2nd ed. *The New Humanities Reader.* Boston: Houghton, 2006.

Spinner, Jenny. "On Women and the Essay: An Anthology from the Seventeenth Century to the Present." Diss. U of Connecticut, 2004.

Straub, Richard, and Ronald F. Lunsford. *Twelve Readers Reading: Responding to College Writing.* Cresskill, NJ: Hampton, 1995.

Strunk, Jr., William, and E. B. White. *The Elements of Style.* 1979. 4th ed. Needham, MA: Allyn and Bacon, 2000.

Stuckey, J.Elspeth. *The Violence of Literacy.* Portsmouth, NH: Heinemann, 1991.

"Students' Right to Their Own Language." *College Composition and Communication* 25 (Fall 1974). Rpt. Urbana, IL: NCTE, 1974.

Sullivan, Patricia. "Passing: A Family Dissemblance." Shepard, McMillan, and Tate. 231–51.

Sullivan, Patrick. "What Is "College-Level" Writing?" *Teaching English in the Two-Year College.* 30.4 (May 2003): 374–90.

Swales, John. *Genre Analysis: English in Academic and Research Settings.* Cambridge: Cambridge UP, 1990.

Tannen, Deborah. *You Just Don't Understand: Women and Men in Conversation.* New York: Ballantine, 1990.

Thoreau, Henry David. *Walden and Other Writings.* Ed. William Howarth. New York: Modern Library, 1981.

Tompkins, Jane. "Me and My Shadow." 1987. Rpt in *Feminisms: An Anthology of Literary Theory and Criticism.* Ed. Robyn R. Warhol and Diane Price Herndl. 2nd ed. New Brunswick, NJ: Rutgers UP, 1997. 1103–116.

Trimbur, John. "Articulation Theory and the Problem of Determination: A Reading of *Lives on the Boundary.*" Olson and Dobrin 236–53.

—. "Taking the Social Turn: Teaching Writing Post-Process." CCC 45.1 (Feb. 1994): 108–18.

Trimmer, Joseph, ed. *Narration as Knowledge: Tales of the Teaching Life.* Portsmouth, NH: Heinemann, 1997.

van Peer, Willie. "Two Laws of Literary History: Growth and Predictability in Canon Formation." *Mosaic* 30.2 (June 1997): 113–32

Vicinus, Martha, and Caroline Eisner, eds. *Originality, Imitation, Plagiarism.* Ann Arbor, MI: U of Michigan P, 2008.

Villanueva, Jr., Victor. "Afterword. Bearing Repetition: Some Assumptions." Allison, Bryant, and Hourigan, 176–79.

—. *Bootstraps: From an American Academic of Color.* Urbana, IL: NCTE, 1993.

"Cho Seung-Hui's Plays - Mr. Brownstone." UmmYeah.com. n.d. . 26 March 2008 <http://ummyeah.com/page/Cho_SeungHuis_Plays_Mr_Brownstone>.

Wallace, David Foster. "Getting Away from Already Being Pretty Much Away from It All." *A Supposedly Fun Thing I'll Never Do Again: Essays and Arguments.* Boston: Little, 1997. 83–137.

Webb, Suzanne S. "Bibliography of Writing Textbooks." *WPA* 14.3 (Spring 1991): 84–108.
—. "Bibliography of Writing Textbooks." *WPA* 15.3 (Spring 1992): 78–98.
Ween, Lori. "This Is Your Book: Marketing America to Itself." *PMLA* 118.1 (Jan. 2003): 90–102.
Westfall, Julie. "The Rate of (Grade) Inflation." *Daily Illini* 6 Dec. 2000. 26 March 2008 <http://web.archive.org/web/20040517062942/http://www.dailyillini.com/dec00/dec06/news/news01.shtml>.
White, E. B. "Foreword." *Essays.* vii-ix.
—. *Essays of E. B. White.* New York: Harper, 1977.
—. "Once More to the Lake." 1941. Rpt. *Essays.* 197–202.
—. "The Ring of Time." 1956. Rpt. *Essays.* 142–49.
Widmer, Ted. "So Help Me God." *American Scholar* 74.1 (Winter 2005): 29–41.
Wiesel, Elie. "Why I Write: Making No Become Yes." 1986. Ed. L Bloom, *Essay Connection,* 7th ed. 38–42.
Winnicott, D. W. "The Relationship of a Mother to her Baby at the Beginning." *The Family and Individual Development.* New York: Basic Books, 1965. 15–20.
Winslow, Rosemary. "Poetry, Community, and the Vision of Hospitality: Writing for Life in a Women's Shelter." *The Literacy Connection:* Ed. Ronald A. Sudol and Alice S. Horning. Cresskill, NJ: Hampton P, 1999. 181–204.
Witte, Stephen P., and Lester Faigley. *Evaluating College Writing Programs.* Carbondale: Southern Illinois UP, 1983.
Wolfe, Tom. "The New Journalism." *The New Journalism with an Anthology.* Ed. Tom Wolfe and E. W. Johnson. New York: Harper, 1973. 3–52.
Woolf, Virginia. "Jane Austen." *The Common Reader.* First Series. 1925. New York: Harcourt, 1953. 137–49.
Yagelski, Robert P., and Scott A. Leonard, eds. *The Relevance of English: Teaching That Matters in Students' Lives.* Urbana, IL: NCTE, 2002.
Yancey, Kathleen Blake. *Reflection in the Writing Classroom.* Logan, UT: Utah State UP, 1998.
Young, Art. *Teaching Writing Across the Curriculum.* 3rd ed. Upper Saddle River, NJ: Prentice-Hall, 1999. Also <http://wac.colostate.edu/aw/books/young_teaching/>.

About the Author

Lynn Z. Bloom is Board of Trustees Distinguished Professor and Aetna Chair of Writing at the University of Connecticut. She learned from great writing teachers: Dr. Seuss, fun; William Strunk and E. B. White, elegant simplicity; Benjamin Spock, precision. "If you don't write clearly, someone could die," he advised when she was writing *Doctor Spock: Biography of a Conservative Radical* (1972). These precepts have governed her teaching and administrative work—at Butler University, the University of New Mexico, the College of William and Mary, Virginia Commonwealth University, and as president of the Council of Writing Program Administrators. They also inform the heart, soul, and human voice of her writing: autobiography—*Composition Studies as a Creative Art* (1998), *The Seven Deadly Virtues* (2008); textbooks such as *The Arlington Reader* (2008) and *The Essay Connection* (9th ed. forthcoming); and composition studies research, including *Writers Without Borders*, two volumes of *Composition Studies in the 21st Century* (1996), and "The Essay Canon" (1999) and "Consuming Prose: The Delectable Rhetoric of Food Writing" (2008), both in *College English*. "(Im)Patient" was named a Notable Essay of 2005. She has received research awards from the National Endowment for the Humanities, NCTE, and the U.S. Department of Agriculture.

Credits, continued from page viii.

"The Good, the Bad, and the Ugly: Ethical Principles for (Re)Presenting Students and Student Writing in Teachers' Publications" was originally published in *Writing on the Edge* 13.2 (Spring 2003): 67-82. Used by permission.

"The Ineluctable Elitism of Essays and Why They Prevail in First-Year Composition Courses" originally appeared in *Open Words: Access and English Studies* 1.2 (Spring 2007).

"Insider Writing: Plagiarism-Proof Assignments" originally appeared in *Originality, Imitation, and Plagiarism: Teaching Writing in the Digital Age.* Ed. Caroline Eisner and Martha Vicinus. Ann Arbor: U of Michigan Press, 2008. © 2008 by the University of Michagan Press. Used by permission.

"Negotiating the Grading Contract: No More Lobbying, Bullying or Crying" appeared originally in *Teaching Ideas for University English: What Really Works.* Ed. Patricia M. Gantt and Lynn L. Meeks. Norwood, MA: Christopher-Gordon, 2004. 93-103. Used by permission.

Index

Aaron, Jane, 39
academic virtues, 124, 133
academic writing, 4, 12, 17–20, 30, 63, 67, 69, 111–113, 120, 123, 125–127, 131, 167; personal style, 22, 69
Ackerman, Diane, 66
Adler-Kassner, Linda, 165
Adorno, Theodor, 28, 111
Alexie, Sherman, 66
Allison, Libby, 97
Als, Hilton, 46
Altieri, Charles, 27
Angelou, Maya, 30, 31, 44, 57, 60, 110, 184; I Know Why the Caged Bird Sings, 30, 60
Annan, Kofi, 88, 89, 91
Arendt, Hannah, 58
argumentation, 68, 84, 115
Aristotle, 61, 93, 125, 199n
Arlen, Michael, 58
Arnold, Matthew, 106, 132
Arnold, Matthew L., 27
Asimov, Isaac, 22, 184
Atwan, Robert, 36, 38, 39, 46, 53, 54
Atwell, Nancie, 96, 198n, 199n
Auden, W. H., 79–80, 91
Aung San Suu Kyi, 89
authorial presence, 15, 58, 60, 61, 62, 65, 66
autobiographical writing, 4, 42, 60, 62, 109, 115–116, 135, 168

autobiography, 17, 30, 31, 37, 43, 60, 82, 88, 101, 110, 116, 166–168

Bacon, Francis, 35
Baker, Russell, 57, 110
Baker, Sheridan, 42
Baldwin, James, 57, 110, 116, 184
Barker, Robert L., 158
Barron, Monica, 203n
Barry, Lynda, 46
Barthes, Roland, 14
Bartholomae, David, 66, 96, 127, 134, 151, 198n, 200n
Bartlett, Thomas, 159
Barzun, Jacques, 39
Basset, Rachel Hile, 54
Bean, John, 169
Beaufort, Anne, 106
Behar, Ruth, 14, 22, 112
Benedict, Ruth, 14, 151
Berkenkotter, Carol, 95, 104
Berlin, James A., 97, 196n
Berry, Wendell, 87
Berubé, Michael, 202n
Best American Essays, 35–36, 38, 54
Bettelhein, Bruno, 184
Biography, 55, 56
Birk, Lisa, 204n
Birkerts, Swen, 22
Bishop, Wendy, 54, 67, 199n
Bizzell, Patricia, 66, 97

Black, Laurel Johnson, 114
Bleich, David, 23, 148, 198n
Bloom, Allen, 25
Bloom, Harold, 25, 26, 29
Bloom, Lynn Z., 47, 57, 81, 82, 84, 85, 87–88, 90, 109, 118, 134, 181, 192, 196n, 201n, 203n
Bradshaw, Andy, 200n
Brady, Judy, 41, 185
Brand, Alice Glarden, 106
Branson, Robert L., 158
Brereton, John, 116
Britton, James, 198n
Bronowski, Jacob, 185
Brueggemann, Brenda Jo, 105, 116
Bryant, Lizbeth, 97
Buell, Lawrence, 188
Buranen, Lise, 135
Butler, Judith, 19
Butrym, Alexander J., 35

canonicity: and study questions, 50, 51, 52, 118
Capote, Truman, 15
Carlyle, Thomas, 27
Carnes, Mark C., 169
Carson, Rachel, 31, 185
Carter, Jimmy, 89
Catton, Bruce, 184
Chan, Sucheng, 46
Chevalier, Tracy, 54, 109
Cho, Seung-Hui, 8, 140, 152, 158
Ciardi, John, 185
Clifford, John, 23, 41, 49, 87, 95, 101, 102, 123, 148, 191, 203n
Cofer, Judith Ortiz, 116
College Composition and Communication (CCC), 120, 140, 198n
Comley, Nancy R., 120, 134
community: and student writing, 69, 76, 113, 121, 123, 135, 156, 170, 172; extracurricular writing, 105; interpretive, 48, 106;

service learning, 69, 121, 122, 135, 169, 170
community colleges, 32, 201n, 204n
composition, 6, 36, 69, 93–94, 97, 103, 108, 116, 118–119, 121, 128, 135, 139–141, 143, 174, 181, 182, 199n–201n; and diversity, 33, 42, 67, 68, 93, 116; and middle class values, 6, 117–118, 120; and personal voice, 128; classroom practice, 108, 115; freshman, 6, 25, 29, 31, 35, 45, 50, 108–109, 118, 120, 176, 180; problematic writing, 8, 127, 139, 141, 145, 148–152, 155, 157, 160; research, 29, 118, 125, 132, 140–141, 148–150, 152; placement tests, 127, 141, 149–151
Conference on College Composition and Communication (CCCC), 8, 54, 120, 126, 139, 140, 144, 148, 150, 152, 154, 156, 158, 201n
Confucius, 169
Connors, Robert J., 103, 116, 118, 126
Cook, Devan, 149
Cooper, Marilyn M., 105
Couture, Barbara, 95, 104
creative nonfiction, 37, 53, 54, 67, 72, 75, 76, 81, 109, 147
creative writing, 24, 124, 126, 132, 140, 159, 161, 167, 203n
Crews, Frederick C., 50
Crick, Bernard, 62
Crooks, Robert, 165
Crowley, Sharon, 94, 103
cultural studies, 104
curricula, curriculum, 6, 25, 27, 28, 31, 32, 103, 105, 108, 113, 116, 121, 124, 139, 168, 195n,

197n, 199n, 200n
Cushman, Ellen, 105, 121, 148, 169, 171, 195n

Daiker, Donald 198n
Darwin, Charles, 48
Deans, Thomas, 69, 105, 121, 135, 169, 170
Decker, Randall, 29, 32
Declaration of Independence, 29, 43, 44, 49, 57, 68, 122, 183
DeJoy, Nancy, 103
DeLillo, Don, 85
deMan, Paul, 13
Derrida, Jacques, 13
Dettmar, Kevin J.H., 44
Dewan, Shaila, 159, 160
Dews, C.L. Barney, 22
Didion, Joan, 5, 35, 57, 58, 59, 65, 67, 80, 109, 183
Dillard, Annie, 5, 15, 36, 53, 57, 110, 135, 166–167, 183
Dixon, Kathleen, 69
Douglass, Frederick, 31, 49, 166
Downing, David B., 165, 195n
Dubus, Andre, 116
Dunmire, Patricia, 105
DuPlessis, Rachel Blau, 53, 111

Eastman, Arthur, 30, 32, 51
Ede, Lisa, 97, 118, 199n
Eggers, Dave, 66
Ehrenreich, Barbara, 117
Ehrlich, Gretel, 36
Eiseley, Loren, 14, 57, 184
Eisner, Caroline, 104
Elbow, Peter, 6, 61, 69, 96, 103, 154, 176, 180, 189, 198n–199n, 201n
Eliot, T.S., 12, 27
elitism, 6, 19, 26, 108, 109, 111, 113, 116–117, 119, 121–122, 198n

Emerson, Ralph Waldo, 12, 36, 67, 82, 112
Emig, Janet, 95
Epstein, Joseph, 26, 36, 54
Ervin, Elizabeth, 95
essay: belletristic, 109, 113; canon(s), 25, 26, 27–29, 31, 34, 37–39, 45, 47, 55; canonical essayists, 4, 32, 34–35, 39, 44, 46–47, 56, 57–60, 65, 67, 68, 109–112, 117, 200n; canonical essays, 32, 39, 43, 44, 46–47, 56, 57, 60, 109, 111–112, 118; canonicity, 25, 31, 33, 34, 37, 39, 40, 42, 45, 47, 54, 68; definition(s), 72; models for student writing, 29, 32, 67, 119, 196n
Estvanik, Nicole, 48
ethics: CCCC Guidelines, 140, 141, 148, 149, 158; censorship, 146, 161; deontological perspective, 141; informed consent, 148–150; instructional materials, 144, 145; publishing student writing, 140, 145, 146, 152; representing student writing, 140; Tarasoff case, 156, 202n; teaching and writing, 8, 41, 85, 140, 151, 170
Evans, Bergen, 39
Evans-Pritchard, E.E., 14, 151

Fadiman, Anne, 37, 66
Faigley, Lester, 50, 52, 96, 103, 105, 200n
Federman, Raymond, 14
Fendrich, Laurie, 86, 87
Flaubert, Gustave, 14
Flower, Linda, 6, 95, 103, 105, 121, 135, 165, 170
Foehr, Regina Paxton, 106
Foer, Jonathan Safran, 196n

Fontaine, Sheryl I., 106, 140
Forster, E. M., 57, 184
Fox, Patricia Shelley, 115
France, Alan W., 108, 119–120
Franklin, Benjamin, 166
Freedman, Diane, 23
Freedman, Sarah Warshauer, 127
Freire, Paolo, 96, 112, 115, 170, 198n
Freud, Sigmund, 47, 58
Frey, James, 128
Frey, Olivia, 23
Friedrich, Dick, 201n
Friend, Christy, 169
Fussell, Paul, 113–114

Gansberg, Martin, 30
Gardner, Howard, 22
Gass, William H., 4, 12, 28, 38, 67, 111, 125, 130
Gates, Jr., Henry Louis, 37, 66
Gawande, Atul, 37
Geertz, Clifford, 14, 15, 22, 151
genre, 53, 104, 109; belletristic essay, 109, 113; creative nonfiction, 37, 53–54, 67, 72, 75–76, 81, 109, 147; nature writing, 54, 109, 187
Gere, Anne, 105, 155
Giroux, Henry, 121
Glenn, Cheryl, 202n
Golding, Alan, 26–27, 29, 38, 45, 47
Goodman, Ellen, 57, 184
Gorman, James, 195n
Goswami, Dixie, 95
Gothard, Sol, 156, 158, 202n
Gould, Stephen Jay, 22, 47, 184
grade inflation, 204n
Graff, Gerald, 13, 115
Graves, Donald, 95
Graves, Richard L., 106
Gregory, Dick, 58

Griffith, Marlene, 32
Grobman, Laurie, 165, 169
Gusdorf, Georges, 60

Hacker, Diana, 202n
Hairston, Maxine, 42, 92, 94, 196n, 197n
Hall, Donald, 39
Hardwick, Elizabeth, 109
Harris Wendell, 28
Harris, Joseph, 96, 97, 103
Harris, Sidney J., 58
Harris, Wendell, 110
Hartley, Matthew, 201n
Harvey, Gordon, 60, 62, 64, 67
Hayakawa, S.I., 184
Hayes, John, 95
Heaney, Seamus, 5, 79, 80, 85
Heath, Shirley Brice, 22
Highet, Gilbert, 185
Hogan, Linda, 116
Holdstein, Deborah H., 23
Holmes, Oliver Wendell, 36
Holzman, Michael, 105
Hourigan, Maureen, 97, 198n
Howarth, William L., 187
Hoy, Pat, 199n
Hughes, Langston, 184
Hunter, Susan M., 106, 140
Hurlbert, Claude Mark, 165
Hutchings, Maynard, 39
Huxley, Thomas H., 185

Inge, M. Thomas, 22
intellectual property, 7, 104; plagiarism, 7, 104, 135, 163–164, 171, 175, 192, 203n
Internet, 3, 4, 7, 12, 17–18, 32, 33, 83, 86, 104, 111, 145, 152, 163–164, 174, 175, 179, 189, 195n, 197n
Iser, Wolfgang, 71, 72

Index

Jacobs, Harriet, 166
Jacobs, Jane, 58
James, William, 47
Jefferson, Thomas, 57, 110, 183
Joseph, Chief, 117
Jung, Karl, 47
Juregensmeyer, Mark, 87

Karr, Mary, 37
Kaufer, David, 105
Kazin, Alfred, 58
Kennedy, X.J., 39, 117
Kent, Thomas, 92, 98
Kerek, Andrew, 198n
Kermode, Frank, 26
Kincaid, Jamaica, 38, 66, 116
King, Jr., Martin Luther, 5, 49, 57, 65, 90, 110, 183; "Letter from Birmingham Jail," 30, 37, 43, 47, 68, 90, 122
Kingsolver, Barbara, 66
Kingston, Maxine Hong, 110, 116, 166–167, 185
Kirklighter, Cristina, 112, 114, 115
Kirsch, Gesa E., 106, 140, 148
Kleege, Georgina, 116
Krutch, Joseph Wood, 185
Kubler-Ross, Elizabeth, 30
Kuester, David, 201n
Kuhn, Thomas, 46, 99, 118
Kumin, Maxine, 38
Kytle, Ray, 198n

Lacan, Jacques, 13
Lahiri, Jhumpa, 66
Lakoff, Robin, 58
Lamb, Charles, 27, 35
Langer, Susanne, 48
Lankford, Scott, 152–155, 158
Lauter, Paul, 27, 52
Law, Carolyn Leste, 23
Lee, Chang-Rae, 46
Leggo, Carl, 61

Leonardi, Susan J., 21, 22, 23, 24
Levin, Gerald, 32
Lévi-Strauss, Claude, 14
Lewiecki-Wilson, Cynthia, 105
Lewis, Bernard, 86
Lewis, C.S., 184
Lipka, Sara, 161
literacy, 140, 198n
literary criticism, 12, 14, 22, 27, 29, 53, 99, 166, 202n
literary theory, 13, 52, 120
Loomis, Kate, 203n
Lopate, Phillip, 28, 54
Lunsford, Andrea, 103, 126, 131
Lunsford, Ronald F., 151

MacDonald, Susan Peck, 18, 19
Mailer, Norman, 14
Mairs, Nancy, 48
Malcolm X, 31
Malinowitz, Harriet, 105
Malinowski, Bronislaw, 14, 151
Mandela, Nelson, 88, 89
Mandell, Barret J., 60
Mandell, Jonathan, 160
Mandell, Stephen R., 202n
Mannes, Marya, 185
Mansfield, Harvey, 204n
Marius, Richard, 129, 131
Marshall, Paule, 116
Martin, Eric, 45
Mathieu, Paula, 165
McCloud, Scott, 46
McCrimmon, James, 103
McGuire, Megan, 203n
McLeod, Susan H., 199n
McMillan, John, 114
McQuade, Christine, 104
McQuade, Donald M., 26, 104
Mead, Margaret, 184
Mencken, H. L., 110, 185
Milgram, Stanley, 30
Mill, J. S., 27

Miller, Nancy K., 20
Miller, Richard, 69, 139–140, 152, 157, 158, 160
Miller, Susan, 92, 99, 197n
Millett, Kate, 116
Mitford, Jessica, 185
Moffett, James, 198n
Momaday, N. Scott, 185
Montagu, Ashley, 58
Montaigne, Michel de, 28, 35, 59, 112
Morenberg,, 198n
Mortensen, Peter, 106, 140
Mumford, Lewis, 39
Murphy, Jr., Richard J., 54, 199n
Murray, Donald, 6, 69, 92, 94, 96, 198n–199n
Muscatine, Charles, 32
Myers, Kimberly, 54

Nafisi, Azar, 46
nature writing, 54, 109, 187; Thoreau, 188
Naylor, Gloria, 58
Nesteruk, Jeffrey, 23
New Criticism, 12, 20, 50–51, 95, 120; and writing assignments, 120
New Journalism, 12, 14, 15, 109; influence of, 16
Newman, Katherine S., 161
Nobel Peace Prize lectures, 5, 88–89, 196n
North, Stephen M., 36

O'Hare, Frank, 198n
Odell, Lee, 95, 105
Olsen, Tillie, 36
Olson, Gary A., 94, 197n
Orbinski, James, 90
Orwell, George, 4, 19, 27, 43–44, 49, 57–59, 62, 65, 67–68, 109, 112, 117, 122, 131, 183; "A Hanging," 62; "Marrakech," 58, 68; "Politics and the English Language," 19, 43, 57–58, 68, 112, 122, 183; "Shooting an Elephant," 27, 43, 57–58, 62, 68, 111

Palchik, Anna, 105
Paley, Grace, 38
Parks, Stephen, 119, 120
pedagogy, 5, 7, 23, 27, 54, 66–67, 72, 77, 97, 103, 105, 137, 169, 198n–199n; and canonicity, 67; college-level writing, 123–124, 153, 201n; current-traditional paradigm, 94, 103, 196n–197n; current-traditional rhetoric, 93, 97; grades and grading, 7, 49, 97, 127, 144, 173–180, 189, 192, 198n, 201n, 204n; grading contract, 173, 176–180, 189; process-oriented, 67, 96, 97, 199n; writing assignments, 6, 101, 121, 127, 134–135, 164, 165, 166, 169, 171
Pelz, William A., 114
Perl, Sondra, 95
Peterson, Linda, 31, 117
Petraglia, Joseph, 97, 99,–105
Petrosky, Anthony, 200n
Petrunkevitch, Alexander, 37, 185
Pianko, Sharon, 95
Piper, Deborah, 114
plagiarism, 7, 104, 135, 163–164, 171, 175, 192, 203n; Internet, 175; plagiarism-proof assignments, 163
Plato, 57, 169, 184
postmodernism, 129
Pound, Erza, 27
Pratt, Mary Louise, 152–153, 157
process: definition, 93, 96; paradigm, 92–93, 98; post-process

Index

theory and practice, 98–99; process-oriented pedagogy, 67, 96–97, 199n; writing, 32, 94, 95, 97–98, 100, 106, 131–132, 147, 193, 197n
Pullman, George, 93

Rabin, Yitzak, 89
Rasula, Jed, 26–27, 29, 38, 109
Ray, Ruth, 105
reader response theory, 49, 72
Readers, 25–35, 37, 39, 42, 43, 54, 109; *Norton Reader*, 30, 32, 33, 37, 39, 44, 48, 50–52, 54, 110, 117, 182; *St. Martin's Handbook*, 103, 131, 202n; *The Brief Handbook*, 202n; *The Writer's Harbrace Handbook*, 125, 127, 128, 130, 132, 182, 202n; *Ways of Reading*, 30, 40, 48, 134, 182, 200n
Reamer, Frederic G., 141
rhetoric, 19, 21, 23, 34, 41–42, 48, 52, 61, 84, 97, 103–105, 125, 152, 182, 196n
Rinaldi, Jacqueline, 105
Rinaldi, Nicholas, 196n
Rodriguez, Richard, 30, 31, 44, 57, 60, 110, 116, 117, 184, 200n; "Aria," 31, 44, 117, 184; *Hunger of Memory: The Education of Richard Rodriguez*, 30, 60, 117
Roney, Stephen K., 19
Rose, Mike, 6, 22, 30, 54, 69, 93, 95, 96, 100–102, 110, 116, 127, 141, 150–151, 198n, 199n
Rose, Phyllis, 13
Rosenblatt, Louise, 95
Rosovsky, Henry, 201n
Rowe, John Carlos, 202n
Roy, Alice M., 135
Roy, Arundhati, 46

Ruskin, John, 27
Russell, Bertrand, 47, 184
Russell, David, 105, 106

Sabine, Gordon A., 33, 44, 50, 51
Sacks, Oliver, 22
Sagan, Carl, 31
Said, Edward, 87, 116
Sanders, Scott Russell, 4, 37, 57, 58–60, 62, 66, 111; "The Singular First Person," 57–58, 60, 111
Sante, Luc, 46
Santiago, Esmerelda, 37, 116
Santora, Marc, 159, 160
Sartre, Jean-Paul, 14, 198n
Schiller, Susan A., 106
Schmidt, Jan Z., 23
Scholes, Robert, 49–50, 53, 119, 134, 164
science fiction, 200n
science writing, 22, 29, 130, 131
Seattle, Chief, 29, 58
Sedaris, David, 66, 116
Selzer, Richard, 22, 35
service-learning, 121, 195n
Sevareid, Eric, 58
Shaughnessy, Mina, 126, 147, 149, 198n
Shaw, George Bernard, 39, 58
Sheehy, Gail, 58
Shepard, Alan, 23, 114
Shuman, R. Baird, 22
Simic, Charles, 38
Slevin, James F., 50, 52
Smart, William, 32, 42
Smith, Barbara, 27
Smith, Barbara Herrnstein, 26
Smith, William E., 155
Smith, Zaidie, 46
Socrates, 169
Sommers, Nancy, 69, 95
Sontag, Susan, 36

Soto, Gary, 116
Spellmeyer, Kurt, 69, 106
Spiegelman, Art, 46
Spinner, Jenny, 54
Spivak, Gayatri Chakravorty, 19
Spock, Benjamin, 56, 62, 66, 70, 130, 134
Stafford, William, 58
Standard English, 6, 108, 114, 117, 119, 120, 122, 124, 126, 133
Stanton, Elizabeth Cady, 116
Staples, Brent, 37
Steele, Shelby, 46, 66
Steinbeck, John, 58
Steinem, Gloria, 116, 186
Straub, Richard, 151
Strunk, William, 71–72, 76, 129–131; *The Elements of Style*, 71, 72, 76, 129, 130, 131
Stuckey, Elspeth, 198n
Stuckey-French, Ned, 44
student writing, 127, 133, 200n; and compression, 75
Sullivan, Patricia A., 6, 108, 113
Sullivan, Patrick, 201n
Swales, John, 104
Swift, Jonathan, 27, 57, 110, 183; "A Modest Proposal," 27, 37, 43–44, 48, 58, 68, 122, 183

Tan, Amy, 66
Tannen, Deborah, 22, 31, 45, 46
Tate, Gary, 114
terrorism, 84–85, 87, 88
The 14th Dalai Lama, Tenzin Gyatso, 89
Thomas, Lewis, 14, 36, 47, 57, 109, 183
Thoreau, Henry David, 5, 30–31, 43, 49, 57, 59, 65, 68, 109, 112, 122, 135, 166, 183, 187–188; *Walden*, 58–59, 65, 166, 187, 188

Thurber, James, 29, 44, 57, 65, 82, 110, 183
Thủy, Lê Thi Diem, 46
Toffler, Alvin, 58
Tompkins, Jane, 20, 22, 24
Trimbur, John, 52, 101, 198n, 199n
Trimmer, Joseph, 42, 54, 199n
Truth, Sojourner, 116
Twain, Mark, 30–31, 57, 65, 110, 177, 183

Ulmer, Gregory, 120, 134

Van Peer, Willie, 39
Vicinus, Martha, 104
Vidal, Gore, 58
Villanueva, Victor, 54, 97, 112, 199n
voice, 56, 61–62, 66, 70; and ethics, 151; authorial, 12, 15, 17, 21, 58, 60–62, 65–66, 131, 187; depersonalized, 13; Modernist self-effacement, 12; multiple, 15; personal, 195n

Walker, Alice, 36, 44, 49, 184, 200n
Wallace, David Foster, 15–16, 18, 66
Watson, James, 14
Watters, Ann, 165
Webb, Suzanne Strobeck, 45
Ween, Lori, 202n
Welsh, Patrick, 115
Welty, Eudora, 186
Westfall, Julie, 204n
White, E. B.: *Democracy*, 32, 51–52, 86, 106; "Once More to the Lake," 27, 43, 48, 57, 58, 60, 63, 67, 183; *The Elements of Style*, 71, 72, 76, 129–131; "The Ring of Time," 57, 60

Wideman, John Edgar, 38
Widmer, Ted, 19, 20
Wiesel, Elie, 3, 8, 81
Williams, Betty, 89
Williams, Patricia, 22, 115
Wilson, Edmund, 58
Winnicott, D.W., 124, 201n
Winslow, Rosemary, 105
Witte, Stephen P., 200n
Wolfe, Tom, 14, 185
Wolff, Tobias, 38
Wollstonecraft, Mary, 116
Woolf, Virginia, 4, 30, 49, 57, 62, 65, 72, 110, 183, 200n; *A Room of One's Own*, 30

Wright, Richard, 116, 166, 167
writing assignments, 6, 101, 121, 127, 134–135, 164–166, 169, 171; autobiographical, 167; insider writing assignments, 163–164, 168, 171; plagiarism-proof, 163, 166, 187

Yancey, Kathleen Blake, 105, 199n
Yeats, William Butler, 24
Young, Art, 169
Yu, Ning, 49, 55

Zinsser, William, 184

www.ingramcontent.com/pod-product-compliance
Lightning Source LLC
Chambersburg PA
CBHW032022230426
43671CB00005B/172